DONALD W. TREADGOLD STUDIES
ON
RUSSIA, EAST EUROPE, AND CENTRAL ASIA

Books in the Treadgold Studies series honor the memory
and distinguished contributions of Donald W. Treadgold,
who taught Russian history at the
University of Washington from 1949 to 1993.

Autobiographies in Red was co-edited by *Treadgold Studies* Editors
Glennys Young and Laada Bilaniuk.

RED AUTOBIOGRAPHIES:
INITIATING THE BOLSHEVIK SELF

Igal Halfin

Published by the Herbert J. Ellison Center for Russian,
East European, and Central Asian Studies, University of Washington

Distributed by the University of Washington Press
Seattle and London

Russian, East European, and Central Asian Studies Center (REECAS)
Henry M. Jackson School of International Studies, University of Washington
www.depts.washington.edu/reecas
For more information about the Treadgold Series and previously published
Treadgold Papers, visit www.jsis.washington.edu/ellison/outreach_treadgold.shtml

University of Washington Press
P.O. Box 50096, Seattle, WA 98145 U.S.A.
www.washington.edu/uwpress

Library of Congress Cataloging-in-Publication Data
Halfin, Igal.
Red autobiographies : initiating the Bolshevik self / Igal Halfin.
p. cm. — (Donald W. Treadgold studies on Russia, East Europe, and Central Asia)
Includes bibliographical references.
ISBN 978-0-295-99112-2 (pbk. : alk. paper)
1. Soviet Union—Politics and government—1917–1936. 2. Soviet Union—Politics
and government—1917–1936—Sources. 3. Soviet Union—History—Revolution,
1917–1921—Social aspects. 4. Soviet Union—Social conditions—1917–1945.
5. Rossiiskaia sotsial-demokraticheskaia rabochaia partiia (bolshevikov)—History.
6. Communists—Soviet Union—Psychology—History. 7. Identity (Psychology)—
Soviet Union—History. 8. Group identity—Soviet Union—History.
9. Autobiography—Social aspects—Soviet Union—History.
10. Social psychology—Soviet Union—History. I. Title.
DK266.3.H35 2010
947.084'1—dc22   2010052395

Амалии

The research for this book was funded by the Israeli Science Foundation, grant number 496--09.

CONTENTS

RED AUTOBIOGRAPHIES:
INITIATING THE BOLSHEVIK SELF

Igal Halfin

INTRODUCTION
Revolutionary Conversions

TO DISCOVER THE SELF, to change the self, to perfect the self—the Soviet regime took these as its most essential duties after 1917. The Bolsheviks looked inward, struggling to understand the meaning of their lives, their social roles, the notions of justice and truth they wanted to live by. They spoke about freedom and equality, and counted on their own initiative, their own resourcefulness, to realize their ideals. Bolshevik identity was malleable, shaped by inner labor, not assigned by law or convention. Rather than reading the Bible or another sacred text to understand who they were, Party members, like any other adherents of modernity, preferred to count on their rationality, their intellectual rigor, and their inspiration. Tradition meant nothing: every citizen of the young Soviet republic was enjoined to break with the past, to work on himself or herself as a free agent.[1] The Party perceived itself as a vehicle of emancipation precisely because it claimed to be a new type of political institution, one that was not coercive but expressive in nature. Official rhetoric emphasized spontaneity and enthusiasm, not fear and constraint.[2]

Recent research into how the self comes into being, how it articulates itself, and how it reflects upon itself suggests that the revolutionary transformation of subjectivity—not only one's life narrative and self image but also the social and political apparatuses monitoring one's social usability—poses fascinating questions.[3] In the field of Soviet history, new theoretical approaches to the self became available just as the Party archives were opened to serious research.[4] I was excited to be among the first Western scholars to work in the Leningrad Party archive in the early 1990s, with Lenin's portrait hanging behind me, and a discolored patch of wall where Gorbachev's portrait had hung only weeks before in front of me.[5] What struck me most in the materials I was handed were not the deceptions and manipulations contemporaries supposedly engaged in but the endless series of autobiographies and letters in which individuals dared to speak about themselves, openly and in great detail.[6] Suddenly I saw that the Bolsheviks' plan was far more ambitious than consolidating power and searching for spoils. They had set their sights on emancipating the working class and constructing a new man, a task they clearly took very seriously.

The amount of paper—a very precious commodity at that time—they devoted to documenting the self attested to the seriousness of their purpose.[7]

There has certainly been a great interest in subjectivity in the Bolshevik universe in the years following their seizure of power.[8] To appreciate it, however, it is crucial not to confuse subjectivity with individualism. The Bolsheviks rejected private life, seeing in it an outlet for the narrow-mindedness and selfishness typical of the old, bourgeois Russia. Individual autonomy was a value they despised: a good life was a life in common. Yet if by subjectivity we mean the intensity of the relations of the self, it was this form of subjectivity they believed to be extremely important.[9] Emerging at the nexus of revolutionary lore, Party dogma, and modern techniques of interrogation, the Bolshevik practices of public self-presentation established new rules in the identity game.[10] Unpacking official ideology and clarifying its tenets to themselves, the initiated listened to each other's personal revelations and cross-examined each other. In their own eyes, they did not so much bow to higher power as they were intent on working through their old, myopic dispositions, hoping that a worthy self would eventually emerge.[11] In the spirit of Communist collectivism, the new self had to be a joint piece of work. Those who applied to join the brotherhood of the elect—a laborious process in which one had to amass sufficient recommendations, persuade one's peers one was worthy of a Party card, and then have the Party higher-ups ratify this decision—often modified their life stories based on the comments they received.[12]

Bolshevik autobiographies from the first postrevolutionary years point to an intricate relationship between the Party's blueprint for the narrative of history as progression toward the light, and the individuals' endeavor to replicate this progression in their subjective development. The Communist autobiography was structurally analogous to Christian confession.[13] The achievement of Communist perfection also required an imperfect starting point: an unconscious, ideologically naive state. At the decisive moment, when the Communist autobiographer claimed to have seen the light of Communism, an individual's consciousness and the Party line (which embodied the supra-personal proletarian consciousness) were supposed to be merged. From the moment of conversion, the Communist's consciousness became permanent and perfect, and s/he was now expected to devote him- or herself to the conversion of others.[14]

Whenever a complete conversion to Bolshevism occurred, class origins—normally the alpha and omega of political suitability in the revolutionary universe—became unimportant.[15] "Our Party organization is open to each and every one (*vsem i kazhdomu*)," Evdokimov explained at the Twelfth Party Congress.[16] Even disenfranchised individuals (the offspring of nobles, gendarmes, priests, and other dignitaries of the old regime) could join the brotherhood of the elect provided they publicly renounced their "reactionary" parents, brothers, and sisters, and proved their own commitment to the revolutionary cause. Of course, such inclusivism did not extend to conscious individuals who deliberately made what the regime considered to be unforgivable political choices—active political support of "counterrevolutionary forces," which included Constitutional Democrats (Kadets) and Mensheviks on the right and Social Revolutionaries and Anarchists on the left. As long as the autobiographer dwelt on that part of his life that had preceded his conversion he blamed his mistakes on political immaturity. When he discussed violations that postdated his conversion, however, this narratological strategy was shut before him. Given the golden rule of the eschatological narrative that advance toward the light had to be unidirectional and that enlightenment promised full consciousness, no autobiographer could easily explain how she or he could reject the truth when already a Party member. Deliberate injury to the revolutionary cause could be perpetrated only by a traitor.

What were the antecedents of the Bolshevik autobiographies? The relationship between self-writing and introspection is an ancient one, traceable at least to Stoicism.[17] The eschatological motifs so prominent in the Bolshevik autobiography certainly permeate Christian confessions after the Fourth Lateran Council.[18] Even the adversarial context has obvious antecedents in the late medieval inquisition.[19] What made the Bolshevik autobiography modern, however, was the self-reliance of its authors.[20] Soviet civilization was able to break out of the Christian orbit only when it learned to found subjectivity not on sacrifice of the self but, on the contrary, on its positive affirmation.[21] Of course, liberals knew how to do this long before Lenin, but if their discourse construed a positive self through juridical institutions (the self as subject of rights), the revolutionary project relied on Marxism (the self as the seat of consciousness) and the Party (the self as the source of value) to foster self affirmation.[22]

The Bolshevik self was imbued by a unique, richly elaborated system of meanings that must be studied on its own terms. The assumption present in so many historical studies, that people always think the same, and that when evidence suggests otherwise it is only because their self-expression is constrained by a hostile environment, is wrong both ethically and empirically. Ethically, because it universalizes the liberal self as an entity driven by a desire for power and money and denies the other his or her language. And empirically, because such a view of historical agency does not offer a plausible explanation for the longevity of the illiberal regimes in twentieth-century history.[23]

Autobiography Interrogated

We can cast a glance at the new self asserting itself in a brief document from a provincial archive: the record of the interrogation of a young Soviet student, a certain Kovalev, from 1921, a pivotal year in Soviet history— Bolsheviks had faced a supreme test in the Civil War, and, now victorious, embarked on creating a socialist society.[24] On October 17, Kovalev stood before the members of the Party cell at the Smolensk Technological Institute, trying to salvage his Bolshevik credentials. A purge was taking place: the Party was cleansing its ranks and many students—a problematic segment of revolutionary society, under suspicion for its intellectual pursuits and its detachment from labor—were shown the door. Worse still, the defendant was a newcomer: he had joined the Party only some eighteen months earlier, after the Reds had already withstood the pressure of the White generals and possession of a Party card had ceased to be perilous. But Kovalev vehemently insisted that his "revolutionary mood" (*revoliutsionnoe nastroenie*), not utilitarian calculations, had led him to join the Bolsheviks. According to him, he was one of the most dedicated revolutionary activists in the locality.

A highly self-conscious transformation of the self provided the central pivot in Kovalev's life story. Family and village had to be rejected so that the international proletariat could be embraced. After a sequence of personal crises and unexpected revelations, the narrator experienced a moment of utter clarity and came to embrace the Bolshevik truth without reservations. Judging by the transcript, Kovalev had detached himself from his religious moorings, embraced the Bolshevik ideology, and hoped to realize himself in the Party, through the Party. As someone who identified with the Revolution, he had gained his bearings in the new, Bolshevik world. He knew what the institutions of Soviet power were and why they were better than the old, tsarist institutions.

Who was Kovalev in class terms? Was he a worker or a poor peasant by birth and as such the best material for Party membership? Or was he a repenting exploiter who could be enrolled with difficulty if at all, or perhaps a member of the intermediary groups who switched between the camps depending on the political wind? If the range of class identities on the questionnaire he filled out as part of the interrogation process was finite, there was still a certain degree of flexibility in answering the question. Kovalev could ignore his parents' petit-bourgeois background (they owned some property and possibly even hired labor) and describe himself as a peasant, on account of his village origins, or he could call himself a proto-proletarian, since he had volunteered for a Bolshevik paramilitary organization. But he could not call himself a real worker (he would not be believed) or a member of the intelligentsia (he would effectively ruin his case, as the intelligentsia was believed to be cut off from revolutionary activity, pretentious and politically unreliable). The official discourse left enough room for an elaborate identity maneuver: Kovalev could listen to how others characterized him, play one class label against another, embrace identities that portrayed him in the most favorable way, and automatically reject those that excluded him. The opinion of Party members and local industrial workers who mediated the process could be played against the expertise of emissaries from the center who came to supervise the purge procedure assuring him that he would not be rejected outright. Unfortunately for Kovalev, however, his autobiography, which he presented in brief, was too alarming for the issue of origins to be glossed over: in 1916 Kovalev had been a student in a theological seminary and, as such, a likely candidate to be stripped not only of his Party card but of his civilian voting rights as well. In disenfranchising "servants of the cult," the new regime expressed Marxism's hostility to religion and Lenin's militant atheism in particular.

The tension between Kovalev's clerical past and his Bolshevik present surfaced in the early stages of his interrogation. When asked about his attitude toward religion Kovalev responded resolutely: "Negative." The next question was a trap: "Did you enroll in the seminary because of a calling for the priesthood?" A hesitant, let alone an affirmative answer, would have exposed him as a mock revolutionary, at best someone subject to the winds of politics, at worst someone who was trying to undermine the Party from within. Kovalev's dry response proved he was equal to the task: "Studies at the seminary didn't cost anything." He had only wanted an affordable education. If Kovalev had fully reinvented himself, he must have clashed with his deeply religious family. Indeed, comrades wondered how he was getting along with his parents these days. "My relations with them are fine," he admitted. "My mother does not understand the movement." Ideology was something transmitted through the masculine line, and here Kovalev had assurances: "My father sympathizes [with the Bolsheviks]." To seal his claim that he was an authentic convert, Kovalev had to show that he was abreast of current official policies toward the Orthodox Church and whole-heartedly endorsed them. Someone asked, "Why is education separated from the church in our country?" "Because there is no reason to support elements who oppose Soviet Power," the unabashed Kovalev explained. As far as he was concerned, clerical brainwashing was a matter of the past. "Divine Law," the linchpin of the tsarist school curriculum, should not be part of the school curriculum.

Students searched for a question that would directly probe Kovalev's conscience. They reckoned that any lingering Christian ethics would be revealed by a question about the killings carried out by Bolshevik detachments during the Civil War—wholesale death sentences and other controversial acts of class revenge carried out by the Cheka (the Chrezvychaynaya Komissiya or Extraordinary Commission, the first Soviet state security organization) in 1918–1920. When asked "What is your attitude toward summary executions?" Kovalev replied, "If someone deserves it, why not shoot him?" [esli kto zasluzhil, to pochemu by i ne rasstreliat'?]. He was almost nonchalant.[25]

Here the Party's plenipotentiary, an emissary from Moscow present during the purge hearings, entered the scene. Kovalev had to be subjected to meticulous political questioning. When asked "What is our supreme power?" he knew to say this was the "Central Executive Committee of the Soviets." He also knew that it is the Party that "runs politics." Two other questions—"Why are we called Communists?" and "When was the 3rd International organized?"—Kovalev found "too difficult to tackle." Clearly, even if he was a true Bolshevik, he scarcely understood what made Lenin's party unique, and why it was superior to its "petit-bourgeois" rivals, chief among them the Mensheviks and the Socialist Revolutionaries. Although some believed that Kovalev was "politically, completely illiterate," others insisted that he had acquitted himself fine overall. A youngster did not have to know everything right now—he would learn more soon enough by joining in political literacy circles. What mattered was Kovalev's desire to learn, and there was plenty of that. Ultimately the cell reached a compromise resolution: Kovalev was reduced from a full Party member to a candidate.

But suspicions lingered. Could Kovalev simply be enthusiastically playing a part in revolutionary theatricals? Did he say what he thought and think what he said?

A number of historians interpret what is spoken publicly in Bolshevik Russia as an expression of the speakers' involvement in relations of unequal power, as signs of tacit resistance to dominant linguistic forms and the values they encode.[26] In their approach the regime largely controlled what could be said and done. For the weak, they go on to argue, the interrogation is, at most, a dramatization of power relations that must not be confused with persuasion. What we confront in the public transcript is a twisted debate about justice and dignity in which, in James Scott's formulation, "one party has a severe speech impediment induced by power relations."[27] Must we conclude then that the self appearing on the Bolshevik public stage expressed nothing but the dry letter of the official dogma?

To be sure, the transcript does not tell us how someone such as Kovalev experienced the downfall of the Romanov dynasty and the organized Church and the consolidation of Soviet power, if we are intent on finding in it unmediated contact with an "authentic person." It is futile to search for Kovalev's true voice, to attempt to return his voice to its pristine condition—one cannot escape the filter of the official language that produced the voice in the first place. What is important here, however, is not whether Kovalev was sincere or not according to our present-day truth criteria, but that the ritual of the Bolshevik interrogation constructed every deposition as the revelation of an interior truth. Kovalev's autobiography, like all of the autobiographies examined over the course of this book, must be examined as a locus of discourse, not of a fixed selfhood.[28]

Discursive Construction of Selves

The work of the sociologist Ervin Goffman is relevant here. Whereas moral and psychologistic approaches tend to treat self-deception and insincerity as weaknesses generated within the deep recesses of the individual personality, Goffman suggests we start from outside the individual and work inward. "We may say that the starting point for all that is to come later consists of the individual performer maintaining a definition of the situation before an audience."[29] Focusing on the way the students presented themselves to others I, too, present my heroes as managers of impressions. From this angle, comrades' performances appear to have been designed to prove they were dedicated, conscious Communists. And the self they performed in crafting their autobiographies was akin to the image that an individual on stage induces others to hold in regard to him or her. Yet we must not revert to the language of authenticity. "A correctly staged and performed scene leads the audience to impute a self to a performed character, but this imputation—this self—is a product of a scene that comes off, and is not a cause of it."[30] While Goffman, to whom this citation belongs, mentions performers, audiences, and dramaturgical strategies, he emphasizes that in the final analysis the metaphor of a mask and a stage must be dropped: there is simply no domain outside of theater where real interaction takes place, where true words are spoken.[31]

Bolsheviks knew of no private sphere where their supposedly authentic thoughts could be spilled out. However private the text we find may be, whether a correspondence between friends, a record of family conversation, or even a secret autobiography written by a solitary student in an attic, we always find these texts permeated by official values. It seems more rewarding to dispense with the dichotomy between the authentic and the unauthentic, the spontaneous and the imposed from above, and to study the specific rules that structured the symbolic exchanges in the various spheres of student lives, hopefully arriving at something like the taxonomy of the contemporary speech. The key issue is not whether Kovalev spoke differently in private—subversion as well as appropriation of the official language was an everyday affair—but what he was actually saying when his words counted most.

When in public, Party applicants were repeatedly asked to recite short versions of their autobiographies; as the example of Kovalev suggests, this was the heart of Bolshevik self-presentation. Involving several stages, the evaluation of candidacy was a complicated process designed to penetrate the mind and determine whether one was "conscious" (*soznatel'nyi*) and "developed" (*razvityi*) enough to be trusted with Party duties. Although some guidance was provided, autobiographies were written spontaneously. Following a more or less standard blueprint, the autobiographies described one's class background, education, and the development of one's worldview.[32] If the always present questionnaire was intended to provide information regarding the applicant's background, the autobiography told a story of spiritual transformation. It was less a record of what had actually happened to the applicant than an account of how he had ascribed meanings to what he had experienced.

Some autobiographies were quite long, certainly three to five times longer than an average declaration. The autobiography of Andronov, a Party applicant at the Leningrad State University, concluded with an apology for the "lyrical torrents prompted by a questionnaire that did not give me the opportunity to express myself fully." The narrator had no choice: "I had to explain *why* things happened as they did and *who* I was" (emphasis in the original).[33]

Insofar as the moment of consummation in the autobiography—the conversion to Bolshevism—was related to emancipation, the individual self was connected to the collective story of the proletariat building a classless society. Conversions could be quite smooth, as was the case with Slesar', a student at Smolensk Technological Institute. This was a natural proletarian, half peasant, half worker, who gradually realized that he had to share his life with the Party. He was born in 1899 to a poor peasant family; his father never had more than three or four *desiatinas* (roughly eight to ten acres) of land and supplemented his income by working as an itinerant carpenter.[34] When the narrator was thirteen a poor harvest forced him to move to Petersburg. "I lived with my older brother and had to earn my own livelihood. At first I worked in a bookstore on the old Nevskii Prospekt. But I could not cope with the harsh way things were done there. We helpers were not considered human beings at all." The bookstore clearly figures here as a metonym for the tsarist regime as a whole. The toiler is humiliated and his honor as a human being is constantly trampled.

Young Slesar' was not yet aware that this was a systemic phenomenon, a result of the capitalist mode of production and not of a shopkeeper's bad character. But later experiences soon persuaded him that exploitation was everywhere and that he could not simply run away from it.

> I went to work at a carpentry shop, owned by a certain Bystrov, where picture frames were made. Life in this shop was no better; no, it was a thousand times worse! The masters abused us on a whim. They used to beat us when they felt like it, using whatever fell to hand, with or without reason, simply out of boredom.

After three months of torture in the carpentry shop, Slesar' was again jobless. He tried three more professions but finally fell ill and was sent back home. There he was to learn that agricultural toilers suffered humiliations no less painful than those of their industrial counterparts. "I spent about a year in the village as a day laborer working on neighboring estates, and I also helped my parents with the household economy." At this time his thoughts began turning to larger questions about the human condition. "I acquired a passion for reading." On the advice of a local teacher, Slesar' moved back to the city so that he could attend school. "In between classes I earned my bread."

Still, Slesar' was far from rising up in revolt. "I barely even noticed the February Revolution. Until 1917 I had no contact with politics—all my time went into the struggle for survival." In September 1917, having enrolled in a technical school in Smolensk, he began to think broadly. "Finding myself in a circle of comrades who were better developed than me politically, I began to develop myself gradually." Between his previous life and the news of the counterrevolutionary subterfuges of Kerenskii and Kornilov, Slesar' matured quickly. "I encountered the October Revolution as a fairly conscious Bolshevik." His friends recognized his progress and elected him to the executive committee of displaced people.

For a dedicated fighter such as Slesar', Party enrollment was a mere formality. "When a Party cell was organized in the institute in the second half of 1918, I became a member." From then on Slesar' helped the Party where it needed him most. "I threw myself into political and social activities with the student youth of the city of Smolensk. When Kolchak approached the walls of Viatka, in April 1919, I volunteered for the eastern front."

The autobiography of Slesar' describes a gradual growth of Bolshevik consciousness. Revolutionism was second nature to him and it was only a matter of time until it emerged. When circumstances ripened, Slesar' found the political organization that expressed his inner self. There was no drama in his conversion, and when he describes how he finally got his Party card his language is dry and bereft of any pathos. It is as if the autobiographer wanted to emphasize that he had been a Bolshevik all along, even though objective conditions slowed down the process of his self-realization.

Other autobiographers, especially those who did not come from the depths of the working class, described more circuitous roads to Bolshevism. Their conversions were more dramatic, constituting a break in their lives. In these scenarios, the catalysts were stronger, more concrete.

Rabinovich, a Jewish student from Smolensk Technological Institute, was a less likely candidate for a Bolshevik conversion than Slesar'. His story was one of extricating himself from his environment and eventually understanding that, as a thinking individual, he ought to help the working class acquire theoretical knowledge. "I come from a shtetl [*mestechko*] called Braslava, in Vilna Province," his autobiography began.[35] The socioeconomic background of his family was not as miserable as an aspiring Bolshevik might have wished. Many Jews in the Pale of Settlement were quite poor, but few of them were true industrial workers. When Rabinovich spoke of his father's career, it was with the anxious self-consciousness of a son of a small proprietor. "Having worked in pharmacies for a long time, my father finally opened a private pharmacy of his own; it was not large. Until 1915, father barely could make ends meet. That September, as the Germans advanced towards our shtetl, everybody who was reasonably well-off ran away. Since he lacked the means to leave my father stayed behind, and, as his competitors were gone, his material situation improved." Did that mean the Rabinoviches became bourgeois? The autobiographer did not want to dwell on the subject for long but mentioned, as if in passing, that "father did not accumulate any capital, nor did he exploit the labor of others."

At this point the autobiographer turned to his own life story. The intimate connections between education and class in imperial Russia laid traps for Rabinovich at every narrative turn. "I began my studies at home, then went to primary school, finishing in 1907." Then came a difficult admission: Rabinovich had attended the prestigious Sakharov Gymnasium located in the city of Dvinsk. "I lived with relatives. Father used to send porters every day with food for me. In the upper grades, I gave lessons to cover my own living expenses." In order to dispel any persisting impression that he had been spoiled, Rabinovich hastened to add that "when I graduated from the gymnasium and expressed an interest in attending the university, it turned out that my father could not afford it. I had to give this idea up."

In the beginning of 1915 Rabinovich went to live with his relatives in Vilna, "hoping to find work there as a clerk." But there was no work to be had and he was obliged to return home. "During the summer, I worked for a wealthy Jew, preparing his daughters for the state examinations. In 1916 I applied to Saratov University but was turned down because of the numerus clausus." Only in 1917, once all tsarist restrictions on Jewish education were abrogated, was he able to enroll in Iur'ev University.

The toppling of the tsar coincided with the fulfillment of Rabinovich's educational aspirations. Though he declared that at the time he was terribly naive politically, he could hardly let this momentous event pass without a comment.

Three days after my arrival in Iur'ev the Revolution began. I was not yet a conscious revolutionary at the time but I joined many other students in the street as soon as I heard about the uprising in Petrograd. Despite the provocative rumors spread by the police and the top tier of the officer corps, we shook the university walls with revolutionary songs and organized a rally . . .

In spring 1918 the German invasion "overwhelmed" Rabinovich. With the rest of the proletarian students, the autobiographer is suffering from the invasion of the Prussian barons and fears the worst kind of reactions. He also experiences economic difficulties. "I was utterly bereft and for two months the student assistance committee helped me out." At last, Rabinovich could say something of himself that would dispel his rich-kid image.

This provided a much needed transition to the requisite discussion of class and class struggle: any mention of exploitation earlier in the story would have put the narrator on the wrong side of the fence. Now he could be counted among the poor students who tried to understand the global roots of their sorry predicament. "During the occupation I began to deal with political questions more consciously. I could not remain indifferent to the German treatment of the peasants or to the miserable conditions of my fellow villagers." Trying to do something to alleviate the misery of the people, Rabinovich "worked very hard to organize a theater in the shtetl, the profits from the shows going to the poor." The point is reiterated at a higher level of abstraction: "Already then I was conducting revolutionary activity among my fellow citizens."

Rabinovich spoke of "citizens" (*grazhdane*) and not "comrades" (*tovarishchi*), meaning he was a revolutionary but not necessarily a Bolshevik: apparently he was waiting for the right opportunity to assert his radical self.

As soon as rumors began circulating that the Germans would be leaving the area I began agitating among the population, working to organize a soviet of soldier and peasant deputies. Having discovered where the head of the militia was hiding, I pressed hard to have him arrested and delivered him to the soviet that was organized that very day. [. . .] With the Germans gone, I immersed myself fully in soviet activity, organizing schools and running them. After the assassination of Liebknecht in January 1919, I and a few friends organized [. . .] a club that we named after him. [. . .] In late March of that year I was sent as a delegate to our district's congress of enlightenment activists and became a member of the collegium of the local Department of People's Education. Expenses made it extremely inconvenient for me to live in the district capital but I accepted this position with pleasure.

In early April 1919 Rabinovich decided to join the Reds. In case anyone might suspect his motives, he emphasized that "this happened just when we were having no success at the front." By the time of the Civil War's terrible ordeals he was already a loyal Bolshevik. "I had to work all day and all night because there were so few activists in the area." Now was the time for the Polish aristocracy to invade the young proletarian republic: on August 30 the Poles approached. Rabinovich fled to Smolensk, concerned that he would be recognized as a leading Bolshevik and shot. "Many, some of whom even called themselves Communists, stayed with the Whites." The price of loyalty was high in this case. "My mother begged me to stay but I left her and an ill sister behind." The time had come to go beyond narrow family commitments, to choose sides. "Although I was in the category of Party sympathizers at the time, I had been accepted into the recently organized punitive detachment. Only Communists were eligible for enrollment."

At the end of the story, Rabinovich emerges with a strong sense of who he is. The author depicts himself as an individual fully conscious of the Party goals, someone who is actively shaping reality in the Marxist image. Rabinovich does not speak anymore about the environment that influenced his life decisions. Rather, his consciousness now influences and reshapes reality.

Less the disguise of subjectivity and more the arena in which the subjectivity of Rabinovich is performed, his autobiography cannot be seen as a record of the life of a devout comrade. When we assume that an autobiography registers the perception of events, we assume that reality preceded its interpretation and therefore overlook the mechanism through which its interpretation produced reality. Thus the life of Rabinovich was restructured within a narrative framework meant to convey to the brotherhood of the elect not the dry facts of his existence but the deeper meaning of it all. The form of his autobiography is far more revealing than the content. It is important to note, for instance, that the moment of conversion in this narrative is not dictated solely by the contents of his life; the rupture in Rabinovich's life was less a contingent event than a poetical necessity.

The notion of the autobiographer's journey in itself necessitated a transition from the passive voice of the victim of exploitation to the active voice of the Bolshevik worldbuilder. In displacing the facts onto the ground of literary fictions, Rabinovich effects, in the terminology of Hayden White, a "process of transcodation," in which life events that he recorded in the questionnaire he submitted in the form of a dry list were retranscribed in literary code.[36] The autobiographies of minor Bolsheviks such as Rabinovich are worthy of our attention precisely for their tropes and figures of thought, without which their authors would not have been able to turn the real events of their lives into meaningful stories.

CHAPTER 1
Party Admissions in Paranoid Times

THE INTRICACIES OF THE REVOLUTIONARY WORK on the self come into sharp relief in the Party records at the grassroots level—the main source for the present chapter. Focusing attention on the provinces and drawing material from institutions of higher learning in Petrograd-Leningrad, Tomsk, and Smolensk, I am interested in how the policy of Party admissions and purges was interpreted by the grassroots, not in how the composition of the Party was conceived of by the center. While I do not ignore the peculiarities of the regions from which the material is drawn, my aim is to provide a set of microstudies, not regional studies. Rather than comparing specific geographical areas and their social relations, I intend to examine the ways in which revolutionary identities were disseminated in the primary Party cells—imagined communities that Bolsheviks tried to mould into their human ideal.[1]

A good part of what follows is dedicated to a discussion of the Party admissions and Party purges, which were key Bolshevik rituals in the years immediately after the seizure of power. I distinguish between the "politics" and the "poetics" of these rituals. By "politics" I mean comrades' struggles to defend their Bolshevik credentials when facing representatives of the central Party apparatus, as well as their local denouncers. By "poetics" I mean comrades' construction of their autobiography on the basis of rules prescribed by the official paradigm that demanded the author be constantly growing and learning. The sources for this discussion are not only the minutes of the purge commissions working in 1921, 1924, and 1929, but questionnaires, letters of recommendation, denunciations, and appeals composed by the victims of the purges. A close examination of the construction of Bolshevik identity made possible by these wonderfully rich sources suggests that success or failure was largely determined, not by any "objective" biographical detail, but by a student's ability to defend, in a set of closely monitored procedures, his or her claim to possess true Communist consciousness.

Every Party meeting was carefully recorded by a stenographer. The attentive reader soon becomes familiar with the language Bolsheviks used in addressing each other and can trace fine shifts in terminology. The transcripts detail their self-fashioning, their perception of comrades and foes, their trustfulness and their suspicion—the reader sometimes feels he is reading not Party documents but the field notes of an anthropologist. Because it encompasses such a rich gathering of sources on which to base close readings, the material constantly reminds us, through its standardized language, its silences and its evasions, of the effects of Bolshevik discourse on forming and expressing the new self.[2]

For the Bolsheviks, the primary Party organizations were a microcosm of the young Soviet society. While the Party cells in the universities embodied everything that was new and exciting about the Revolution, including access to education by the lower classes, equality, and dissemination of emancipatory ideology, the difficulties involved in their staffing and everyday operation also point to many of the challenges that still lay ahead.[3] It was one thing to seize the universities and integrate them into the organizational structure of the Commissariat of Enlightenment.[4] It was quite another to transform each and every academic institution in the country into a true center of Bolshevik teaching. The Party marshaled an impressive political apparatus that monitored the new identities produced in the universities. While such traditional bodies as administration boards or professorial committees were delegitimized, the Party district committee and the university Party cells were given a free hand to intervene in student affairs.

The changing criteria according to which students were evaluated (these, of course, had little to do with excellence in academic studies) present in a nutshell the assumptions regarding how the new society was to be organized. Party admissions were conceived as a continuous process, paralleling the social engineering the country was undergoing. While enrolling the most promising individuals, the Party had to take it slowly with others, assessing their progress from time to time and purging the unenlightened dross. The Party apparatus divided the student body into proletarians (workers and peasants), petit-bourgeois, and "class aliens" (*chuzhie*), primarily the aristocracy and the clergy. The first were natural candidates for Party membership, the last were to be driven out of the universities, while those in the middle were stranded somewhere along the road to full consciousness.

The series of micro-studies undertaken below enables us to examine the interaction between Bolshevized students, Party organs, and official language on an everyday basis.[5] Some of the institutions under scrutiny, chief among them the famous "workers' faculties" (*rabochie fakul'tety*)— special schools described in the official press as "siege ladders used by worker and peasant youths to mount the university walls"—were groups of a new type brought into being by the Revolution.[6] Free from prerevolutionary academic traditions, they present us with an ideal Bolshevik community, one unhampered by legacies of the past. While other academic institutions such as the famous Petrograd State University and the Tomsk Technological Institute existed before the Bolshevik seizure of power, changes in their functioning are interesting too, in that they point to the radical transformation these institutions underwent following Red victory.

It is impossible to understand the Bolshevik effort to enlighten the population and bring the best youngsters into the brotherhood of the elect without studying the Party's changing self-perception. In its own eyes, the prerevolutionary Party organization was purely proletarian. It represented the working class, drew on working-class membership, and was the natural carrier of the proletarian revolution in Russia. As a contem-poraneous publicist put it, "our Party was primarily made of workers from the bench. In comparison with the SRs or the Mensheviks the share of intelligentsia in the Party was very low." According to the Party dogma, during the glorious underground epoch and throughout 1917 only committed revolutionaries joined the Party, putting their entire life at stake. The fall from the state of original purity was initiated by the Party's coming to power and its transformation into a ruling apparatus: "after October, the Party organization spread. In localities where the proletarian element was absent the Party could build itself up drawing only on the middle, petty-bourgeois population layers. After its first successes the intelligentsia enrolled into the Party, then the peasantry. At the same time the best workers had to be removed from the factories and sent to the Red Army or to administrative work."[7] In the latter case, they fell immediately under the influence of the alien social milieu "and could not fail to experience its degenerating influence."[8] If prior to 1917 workers comprised 57 percent of the Party's personnel, by late 1918 their share dropped to 44 percent. Inversely, the share of the peasants grew from 3 percent to 17 percent, and the share of clerks and chancellery employees from 16 to 22 percent— alarming data as far as the Bolsheviks were concerned.[9]

During the years 1918–1920 Party membership could already offer some spoils, but since the outcome of the war was not yet certain it still brought many hazards. Placing the issue of the social composition of the Party at the top of the list, the Eighth Party Congress (March 1919) resolved that "the growth of the Party is indeed a progressive phenomenon, but only to the extent that these are the healthy social elements that join us." Local branches were instructed to monitor their membership better and to periodically report data on their social composition. The Party Secretariat took its first steps to achieve uniformity in class statistics.[10] A "uniform Party card" postulated four "social position" categories: "worker," "peasant," "intelligentsia, and "employee." When possible it was suggested that ties to other social groups, such as "worker, the family is in the village," "peasant, seasonal worker in . . . " and so on, would be specified.[11]

The third and most problematic period commenced when the Bolsheviks' final victory over the Whites became certain. The dangers of participation in the Party were reduced to nil and the Party card offered the most lucrative careers to its holders. Toward the Ninth Party Congress (1920), Nikolai Krestinskii, the Party's secretary, had to admit that "the Party was losing some of its ties to the working class [. . .] as a result of the growth of the soviet and professional apparatus."[12] From this stage on, Party membership could be viewed as a privilege and the sincerity of applicants' intentions to serve the Bolshevik cause was more likely to be doubted.[13]

The introduction of the New Economic Policy (henceforth NEP) in March 1921 further exacerbated the problem. Though it was clear that War Communism, famous for its inefficient shock campaigns and incessant requisitions, had to be folded, the Bolsheviks perceived NEP as a set of economic concessions forced on the Soviet republic by the breakdown of economic relations. The recent peasant mutinies, coupled with the rebellion of the Kronstadt fortress, a revolutionary bastion that was indispensable in securing the Bolshevik victory in 1917, forced the Party to reintroduce the market as a mechanism mediating between the city and the village.[14] The Bolsheviks retained control of heavy industry, the army, and the bureaucracy, and their concessions were mild indeed. In their eyes, however, NEP was a regrettable and dangerous step back, however necessary it might be for the time being.[15]

To what extent were the Party interrogations regulated? Did specific guidelines exist for prosecution or defense? What yardsticks were brought to bear, what useful pointers were given? Party referees were supposed to measure an individual in terms of class background, education, and, most importantly, performance during revolutionary ordeals. But interrogation was something special, quite unscientific, requiring a special intuition (chut'e). The Party's courts, Matvei Shkiriatov from the Central Control Commission had explained in 1923, had to get by without abstract criteria:

"It is impossible to compose a circular specifying what offences merit what censure; we cannot purge anyone before we have determined not only that he did indeed commit some sort of moral offense, but also that we know under what circumstances it was done." Ridiculing those provincial organizations that tried to come up with blanket guidelines for the interrogators, Shkiriatov advised comrades to "let their general revolutionary instincts guide them—an individual approach is necessary."[16] All subsequent appeals for clarification were ignored: violations of Party regulations would have to be dealt with on a case-by-case basis.[17]

Indeed, more than applied ideology, Bolshevik discourse was a technique, a set of stratagems for describing and classifying people. The principles of the Bolshevik interrogation, whose practices were uniquely prone to reinterpretation and reconstitution, could be acquired only through apprenticeship. There could always be more than one criterion applied to each case depending on what part of the individual's life was being emphasized. The Party judged one only when one was believed to be fully responsible for one's actions. When did a specific individual became conscious of himself politically and ideologically? History designed specific ordeals for each and every individual. One could have been a youngster during 1917 or the Civil War, for example, in which case one's conduct in this momentous period was inconsequential. On the other hand, if one were already an experienced activist at that time one's actions carried great importance. In the latter case, one's conduct became indicative of one's soul and one was politically responsible for one's actions.

The 1926 investigation of Shergov from the Tomsk Technological Institute fleshes out the connection between the timetable of an individual conversion and the applicant's truthfulness.[18] Shergov's social background was mixed. As a contractor (a second guild-merchant) his father belonged with the class aliens, yet the family was involved in revolutionary activity. The Party organization was trying to determine whether he was a genuine recruit to Bolshevism or an individual seeking the spoils of power.

The discussion of Shergov's Party candidacy revolved around his conduct during the Civil War in his native Siberia, controlled by the Whites until late in 1920.

Q: But how did you end up in the White Army?
Shergov: I was in the east and they mobilized me from school.
Q: You were born in 1901 and mobilized in 1919?

Shergov: An order came to mobilize everyone between eighteen and
    forty years old. I served a mere six weeks [. . .] as a private. [. . .]
Q: Why didn't you become a partisan after deserting from the
    White Army?
Shergov: I was only eighteen. I wasn't up to it.
Q: Why is it that while your brothers and sisters entered the
    revolutionary sphere you trailed behind?
Shergov: [. . .] I didn't think about politics.

The year 1919 divided the wheat from the chaff in Siberia, as far as the
Bolsheviks were concerned, and in the year 1919 Shergov "spent a lot of
time at home." Not a promising beginning.

It got worse. A student named Poroskun, for example, reported that
he had talked to a Bolshevik in the institute who knew a certain Shergov
who had joined a scout organization although a Komsomol cell was right
nearby. Could Shergov have opted for this petit-bourgeois organization and
neglected its Bolshevik counterpart quite deliberately? The applicant denied
it: "I was in a students' cooperative and no other organization whatsoever.
[. . .] Yes, I knew about the existence of the Komsomol but did not join
because I was not fully aware at the time of its political goals."

Zel'manovich, the applicant's benefactor, intervened here: "Let's remember that Shergov was not politically mature at the time." By marking
1919 as a preadolescent stage in Shergov's journey from darkness to light,
Zel'manovich was suggesting that as time passed and Shergov's political
consciousness grew, and he learned to understand what was what. His
present application spoke for itself. But another student retorted: "Shergov
was about to graduate from high school at the time"—he was educated and
his political consciousness should already have been mature.

Finally it was Shergov's turn to take the floor. "I am offended by the
comrades who said that I want to weasel into the Party. I worked conscien-
tiously and had I not been a Communist in my soul [v dushe] I would not
have implemented [Bolshevik] directives."

Although the final vote approved his application seventeen to none
(with eight abstentions), Shergov's chances of remaining in the brotherhood of the elect for very long were quite slim.[19] The Party remained highly
ambivalent about the inclusion of students, that liminal group. The years of
NEP were no time to open the doors wide.[20] The Eleventh Party Congress
(held in spring 1922) raised the standards of admission for everybody

except bench workers.[21] "Let us admit only those comrades who will bring a genuinely healthy spirit into the Party and shut all others out."[22] Lev Kopelev recalled the rationale that convinced the Party to rescind its open admissions policy: "We believed that [. . .] it is only in those countries yet to undergo revolutions and civil wars that one can become a leader of the proletariat irrespective of social origins. [. . .] Since comparable ordeals were absent [in Soviet Russia], only workers and peasants were deemed sufficiently reliable to become Communists."[23]

The amended Party regulations of 1922 established three recruitment categories: "workers and Red Army soldiers from the working class and the peasantry," "peasants (other than Red Army soldiers)," and "employees, nonexploitative artisans, and others."[24] The new policy manifested itself in the variable number of recommendations required, the Party seniority of those offering recommendations, the administrative level at which final approval was made, and the length of the probation period—highly stringent for the last category, stringent for the second, undemanding for the first.[25] Nearly all students fell into unfavorable categories. Even those among them who had been sent to the university directly from the factory lost their former status. They became nonindustrial workers, a category that included couriers, guards, cleaners, and "workers in education."[26] Officials assumed that any student who had not previously worked had to be from the intelligentsia, a rather unattractive condition.[27]

But the transition of young Soviet society from military to civilian life was already fully underway and the pen had to replace the rifle.[28] Revolution in education was a protracted process, Party propagandists explained, but without it true proletarian emancipation was impossible.[29] Though many insisted on the inferiority of the study bench to the factory line, Red Army veterans streamed into institutions of higher education. The following poem by Strogatskii, a Bolshevik pundit, captured this trend:

So, where has our "bearded comrade" gone?
Is he a weary invalid, good for none?
No, he's a strongman,
Struggling on a new front
Fatigue? It's nothing!
At a time like this?
He's college student now - that's what he is![30]

[Nu gde zhe on, 'tovarishch Boroda'? / Ustalyi invalid, negodnyi nikuda?
/ Net, on silach vedet bor'bu, na fronte novom / Ustalost,' Chepukha!
Zhivem v takoi moment. / On nynche vuzovets, student!]

Among Bolshevik leaders, many feared that the flow of Party members
into the universities would precipitate a collapse of collectivist consciousness.
In late 1921, *Pravda* opened a public debate on the subject. A functionary
in the Moscow Party organization named Stukov said early in the debate
that university studies facilitated estrangement and warned that even
the best Party members indulged in "academic isolationism."[31] Stukov's
pessimism elicited a number of replies. Lozinskii's article, entitled "A Normal
Phenomenon," flatly denied "student disillusionment and anomie" and
disputed the assertion that students suffered from a "cowardly urge to flee
real life." Party members, he explained, embarked on the road of demanding
university studies because they wanted to acquire the knowledge that would
help them labor in the factories.[32]

M. Mironov's contribution, "False Alarm," was also upbeat. Communist
youths attended institutions of higher learning "not for the sake of academic
study per se, but to broaden their political thinking."[33] In "Knowledge for
the Proletariat" E. Preobrazhenskii insisted that worker interest in higher
learning was a "continuation of the October Revolution by different means,
a token of the determination to participate in a sphere where the proletariat
cannot count on an instant victory."[34] A group of students from Moscow
Sverdlov Communist University joined in the chorus that equated education
with ideological commitment. "What we do here should be viewed not as
a withdrawal into the self but as a search for a new way to approach the
masses. [. . .] Every day we ask ourselves what forms our ties to the local
proletariat should take and how we can gain maximum knowledge in the
shortest time before going back to production."[35] Eventually the Central
Committee decided that the university Party cells were the most expedient
option after all. There was simply no other way to secure the Bolshevization
of higher education.[36]

Because Siberia was controlled by the Whites for most of the Civil War,
the process there highlights many of the difficulties the Bolsheviks faced in
bringing the universities under their control. In 1920 the Central Committee
instructed the Siberian Party bureau to form academic committees in all
major cities; they were to function under the provincial Party apparatus.[37]
Easier said than done: the situation in Tomsk—a city known as the "Athens

of Siberia" for its long university tradition—was particularly dire.[38] At that time there were no Bolsheviks in Tomsk State University and no more than fifteen Bolsheviks in Tomsk Technological Institute. To cope with the shortage of manpower, an umbrella Party organization was created in the city, uniting the seventy-three student Bolsheviks resident in the city late in 1921.[39] It was not until spring 1923 that Party cells were established in each of the city's academic institutions.[40]

Conditions in Petrograd were only slightly better. Menshevik students heavily outnumbered Bolsheviks in 1917 and 1918, and during the 1921–22 academic year Party cells functioned in only twenty of the thirty-five local universities; sizeable Bolshevik contingents existed only in the Communist universities and the workers' faculties.[41] Once the government established a National Dispatch Commission in 1922, as part of a system for placing Party members in higher education, the tide had turned—the total number of Bolshevik students doubled in the course of one academic year, climbing to 4,250.[42] It must be emphasized, however, that while the Bolshevik presence in the universities grew this was only due to the admission of many incoming students who already possessed Party cards. As the example of the Leningrad Engineering Institute suggests, the number of students who joined the Party while studying at the university remained negligible.[43] Many applied, but the district Party committee demanded that all applicants be regarded as non-proletarians, a state of affairs that, according to the local Party bureau "renders their admissions process very difficult." Furthermore, the bureau was instructed to investigate the motives of those who sponsored students, insisting they carefully consider every recommendation.[44]

Even as they grew into robust entities, the university Party organizations were viewed with some suspicion throughout the 1920s.[45] Separated from the healthy industrial environment before their consciousness was fully developed, exposed to the lifestyle of the reclusive professoriate, students allegedly tended to succumb to "individualism," "philistinism," and "hypertrophy of the mind." Here we witness Bolshevik ambivalence toward mental labor as such. Even as they described it as an indispensable path to salvation, mental labor was perceived as a dangerous competitor to manual labor: excessive study threatened to turn workers into lascivious and weak-willed bourgeois. "Degeneration" (*upadok*) accounted for many anxieties regarding NEP: the revival of capitalism supposedly threw Soviet society backward into an era of unfettered economic competition associated with the animalistic state of human existence.[46]

Recommendations, Denunciations

Suspect from the outset, Party applicants were interrogated by the district committee, the Party bureau, and by the university Party cell. Workers and peasants were invited to participate in discussions, urged to divulge important detail, and to express their opinion on the students' merits and shortcomings. The truth about the self was at the heart of Party ritual; "faked" (*dutye*) autobiographies were dismissed.[47] "Sincerity" (*iksrennost'*) was the ultimate touchstone for a successful autobiographical self-presentation, no less important than "social position" or "revolutionary merits."[48]

According to the famous definition by Lionel Trilling, "sincerity is the avoidance of being false to any man through being true to one's own self." Trilling argues that while this state of personal existence was not to be attained without arduous effort, at a certain point in the history of Western Europe certain men conceived that the making of this effort was of supreme importance. In Bolshevik Russia, this process took a different inflection: the burden of establishing the truthfulness of the individual self previously carried by the church was shifted not onto unregulated agents evenly spread through society but onto the Party.[49]

The truthfulness of life-narratives was frequently challenged. Various autobiographical details reported by Leningrad Communist University students during the 1924 Party purge, for example, were dismissed as unlikely. The autobiography of Reztsov was described as "half true, half untrue."[50] His peers were highly skeptical of the author's claim that he had already possessed revolutionary consciousness at the age of six.

The autobiography of Petrova was subjected to even more careful scrutiny.[51] If Petrova was to be believed, she was "a daughter of an Old Bolshevik who was executed by the Whites in 1919 and a revolutionary almost from birth." Already in her teens she was an activist: she boasted that when in a professional school "the Party was already paying my tuition." In 1913, the autobiographer found employment as a day laborer, then as a seamstress. After the October Revolution she supposedly became an official informer for the Reds. "I combined my duties as the secretary of the Party cell with the work of a secret agent," and this activity carried great risks.

> When Kolchak advanced I had to be evacuated from Kushva [a factory on the Urals] together with my family. Just before we reached Viatka news came that Kolchak was retreating. During our roundabout return

we were captured by the Whites, brought to Kushva and kept under arrest for six months. The Whites whipped us and only the arrival of the Reds saved us from their hands.

According to her autobiography, Petrova moved to Cheliabinsk in 1921 and found employment in the local Cheka. "At that time, I was carrying out Party activity, serving as a secretary of the provincial Woman's Department and attending the local Party school."

Despite—or perhaps because of—so many exploits, Petrova's narrative was "suspicious" (*podozritel'naia*). Trying to undermine the author's proletarian credentials, Goriunov noted that "Petrova could not have become a day laborer at the age of twelve. It seems to me that she studied not until 1913, as she says, but at least until 1914." The episode with her arrest by the Whites was even less credible. "On the rolls of the Bolshevik political department and yet only whipped"—this Goriunov refused to believe. Kolchak's officers executed every Bolshevik they could lay their hands on. And who would believe that "whipping did not even interrupt her pregnancy?"

Additional contradictions were believed to be revelatory of the mendacious character of Petrova's writing: "thus she says she served as a 'responsible secretary' (*otvetstvennyi sekretar'*) in 1918. This position, however, was introduced only in 1919." Voronov found a particularly jarring distortion: "In 1918, Petrova worked in the Cheka, only seventeen years of age. She could not have been a secret agent because she entered the Party only in that year." Khadeev was even more sarcastic: "She was a Cheka secret agent, studied in a provincial Party school, worked with a group of lecturers and was a secretary of the women's department, all this at one and the same time—this is impossible!"

Even with her back to the wall, Petrova would not budge. "I reaffirm everything stated in my autobiography," she insisted. "Yes, I found my way in the Party early on because I always revolved in an exclusively Bolshevik milieu. Yes, I worked as a secret agent in the Cheka. And yes, whipping did not damage me or my child." Petrova mastered enough authority to deflect the charges of fraud. She was described as "intemperate and undisciplined" but not a liar and her Party career went on.

Framing the question of truth strictly in terms of correspondence between text and reality puts the historian of the Bolshevik autobiography in the position of a denouncer—an investigator/interrogator in his own right. Such a historian debunks the text, points to its omissions and lies, unmasks the narrator. According to this approach, truth is obtained by meticulously comparing the author's narrative with the other available records. Here the historian is loyal to the classic, Aristotelian distinction between history and fiction: "The distinction between historian and poet is not in the one writing prose and the other verse, as it would still be a specimen of history; it consists really in this, that the one describes the things that have been, and the other a kind of a thing that might be" (Aristotle, *Poetics*, 1451b).

According to the followers of Aristotle, a truthful autobiography is a critical scholarly biography. A French compendium of autobiographies from 1967 of Bolshevik leaders is indeed such a product insofar as it supplements each autobiography with a critical postscript that provides the reader with a more accurate reconstruction of the protagonist's life. Privileging truth as historical veracity, however, such an approach fails to appreciate truth as a construct: the official discourse produced truth by pitting narratives against each other, whether accurate or doctored, and adjudicating between them. Truth, in this scenario, was a matter of politics, not of a simple fact-finding procedure. "Each society," Foucault explains, has its "general politics of truth": that is, the types of discourse that it accepts and makes function as true; the mechanisms and instances that enable one to distinguish true and false statements, the means by which each is sanctioned. Foucault's additional comment that there is always a struggle over the status of truth and the political role it plays seems to be very pertinent to the Party organizations of the 1920s.[52] To treat Bolshevik poetics seriously, and to argue that— provided certain conditions are met—even the incredible can become truthful, does not mean that one must be blind to the difference between history and literature. Rather, it means that the root of this difference must be sought not in ontology, privileging the opposition between veracity and falsehood, but in practice, in the workings of the composition of the text and the conditions for its reception.

Obviously, students submitting their Party applications were not free to exercise their talents as writers and to come up with whatever stories they felt were most entertaining or most useful. Every narrative they composed was constrained by their need to foreshadow and neutralize damaging counternarratives. What they eventually confined to paper could be called the truth if by truth we understand not an objective state of affairs that precedes the act of writing but a product, a compromise that results from the clash between different versions of one's past put forward in a given place at a given time.[53]

Life stories had to be corroborated, and a student could not hope to enter the Party without strong recommendations from Bolsheviks who knew him or her well. The status of the recommenders was crucial, and after receiving the candidate's autobiography and opening a "personal file" (*lichnoe delo*) on the applicant, the secretary of the Party cell carefully recorded the recommenders' names and Party card numbers.[54] While the applicants were expected to take the initiative in gathering recommendations, conscientious Bolsheviks were duty bound to "draw" (*vovlekat'*) the uninitiated into the brotherhood of the elect.[55] The Party expected members to cast their gaze on the student body and single out the most deserving. Those who chose to support an application had to assume a considerable responsibility: the "recommender" (*poruchitel'*) had to aver that the "personal qualities of the student were absolutely indispensable for the work of the cell." Additionally, the recommender had to answer the following questions:

- How long have you known the applicant?
- How well do you know him?
- Did you meet the applicant at work or on a social occasion?
- What are the applicant's merits and what are his shortcomings?
- What are the applicant's motives for applying?
- Is the applicant motivated by a genuine desire to be a Party member, follow Party directives and abide by Party ethics?
- In what way has the applicant demonstrated his commitment to Communism in practice?[56]

At the end of his letter of support, the recommender signed his full name and specified his length of service for the Party, social position, and occupation.

Throughout the 1920s, Party authorities reiterated that recommendations must not be written "out of politeness" (*iz liubeznosti*).[57] Lenin proposed that letters be accepted only from persons who had observed the work of the applicant for at least one year; the suggestion was accepted and entered into the Party Regulations.[58] After a secret circular from the Siberian Control Commission informed the Tomsk Technological Institute that local Bolsheviks had "recommended socially alien individuals to the Party," the bureau demanded notification regarding each and every recommendation issued.[59] And it was officially stipulated that recommenders "carry full responsibility for their protégés (here & below)," and that cases of "irresponsible support of a candidate" would lead to recommenders being either reprimanded or even purged from the Party, "depending on the severity of their mistake." [60]

That this was not just bluster was demonstrated in the case of a certain Ershov. On April 10, 1924, this student from the Petrograd Agricultural Institute was arrested. After nearly three months of detention GPU (General Political Department, heir to the Cheka) released him on the condition that he was not allowed to return to Petrograd. Ershov found this stricture unjust: "My conviction was obviously based on a misunderstanding or on malignant libel." Announcing to everybody who would listen that he planned to take his appeal as high as the Supreme Soviet, if necessary, Ershov requested a recommendation that would "say the truth about my work in the student organizations as well as my general political profile." Three of the institute's Party members obliged, submitting recommendations that Ershov's case be reevaluated. With an audacity he was to regret, Ermolov, the most outspoken among Ershov's supporters, wrote:

> The fact that Ershov had the civic courage to question several truisms was interpreted by some as an anti-Soviet stance. But we should beware of citizens who unthinkingly accede to Party directives; they are as bad for the Reds as they are for the Whites. [. . .] In my view, the groundless arrest of Ershov and his expulsion from Petrograd are unfair. Better to let two criminals free than to convict one innocent person, let alone a worker or a peasant.

This sort of remonstrance was nipped in the bud. Ermolov was promptly summoned to the Party bureau where he was severely reprimanded "for defying GPU." He had questioned the authority of "the scourge of the counterrevolution" and this was duly noted by the local Party district committee; an entry to that effect was made in Ermolov's personal file and he was deprived of the right to recommend anybody else in the future. [61]

Writing a recommendation letter was an art. Since consciousness had superseded class as the principal criterion for admission to the Party, those who wrote letters emphasized, first and foremost, that their recommendees had completed the journey toward the light. Working-class origins alone were enough to guarantee admission to the proletarian university but were, by themselves, insufficient to ensure enrollment into the university's Bolshevik organization. As the following examples drawn from recommendations written for Party applicants at Leningrad State University suggest, only after political trustworthiness was ascertained could mention be made of the applicant's class background:

(1) "a member of the Komsomol since 1920, comes from working class family. In the university showed himself as a disciplined activist." (Zil'berova);

(2) "a member of the Komsomol since 1920, comes from a poor peasant family;" "served in the Red Army and was wounded" (Shkrabo);

(3) "a member of the Komsomol since 1922 who served as a volunteer in the Red Army. Now active in public work; recently contributed to the work of our purge committee. Has a drawback—mediocre political preparation" (Karpitskii);

(4) "*intelligentka*, disciplined" (Limberik)[62]

The last and rather laconic recommender implied that his protégé had overcome the imprint of petit-bourgeois background, and was now worthy of the Party card. Writing in support of the membership application of Smirnov to the Party cell of the Leningrad Agricultural Institute in 1927, his peer also masterfully played class and consciousness against each other to the applicant's benefit:

Having known Smirnov since 1921, I recommend him to the Party. Smirnov's dedication to his work as a tailor, as well as his proletarian psychology are so obvious that they illuminate his public life and his everyday conduct. Smirnov's proletarian convictions surface constantly in his contacts with his clients and in his family life, often leading to bitter disagreements on questions of religion.[63]

Though the recommender could not entirely dodge the issue of Smirnov's petit-bourgeois vocation, he ingeniously diverted attention away from the applicant's economic activity, portraying the applicant as a person with a "proletarian psychology." This flexibility was built into the Bolshevik discourse: the recommender had to decide whether to emphasize the economic activity of his protagonist or dwell on the applicant's ideological purity.

Soldatenkov's 1923 recommendation suggests that it was absolutely crucial to establish the applicant's political loyalty. In this case, the recommender alluded to the proletarian social origin of his protégé only in passing. The bulk of the text was dedicated to Soldatenkov's active engagement in the struggle for Bolshevik political supremacy in the university: "In 1921 and 1922, when Mensheviks, SRs, and Anarchists sabotaged student gatherings, Soldatenkov assisted our tiny Party cell in pushing through its resolutions. Today Soldatenkov works at Zinoviev University and spends his time only with Party members."[64] Similar stress is evident in the letter given in the mid-1920s to Malakhovich, a student at a technical school in Novgorod, when he applied to Leningrad Agricultural Institute. "I vouch (*ruchaius'*) for Malakhovich's loyalty," the recommender stated. "He stands fully on the Soviet platform."[65]

Subsequent to prominently posting the list of fresh Party applicants on its announcement board, the bureau appealed to all who knew the students in question "to advance oral or written statements against them." Admissions protocols always specified whether any denunciations against a given applicant had been received, and, if so, how many. Those who spoke up could choose not to reveal their names. The contents of the letter, however, had to be made available, both to the applicant and to the cell.[66]

While the recommendation was designed to measure the applicant's purity, denunciation, which in the official language was called "derailment" (*otvod*), unearthed the dark side of his biography.[67] Making perfect sense within the Bolshevik narratological framework, the literal sense of the term "derailment" suggested that the applicant had been "derailed," led astray or diverted from the normal progression to the light and that he therefore did not deserve to join the Party. Gusev, a secretary of the Central Control Commission stated during the Fourteenth Party Congress (December 1925): "I do not suggest we institute a Cheka within the Party. The Central Commission and the Central Control Commission should suffice; but I do think that every Bolshevik should be engaged in derailing the untrustworthy. If we have a problem it is not too many derailments but too few."[68]

The public nature of the derailment process is evident in the strongly worded derailment against Chumakov, a student at the Leningrad Agricultural Institute. What makes this letter, sent by the Kostroma Party organization and accusing Chumakov of a "gruff attitude toward workers," especially interesting is the threat with which it concluded: "When considering Chumakov's application please take our letter into account and think about inviting us to send a delegation to the relevant meeting of the institute's cell. In case you decide to do without us please promptly inform us of your decision so that we will have ample time to protest in front of the highest Party organs." Since the Party cell of the Agricultural Institute did not exist in a vacuum this letter could not go unnoticed. If enrolled, Chumakov would have had to be approved by the Leningrad district and provincial Party committees, which would have had to be attentive to derailment letters signed by eight Bolsheviks, two of whom had considerable length of service for the Party.[69]

Submitting a derailment was perceived neither as an ignoble betrayal of a colleague nor as an illegitimate tampering with someone else's private affairs.[70] It was common for Bolsheviks to be called on to comment not only on the public but also on the personal behavior of their peers.[71] (The Tenth Party Congress stipulated that denunciations against Party members may be accepted not only from their comrades but also from non-members.)[72]

Party authorities acknowledged that incessant meddling in the affairs of others could undermine the social fabric of the brotherhood of the elect. Bakaev, a member of the Central Control Commission, condemned the "unhealthy" growth of denunciations that prevented "a friend from telling his friend a sincere thought."[73] There were special terms for unfounded accusations—"slander" (*kliauza*) or "libel" (*nagovor*) were negative acts because they created "squabbles" (*skloki*) that undermined the collective.[74] The Party press periodically criticized such destructive practices as "dismembering" (*raznos*) and Lenin demanded that false denunciations be punished with death.[75] But in general letters of derailment were seen not as sources of discord within the Party cell but as remedies for it.

To be effective, such a letter had to be written by a proper Party member and aimed at a political alien. That many such letters were signed by anonymous "Communists" attests to the general understanding that only members in the brotherhood of the elect were experienced diagnosticians of consciousness.[76] The outcome of the contest between denouncers and recommenders depended on the reception of derailment efforts by the purge commission. If the detractor had made a convincing case in his accusation, his derailment was deemed truthful and he was declared a "loyal comrade." Conversely, if his charges were overturned, the detractor stood the risk of emerging as a class alien, his letter automatically classified as "libelous wrecking" (*vreditel'stvo*).

Schematically speaking, letters of derailment were inverted recommendations. Where the latter saw proletarian universalism, the former found only petit-bourgeois narrow-mindedness. The brief but stinging derailment against Gets, a Leningrad student, should be read in this light: "Gets's philistine upbringing is foreign to us—he comports himself like an old master."[77] An anonymous derailment letter had "unmasked" another Leningrad student applicant named Burdanov: "Burdanov's consciousness resembles the consciousness of a callous and uneducated kulak. When I asked him for a piece of bread (Burdanov had plenty back then) he rudely refused me. He is a negative type, aloof and vain." The narrative so carefully constructed by the applicant's recommenders—that their peasant protégé worked first as an "unskilled laborer in the wood industry" and then in a "private smithy," that he had tasted exploitation firsthand and therefore had recognized the Bolshevik truth—was completely shattered and Burdanov was rejected.[78]

The derailment against Pervutana from the Leningrad State University shows that the surest way to doom a Party application was to frame the applicant as one who sought admission because he wanted to get ahead in life.[79] Written by Maslenkov, a student at the Leningrad Mining Institute and a "Party member since 1918 who had realized that writing this letter is my Communist duty," the derailment letter stated: "We have to be especially cautious with Pervutana. Last year this daughter of a merchant tried to take advantage of my position as a secretary of the Party History Commission, repeatedly asking me for all kinds of papers [. . .] which she intended to use for personal gain." If Pervutana possessed any awareness, the letter implied, it was an awareness of her selfish, petit-bourgeois interest.

Charges against Party applicants' consciousness were intrinsic to the derailment genre. In June 1924, the Party cell of the Leningrad Engineering Institute issued personal evaluations to students that amounted to derailments: "politically colorless," "philistine," "politically not determined" (ne vyiasnen), "though a good expert, exhibited an anti-soviet deviation," "full of old traditions, active opponent of the proletarianization of the universities."[80]

The events at Leningrad State University surrounding the case of Knupt illustrate what happened when an application procedure degenerated into an all-out showdown between recommenders and denouncers.[81] On November 24, 1926, the local Komsomol organization turned down Knupt's application. The dry phrasing of the rejection—"Knupt failed to attend the three cell meetings during which her application was heard and her case was therefore dismissed"—hints that in this case that the balance of power between benefactors and detractors may have predetermined the upshot of the case. Indeed, the candidate's public hearing was in some cases entirely dispensed with (when, for example, the bureau received too much negative material) and in others rendered brief and automatic (when the letters of support were very strong); it all depended on the credibility of those who stood behind him or her.

Knupt was a daughter of an employee, and occupationally classified as a "student." Two strong recommendations maintained that Knupt "had proved to be dedicated to public work" and that she could be "only of benefit to any Communist cell." A third recommendation, signed by Stepanov, who was a sometime member of the local Party organization, said that Knupt was an "energetic comrade who can positively contribute to our work." But after the passage of a few months Stepanov withdrew the recommendation he had written on Knupt's behalf. Now he believed that Knupt was "ideologically immature." Another rumor, that Knupt "told the non-Party students that public work is carried out there by the least capable and the most stupid Party members," confirmed Stepanov's belated suspicions.

Finally, there was a letter of derailment signed by a certain Volkova; this especially extensive text flipped the applicant's "How-I-reached-Communist-consciousness" narrative on its head:

Having received the news that Knupt is trying to infiltrate our ranks, I feel it is my Party and Komsomol duty to forward some information that shows the person under discussion to be one whose place is not in our proletarian family. I have known Knupt since 1923. There is no need to explain here in detail what our universities were like in those years. [. . .] You all know the creative work our Party carried out in order to reform the universities [. . .] and you know that it encountered staunch resistance from the conservative bourgeois professors and their right arm, the White students. Part of this White scum populated our faculty of chemistry headed by Fainbergs and Verasovs and including students like Knupt. It was at this time, when a small Komsomol group did its best to implement Party policy, that these Knupts, Verasovs, and Co. committed their counterrevolutionary deeds. When we attended student gatherings in our capacity as Komsomol representatives they would yell, "spies!" at us. They would call the Party's cell "Party's dog" [a pun on "komiacheika" and "komiashcheika"]. Most of this putrescence is now outside the university. I say "most" because bits of this largely vanquished body are still with us, Knupt being a case in point. To be sure, in 1924 she and her gang were purged from the university [. . .] but thanks to their persistence they have had found a way back.

Needless to say, this sort of accusation, when credible, made it quite hard for an applicant to insist that she belonged to the proletarian commonwealth. Her denouncer went on to describe the period of organizing Party political groups from 1924 to 1926:

> Guess what Knupt did at the time? She pretended to take part in our work while all the time trying to undermine it from within. Each time Knupt showed up at the circle she would say, "Why the hell do we need all that, we students? Our business is to take from the university all professors have to offer and not to deal with Bolshevik politics."

Knupt's declarations supposedly contributed to the creation of a "sense of passivity among students."

The above letter of derailment was a sort of anti-biography. Volkova carefully preserved the codes of the autobiographical genre but her aim was just the reverse: to prove that Knupt's life demonstrated that she could never be a conscious Party member but in fact was, and would forever remain, an alien element. The letter's conclusion was particularly harsh: "Knupt needs Komsomol membership with which to mask her alien face." The applicant was so totally discredited that Stepanov, who must have been fairly close to Knupt to risk recommending one stigmatized as the "daughter of an employee," had to repent in writing.

Knupt's fate was sealed. Following an abortive attempt to join the brotherhood of the elect, she underwent the humiliation of seeing her status changed from that of nonaffiliated individual to counterrevolutionary. The cell now had a file with incriminating details against her that would be consulted whenever she attempted to reenter public life.

Final Stages

Party enrollment was an important affair, carried out with utmost seriousness.[82] Various Party bodies and potentates monitored the process, and could interfere and reverse it at any moment.[83] A student did not become a Party member until the bureau recommended his enrollment, the cell voted in his favor, and the district committee ratified this decision. At one point, the local Leningrad Party organization begged the Party leadership to make sure that "no more than six Party organs review a single student Party application."[84]

36

The movement of the case of Filatov from Leningrad State University shows how long things could take.

**Table 1. Timetable of the movement of the case of Filatov
from the Leningrad State University, 1924–1926**

Filatov submitted an application	April 5, 1924
The bureau of the Party cell at Leningrad State University discussed Filatov's application	October 22, 1924
The cell's general meeting declined his application	November 10, 1924
The bureau discussed his appeal	April 14, 1925
The general meeting of the cell accepted the bureau's recommendation to accept Filatov	April 16, 1925
Vasil'evsk Island Party district committee ratified the decision of the Leningrad State University Party cell	August 19, 1925
The Leningrad provincial party committee asked for additional personal evaluations on Filatov	November 2, 1925
Leningrad State University Party cell submitted additional personal evaluations on the applicant	December 15, 1925
The district committee approved Filatov's candidacy	March 17, 1926
The provincial Party committee voted down Filatov's application	June 7, 1926

It took over two years to reject this Leningrad university student. For the sake of comparison, it is worth noting that the status of full Party members was conferred on industrial workers (who were relegated to the first category, barred before students) after only six months.[85]

No candidate could skip the stage of Party candidacy—a period of probation during which the Party tested the loyalty and maturity of the newcomer.[86] According to the instructions of the Leningrad Party committee from March 1923, the university Party bureau had to ascertain that every individual promoted to full membership was on probation for a period stipulated in the Party regulations (the exact duration depended on one's class position), had completed a course of studies at a school of political education, and had procured fresh recommendations.[87]

The student who was found to be hostile to Communism was turned down flat. His futile attempt to win admission was carefully recorded and generally functioned as a guarantee that other Party organizations would also reject him. Those students who were seen as on the right track but still requiring considerable spiritual development were counseled by the Party to reapply at a later date. In such cases, it was said that "the applicant is not fully developed" (*nedostatochno razvit*)—the soil was fertile but the fruit had not yet ripened. Thus, for example, the Leningrad State University Party organization rejected Burdanov as someone who "has not yet demonstrated his worth" (*sebia ne proiavil*).[88]

Student applicants knew they were expected to apply to the Party only when their inner self was ripe for Communism. Although Konstantinovskii, a student at Leningrad Communist University, acted as a Bolshevik early on and in 1918 sided with the Reds during the Ukrainian Civil War campaigns, he joined the Party ranks only when "he took his final shape" (*okonchatel'no oformirovalsia*). The timing of Konstantinovskii's admission—the November 1919 "Party Week"—which coincided with the transporting of fresh recruits to the front—proved that he was truly "conscious" (*soznatel'nyi*). Only conscious Bolsheviks, so the assumption went, would risk their life for the embattled proletarian republic.[89]

"Transfers" (*perevody*) to full Party membership indicated perseverance, discipline, and respect of Party regulations. The Leningrad Party committee instructed in March 1923 that before handing one a permanent Party card, the bureau had to ascertain whether the candidate was on probation for a period stipulated in Party regulations and whether he had procured fresh recommendations.[90] When granted full voting rights such a person was supposed to be well versed in social and political questions, domestic as well as international. To ascertain the level of his "political maturity" (*politicheskaia zrelost'*) bureau members questioned him in detail.[91]

When Sobolev faced the Party cell at the Smolensk Technological Institute in 1921 it was soon clear to all that he had been a Party candidate for a suspiciously long time. Could it be that he was waiting to see whether the Reds would win before finally tying his fate with theirs? Sobolev introduced as a character witness a veteran who had served with him in a special detachment of the 53rd Red Army Division, a certain Khoroshkin. Noting the candidate's proletarian origins, "his service as an excellent military specialist" and "his participation in the suppression of Kronstadt,"

Khoroshkin persuaded the cell that Sobolev had not opportunistically postponed his transfer to full Party membership.[92]

Even more contentious, the debates concerning the promotion request by Vinichek, a student at Tomsk Technological Institute, give a good view of the centrality of procedure in Party enrollment. We are helped by an unusually rich transcript in this case: the importance of strong recommendations, the authority of the bureau, and the role of the rank and file in judging an applicant all come into sharp focus.

Following official regulations, Vinichek's application was first examined by the cell's bureau on January 30, 1926. His autobiography told the story of a thirty-four-year-old peasant who applied for Party membership in 1920 while serving in the army. As six years had elapsed and a Party candidate could be on probation for no more than two years, Vinichek's indeterminate status was an embarrassment to the bureau. The jokes that ensued suggest a certain uneasiness:

Petukhov: Why are you still a candidate after five years?
 This is far too long!
Vinichek: [Since I have been constantly in transit,] I've had no one
 to vouch for me.
Petukhov: What are you, a migratory bird [*pereletnaia ptichka*]?
Kaziukin [looking into the questionnaire]: What kept you from
 becoming a full member in the workers' faculty? [. . .]
 Are we supposed to believe that no one came to know you
 during your two years of studies there?
Vinichek: Comrades in the Omsk workers' faculty barely knew
 my character.
Kaziukin: And in the army?
Vinichek: There were very few Communists in my unit.

The dilemma of the bureau members was articulated most clearly by Kuznetsov: "On the one hand, the grounds for promoting Vinichek to full membership are weak. On the other hand, we cannot keep him as a candidate any longer." At this point, Klikunov, the secretary of the Party organization, consulted the recommendations again: "Two letters have a minus, two a plus, and one is indeterminate." At this point the transcript reads "Thinking," meaning that there was a pause in the discussion. "Heavy is the cap of Monomakh," Kaziukin joked breaking the silence with a reference to a proverbial Russian expression indicating that authority comes with heavy responsibility.

Klikunov solicited suggestions on how to vote. Soloviev proposed to abstain, but this suggestion was ridiculed: "What does 'abstaining' mean?" The implication would be that the bureau had refused to do its duty. Klikunov wanted to know who had persuaded Vinichek to submit his belated application: "Did you apply only when Comrade Andrianov approached you?" When Vinichek replied in the affirmative, Klikunov said he had been prodded by others, implying that he had no real interest in the Communist Party. Kaziukin lunged: "Let's purge him!" And that is what the bureau put as its final recommendation.[93]

Three months later, on May 4, 1926, Vinichek faced the Party cell assigned to look further into his case. Students confronted him with miscellaneous questions about his autobiography:

Q: What did you do for the working class during your studies at Omsk?
Vinichek: I did no public work because I was simultaneously a student and a Red Army serviceman.
Q: What were your army duties? Did you choose them or were they forced on you?
Vinichek: I was nominated to be the secretary of a military committee.
Q: How do you explain your constant redeployment?
Vinichek: Strategic considerations.

Then students asked the bureau to explain why it had voted in favor of purging Vinichek. Klikunov spoke up:

We discussed this case endlessly. Our impression was that Vinichek did not apply for full membership because he was alienated from the Party. Comrades who recommended him depicted him in strong colors, arguing that they knew his "psychology" and "ideology." I think it's all bogus. Further on, his work in the institute's professional committee was not great. [. . .] He did not prove himself a disciplined comrade.

Heated debates ensued, with the speakers constantly interrupting each other. Citing the importance of Party democracy, everybody claimed to have something important to say:

Subotin: Vinichek is an awful individualist.

Kusanov: Vinichek was in the Red Army for five years and now we
    want to get rid of him with the stroke of a pen—this is wrong!
    [. . .] Regarding his alleged individualism: I approached him more
    than once in difficult times and he never turned me down.

Brukner: I remember Vinichek from the workers' faculty as someone
    who could not care less about Party activity. [. . .]

Gliukin: I was in the Red Army and know how difficult it is to join
    the Party there. The transitory nature of the service prevents one
    from making friends or getting acquainted with the environment.
    The army makes one unapproachable. [. . .]

Shcherbakov: Remember, Vinichek volunteered for the Red Army!

Voice from the audience: I thought volunteers were at the front rather
    than sitting in headquarters and offices.

The debate recapitulated the points already voiced at the bureau meeting.
Still, the sticking point was timing: was Vinichek's failure to transfer to full
Party membership a token of his army-bred alienation, or was he an unjustly
persecuted veteran haunted by the undependable social fabric of military
life? Enter Zaikin:

Although I am a bureau member, I missed the meeting where Vinichek's
candidacy was discussed. [. . .] I know Vinichek from the Omsk workers'
faculty as a loyal comrade. When famine raged and people tore up their
Party cards, he applied to the Party. Surely this means he has strong
convictions. [. . .] Vinichek did not want to make a nuisance of himself
and the bureau ignored him.

With Zaikin now siding with Vinichek, the authority of the bureau was
shaken. The applicant's supporters launched an offensive, determined to
shift the burden of proof from the candidate to the leadership of the cell.

Dolgov: The bureau paid insufficient attention to Vinichek and
    failed to notice his political development. How can it assign tasks
    to Vinichek if it's not even aware that he exists?

Kostyliuk: None of those who are speaking against Vinichek today
    had the guts earlier to denounce him for failing to execute his
    Party duties properly. They tried to frame him; they collected

material to attack him.

Polonskii: The Party purges people from the following categories: aliens, hangers on, and those deemed organizationally inadequate and passive. Even if Vinichek somehow fits the last category, what is the Party supposed to do with passive people? It must attempt to make them active, not rush to purge them!

Sensing a certain shift in the cell's disposition, Klikunov tried to wrap up the hearings with a final speech on behalf of the prosecution. "Comrades have appealed to unsubstantiated facts in their efforts to defend Vinichek. Though this student may have heroic achievements to his credit, this does not mean that he cannot be expelled from the Party." Taking the laudatory comments one at a time, Klikunov debunked the case for Vinichek:

- Shcherbakov adds little when he talks of Vinichek's bogus glory in the army.
- And Zaikin is wrong to say that [Vinichek applied to the Party just as the Soviet regime ran into trouble and] others were tearing up their Party cards. The Red Army was chasing down the last of the White dogs at the time. Vinichek is a small contributor to the collective if all this means is that he helped Zaikin and Shcherbakov solving problems in arithmetic.
- Yes, about Polonskii: he has no idea what he is talking about! Classifications will get him nowhere. Yes, we regard Vinichek as a passive comrade. Did he ever prove he is anything else?

But protocol assigned the final word to the applicant: Vinichek had been recognized as an enfranchised individual, a self-possessed actor who could defend his own interpretation of the Bolshevik symbolic order. And he did not hesitate to criticize his critics:

- During his time on the professional committee, Akimov did nothing himself. He has a personal grudge against me.
- Then there is Klikunov. Where on earth did he come from? If we had not stood firm in 1918 he would not be standing here talking to us!

By speaking bluntly and fashioning himself as an uncouth but authentic worker, Vinichek carried the day: sixty-one students supported his promotion to full Party membership against only twenty-eight who wanted to see him purged.[94]

The odds had been against the bureau from the beginning of the Party cell meeting. Though bureau members had never been confident of their characterization of the applicant, they believed they were obliged to present the grassroots with an authoritative evaluation of Vinichek's social physiognomy. Facing an accusation that hinged almost exclusively on his alleged carelessness about rules, the defendant nevertheless found a way to turn Party regulations against his high-standing detractors. It was not he who shunned Party activity; the fault lay with the bureau that refused to assign him duties befitting his level of political development. Of course, procedural matters seldom dominated the discussion of an applicant's candidacy to this extent. In most cases the bureau, functioning in its usual role of reader of the applicant's soul, asserted its authority and had its recommendation rubber-stamped.

The date of one's admission was marked as the apotheosis of one's moral, theoretical, and political mind.[95] The crucial date was that upon which one's full membership was ratified, and it became the basis for calculating one's "length of service for the Party" (*partiinyi stazh*).

Bolsheviks with length of service for the Party harking back to the years of the underground enjoyed a special prestige. They were assigned to check-up teams, as well as verification and purge commissions, and were invited to "evenings of remembering" held by the Party's history department. Apparently some treated their Party seniority as a source of overweening pride, and Zinoviev felt obliged to curb comrades' ardor at the Eleventh Party Congress: "Seasoned Party members must be more tactful and will please refrain from bragging that 'I can work better than you—look how long my Party beard is!' Younger comrades naturally get upset over this kind of taunt and there's little they can do but retort with, 'Fine, but do not push it in my face!' "[96]

Some Bolsheviks maintained that their contributions to the Party were so obvious and so well known that they resented having to undergo a process of certification. Piotr Zalutskii refused to exchange his untainted charismatic authority for a piece of paper, though this Party record would have been impressive. From a worker background, this overseer of the Party's education activities in Leningrad until the mid-1920s had risen to fame as a member of the Petrograd revolutionary committee during the Bolshevik seizure of power. When D. Sarkis, the deputy head of the Leningrad Provincial Committee, asked him to report to the Department of Cadres in 1925, Zalutskii brusquely replied "I do not want to turn in any questionnaires or personal evaluations to Party clerks. They should know me without such formulaic documents." Writing in the third person singular, this resplendent hero of the Bolshevik underground wrote across the otherwise blank questionnaire: "The Party is quite familiar with Comrade Zalutskii."[97]

But this was an exceptional case. By the mid-1920s, mighty efforts had been made to regularize the way personnel were accounted for. In May 1924 the Leningrad Party apparatus called for all Communist students to register. The universities were to prepare a letter of evaluation for each student, sending one copy to the district committee and another to the provincial committee. The Party cell was to prepare two copies of each personal file, keeping one in the cell's bureau, the other at the district Party committee.[98]

Kvachko, a student at Leningrad Communist University, grew irritated when asked to report on his past Party activity for a second time. "When I enrolled at the university in September 1923," he complained, "I delivered my personal file to the head of the university secretariat. [. . .] Five months later, however, I was invited to the Party offices again to fill out the paperwork again. [. . .] Such an attitude toward comrades' documents is unacceptable!" When something similar happened to Golubeev, a student at the same university, in February 1924, he took a resolute stand. "I see no need to produce a duplicate of my personal file," he stated in a letter to the Party bureau.

> Copies of such a file must exist somewhere. [. . .] When I first arrived at the university in September 1922 I handed it to the bureau, including the certificates regarding my previous Party activity. The district committee made a second copy of my personal file when I was given a new Party card on October 25, 1922. I am sure that you will be able to find this file at least, especially since when I was summoned to the control commission in December 1923 I saw my file lying on the table."[99]

Obliged to ensure that the information it had on each student was accurate, the university Party cell checked and rechecked the relevant materials. In fall 1923, Ivanov, the local Party secretary, sent the following letter to the Odessa Party committee: "Shkol'nik's Party card does not state whether he went through the 1921 check-up. This student claims that he reregistered in Moscow. [. . .] We sent a request for information to the address he specified but no response was forthcoming. Can you shed light on this matter?"[100] In a similar case, the local bureau asked the Nizhni Tagil regional

Party committee for clarification about the student Krasilova (October 4, 1923). "In the Party card you issued, her name and surname were originally written in red ink and then written over with black ink" and forgery of identity could not be ruled out.[101]

No matter how bureaucratized, Party induction was the most important rite of passage in the early Soviet society. Once his or her status was approved by the Party offices, the inductee had joined an elite order of dedicated builders of the future. Such a convert was believed to have exceptional epistemological capabilities—he or she had an intimate understanding of the historical process and its impact on the progress of the human mind. This lofty status involved serious responsibilities: unlike the non-missionary religious virtuosos, permitted to bask in the light of the perfection they had attained, Bolsheviks had to seek out the citizens of the young Soviet Republic and open their eyes to the truth of Communism.

CHAPTER 2
Workers Toward the Light

THE DISCOURSE OF CLASS PERMEATED ALL SPHERES of Bolshevik academic life. This was true of the vocabulary of university Party cells, intermediary state and academic bureaucratic bodies, sociologists, psychologists, and, most importantly, students themselves. In the daily life of the brotherhood of the elect, class was a complex network of significations that had to be handled with extreme care. It took the form of a ritual of words and deeds that had to be performed faultlessly. Although students could disagree with this or that aspect of the official policy, they were obliged to appeal for membership in the name of class.[1]

From the Marxist perspective, capitalist economy polarized society into proletarians and bourgeois. Following the withering away of the distinction between mental and manual labor (the intelligentsia and the workers) and between agricultural labor and industrial labor (the peasantry and the workers), intermediary classes were destined to disappear. But in the meantime NEP economics preserved a wide spectrum of classes, class-groupings, and class layers, related to the somewhat amorphous petit-bourgeoisie.[2] "During the Civil War we divided society in two, those with us and those against us," wrote Vinokur, a contemporary language theorist. "But NEP came and disrupted all. No longer waging an open war against each other, good and evil coexist today within the same collective."[3]

The lingering of "intermediary classes" (*promezhutochnye klassy*) on the historical scene, chiefly the peasants and the intelligentsia, was held to be the result of the relative backwardness of the Russian economy. These social groups were not necessarily antagonistic to the working class; should they understand the inexorable course of historical development, so the Bolsheviks were saying to themselves, intelligentsia and peasants were bound to join workers in their rightful struggle for the abolition of exploitation on earth. In fact, in Lenin's analysis from 1921–22, their collaboration with the workers was vital for the successful completion of the revolution and the building of classless society. In the end, they were destined to merge with the working class.[4]

The ambivalence regarding proletarian allies was reflected in the ever-changing admission clauses appearing in the Party regulations in the 1920s.

At times, the enrollment of anyone other than "workers from the bench" was prohibited. In other periods, the "non-exploiting peasants" and the "toiling intelligentsia" were welcomed in. But no student appeared before the Party organization as socially undetermined. One of the first queries in the questionnaire an applicant had to fill out addressed the issue of his or her class affiliation.[5] One's recommendation letters, declaration, auto-biography, all the material in one's application dossier, revolved around that subject. A worker would typically argue that it was natural for him or her to join the Party because it embodied the will of his or her class. A peasant or a member of the intelligentsia explained that he or she wished to assist the working class struggle for emancipation.

The tension between the notion of a party as a uniform and united brotherhood and a notion of a party as a bunch of individuals belonging to different classes was not resolved during NEP.[6] On the one hand, Lenin maintained already in 1902 that, due to the professional revolutionaries' supreme consciousness, "all distinction between workers and intelligentsia must be utterly obliterated."[7] The message of the Ninth Party Conference (1920) emphatically reiterated his position: "Party members may be distinguished solely in terms of the level of their consciousness, loyalty, temperance, political maturity, revolutionary experience, and their readiness for self-sacrifice. No other basis of discrimination between Communists will be tolerated."[8] Iakovleva explained a few months later that "the division of people into classes, which we Marxists are obliged to carry out, is impermissible and illegal within the Party itself. If we enroll someone, that person must be granted rights equal to those of everybody else, regardless of their class origins."[9] But the Party never succeeded in becoming the melting pot it tried to be. Summarizing a comprehensive Party purge that had just came to an end, the Twelfth Party Conference (August 1922) lamented "the unevenness in the class composition of the Party, particularly in times of NEP."[10]

But how was class identity to be determined in individual cases? Insofar as it dismissed the "individual" as little more than a bourgeois fetish designed to conceal the reality of class relations, the official theoretical canon provided little insight into this question.[11] When the Bolsheviks needed to apply Marxist analysis to concrete Party members they found nothing better to consult than personal biographical narratives. Economic analysis alone was unable to determine what in the life circumstances of this or that individual was decisive for the determination of class interest; was it family background, material well-being at the moment, profession and employment prospects? Clearly, political and cultural aspects of the self had to be considered as well.

Class taxonomies could be controlled by the ideological apparatus; their application could not be. Identities were constituted through micropractices that interpreted, modified, and sometimes even subverted the official lexicon. The Party cell was on its own when it came to adjudicating the social characteristics of this or that student. In establishing the boundary between the ins and the outs, the grassroots not only made ad hoc pronouncements in the realm of theory but also deployed controlling techniques that delineated the implications of the various identities the subjects took. From this perspective, class may be seen as an index of shifting power relations within the brotherhood of the elect.

Party admission statistics, which have so much to say about class, will occupy us in this chapter. The significance of these data, however, is not self-evident. It is not that admission figures were somehow fraudulent, or failed to capture the objective reality they supposedly aimed at; the more urgent problem is that a preoccupation with quantities leads to a neglect of the qualities that admission figures were supposed to represent. If we focus on the validity of the data, we leave unquestioned the paradigm that drove their collection in the first place. Since I prefer to concentrate not on measuring the success of the proletarianization of the Party but on the logic that originally set the parameters of this policy, statistical tables are scrutinized below not as (quantitative) data but as (qualitative) texts.[12]

By dwelling on the indeterminacy of the Party's methods of class categorization I hope to demonstrate the constructed nature of the Communist class typology. Statistics, then, become less a presentation of reality than an active force in its shaping. Rather than simply casting their nets and drawing in the proletarians, what the Party statisticians were actually doing was turning individuals who belonged to specific prerevolutionary occupational, estate, or ethnic categories into proletarians. By establishing the criteria for admission, statistical tables taught students which categories of people were welcome into the brotherhood of the elect and which had no place there.

The social makeup of the individuals dispatched to the Siberian Communist University in the fall of 1923 demonstrates the improvised nature of this social classification. The university bureau used categories in a lax manner, often confusing "social origins," "estate," and ideological characteristics in its description of students. Laptev, an "employee," was described in terms of his "material well-being" (*imushchestvennoe polozhenie*), before the Revolution and at the present. When the secretary of the Party committee addressed the pre-1917 part of Laptev's life, he mentioned "former estate affiliation" (*byvshaia soslovnaia prinadlezhnost'*):[13] the grandfather of the student in question, so the record read, was a "peasant" and his father a "worker." It should be noted that, according to all Marxist class theorists, not only was estate affiliation largely unhelpful in establishing one's class identity but Laptev's father also could hardly belong to the "workers' estate" since such an estate denotation simply did not exist in Imperial Russia.[14]

The estate affiliation of Mashkin's grandfather, to give another example, was listed as "a peasant and a worker"—clearly the bureau could not make up its mind how to describe him. In the social position column Mashkin was said to be a "student"—in this case, class and occupation were confused. Later on, Mashkin was portrayed as a "worker, with a steady proletarian psychology, someone who does not deviate from Marxism. [. . .] No petit-bourgeois inclinations were recorded in his physiognomy."[15] Here it is clear that character and political outlook interfered with what was supposed to be a more technical and objectively established class affiliation. By contrast, Sergeev's class position was defined in close accordance with the book. This student was a "peasant" in terms of his social position and a "poor peasant" (bedniak) in terms of his material well-being. To rule out the possibility that Sergeev was a kulak the bureau was compelled to add that Sergeev had a "good proletarian psychology; he approached economic questions correctly" [i.e., supported NEP].[16]

Of course, most Party members came to the university with an already fixed class identity. The statistician of the cell could not easily change what had figured in the Party card's "social position" rubric.

Whereas most of the Party members accepted into the Tomsk Technological Institute were toilers, in the Tomsk State University non-manual laborers heavily predominated. A cause of great concern to the local Party leadership, the nonproletarian composition of the university's Party cell stemmed from the university curriculum, "attractive mainly to the intelligentsia."

All organizations dispatching Communists to the universities were supposed to prefer individuals with "substantial experience in physical work." It is highly doubtful, however, that "workers" who made their way to the Tomsk Technological Institute (25 out of the total 49 new students), matched this ideal type. A good half of those described as "workers" by the trade unions that sent them were in fact semi-industrial laborers, lower service personnel, or fresh Party recruits carrying out white-collar functions. When we turn to examine the professions of the "workers" dispatched by the workers' faculties, we find "modelers," "gold sewers," "binders," "hat makers"—in short, individuals hardly deserving the title "workers from the bench." [17]

Table 2. Class Composition of Communists Enrolled into Tomsk Universities (1923)

Social Origins	Technological Institute	State University
Workers from the bench	17	4
Peasants from the plow	4	5
Workers' children	8	-
Peasants' children	3	1
Toiling intelligentsia	15	25
The children of the toiling intelligentsia	2	1
Others	–	–
Total	49	36

Source: GANO, f.1053, op.1, d.682, l.23.

Rather than reading statistics of class as a description of social reality and assuming that those sent to study were workers in the sociological sense of the term, we must conclude then that a student became a "worker" if he was dispatched to the university by a "workers' organization." Class, never simply there to be found and promoted, was an ascriptive category. Working-class identity was manufactured by the Bolshevik discourse in a circular fashion: a "proletarian" organization delegated the worker status to its protégés by virtue of classifying them as such.

Declarations—A Synchronic View of the Self

The assignment of a Party member into a statistical category was only the starting point. Class identity was soon elaborated through an increasingly subtle classification of moral and psychological characteristics. Schematically speaking, the practice by which a student became a subject of class took two additional forms that interlocked in ways that we shall presently consider. First, the objectivizing of the speaking subject in the process of interrogation—the student had to justify the identity he chose for himself during the elaborate admission ceremonies and Party purges. And second, self-objectification—by recognizing the properties that went along with a class identity, the student had to turn him- or herself into his or her own object, to be fashioned through autobiographical writings.[18]

We can introduce the issue in a nutshell by utilizing the brief "declaration" (*zaiavlenie*), a cover letter of sorts that every Party applicant was expected to compose. Whereas in the autobiography nothing was supposed to overshadow the narrative element, in the declaration the applicant constructed an abstract argument for his or her admission. This was a portrait rather than a history.

In stating the author's affinity with the Party, a declaration typically consisted of three thematic propositions that could be arranged into a coherent argument. The first proposition argued that one was drawn toward the proletarian Party, the second supplemented it by saying that one had achieved proletarian consciousness, and the third went on to conclude that, having reached proletarian consciousness, one realized that it was one's duty to struggle for the proletarian revolution with the Party—the agency entrusted with the historical task of achieving this goal.[19]

Basking in compliments such as "these youngsters just came from the industrial line," or "the local youth is removed from the ugly phenomena of NEP," the workers' faculty students at Tomsk State University felt entitled to style themselves as the Party's natural raw material. "I applied to the Party," student declarations stated:

- "Out of class instinct"; (Kubanova, a peasant);
- "Spontaneously. On the front I voted the Bolshevik ballot for the sole reason that this was the ballot that opposed war"; (Beliaev, a peasant);
- "Lacking consciousness. A Women's Department was opened and all present in the inaugural meeting were [automatically] enrolled as candidates into the Party"; (Skurikhina, a peasant);
- "After demobilization. I did not join any other party because on the front only officers joined the SRs while workers joined the Party"; (Arkhipov, a worker).

In all these declarations the motivation to become a Party member was couched in terms of a natural drive, not a rationally mediated decision. The absence of intention was no little matter—it amounted to the applicant's confession that his or her consciousness was rudimentary. The overarching assumption was that it was somehow "natural" for proletarian students to seek Party membership even if they could not always explain what exactly attached them to Bolshevism. The declaration of the "worker" Bykovskii shows this point well:

> Employed in a trade union workshop in Biisk in 1917, I sensed in practice the difference between socialized work and work for private owners. The ban on our workshop only increased my antipathy toward Kolchak. My sympathy to the Bolsheviks under whose rule owners were prevented from squeezing the last juice from workers grew. To live under the Bolsheviks one has to help them fight against counterrevolution.

Bykovskii stressed his emotions—his "sympathies" and "antipathies"—his declaration mentioned neither the Party nor its program as catalysts of his spiritual transformation.

Of course, not all Tomsk State University workers' faculty applicants gave up claims for a deliberate decision to enter the Party. Some professed to have occupied an intermediary semiconscious position. In writing that he joined the Party out of revolutionary "feeling and conviction accumulated during Kolchak's reaction," the peasant-student Bakhturov, for example, attributed to himself at least a flickering of self-awareness. Other declarations stressed consciousness (the second proposition in our typology) in an even more straightforward fashion. Students joined the Party

- "out of conviction"; (Kovalev, a peasant);
- "as a worker who became conscious of the Party ideas"; (Belykh, a peasant);
- "following an in-depth view into my class identity"; (Bobylev, Alfred, and Burlakov, all peasants).

Finally, there were a few declarations that stressed awareness of the Party's historical role, thus deploying the entire declaration syllogism. In these cases, the applicants claimed to have applied to the Party:

- "so that I could take an active part in the construction of the Communist society"; (Chukhlov, a peasant);
- "for the sake of participation in an organized struggle against the bourgeoisie"; (Musatov, a peasant who turned into a merchant);
- "because I realized it is the duty of every worker to defend the interest of the toiling masses"; (Silkin, a son of a factory worker and a housekeeper).

How students crafted their declarations clearly depended on the class identity they indicated in the questionnaire. Confident that the Party would enroll them anyway, relying on the milieu in which they revolved to upgrade their consciousness, workers did not have to present themselves as fully self-aware. Students whose social identity was said to be in a state of flux and possibly even degenerating, on the other hand, had to present a more sophisticated motive to become Communists.

The preference shown by students in the highbrow Leningrad State University in claiming advanced consciousness in the present further corroborates the notion that the deeper Party applicants dove into the recesses of the declaration poetics to argue their case, the less likely were they to be a proletarian. "Every additional breath of proletarian air I inhaled," the white-collar Susurin wrote, "improved my understanding of politics. Now I comprehend what the working class struggles for." [20] The declaration of his colleague, Nikonskii, also boasted mastery of the Party credo to compensate for his petit-bourgeois social position: "Since I feel I am prepared to carry out the Party tasks, I wish to become an activist who propagates among the worker-peasant masses." While in declarations submitted by the Tomsk State University workers faculty proletarian identity usually came first, and consciousness only second, the last two examples suggest that applicants from Leningrad State University began with contending that revolutionary consciousness made them proletarian and then concluded that, as proletarians in spirit, their place was in the Party. This reversal of order points to an important difference between a typically proletarian self-fashioning and the self-fashioning of the Bolshevik intelligentsia. We shall see below how this played itself out in the longer student autobiographies. [21]

Proletarian Origins

The Bolsheviks maintained that the workers were the most suitable candidates for the Party. Their experience as laborers in large plants and their wretched living conditions in the overpopulated cities of late imperial Russia supposedly taught them that their predicament could be improved only collectively, through a highly organized state action. "At various times various people have believed themselves to be messiahs called to save the world," Gorky announced in 1919. "These days, History has bestowed this mission on the [. . .] Russian working class—a model for the rest of the world."[22]

Workers were said to possess remarkable epistemological acuity. Separation from the means of production turned them into the first unselfish class history had ever known. Because the bourgeois was guided by greed alone (in the context of class epistemology, the term "bourgeoisie" should be understood to include all property owners, including "artisans" and "peasants"), his perception of reality was distorted. The proletarian was poised to transcend the limits of the individualist mind: "The large factory, where every article passes through hundreds of hands prior to its completion, destroys the spirit of individualism," argued one of the heads of the Bolshevik educational establishment, Martyn Liadov. " 'We create!', 'We produce!', says the worker. Life itself whispers in his ear that only by a collective effort can he improve his plight."[23] Based on that principle, Anatolii Lunacharskii, the commissar of enlightenment, deduced workers' theoretical sagacity: "Nothing but working class affiliation could prepare an individual to embrace Marxism."[24]

Many students insisted on working-class affiliation despite all odds, painstakingly constructing their autobiographies accordingly. Kondrat'ev from the Petrograd State University claimed in his 1923 Party application he was a "worker" although he had been employed in administrative jobs for a number of years by then. His parents gave him even more trouble. "True, by social origin my father is a peasant," his autobiography maintained. "Yet, very young, he became an artisan. He used to work as a hired laborer in privately owned shops." Turning to his mother, the autobiographer wrote that "in terms of her social origin, she is a Petersburg petit-bourgeois (meshchanka) who worked as a tailor in private shops." When Kondrat'ev's father died from consumption (February 1917) his mother married "another baker." In autumn 1921, the couple opened a bakery of their own. "This," Kondrat'ev hastened to add, "was strictly an artisan enterprise, based on family labor and entailing no exploitation whatsoever." By channeling the descriptions of his family background in a proletarian direction and emphasizing his status as a student in the workers' faculty, Kondrat'ev did his best to present himself as a worker of sorts.[25] Apropos such applications, Shkiriatov said at the Eleventh Party Congress (1922), "Many frequently count themselves as 'workers' in the questionnaires. [. . .] One would sometimes state, 'I am a worker,' but in reality it turns out that twenty years have passed since he last held a file in his hand."[26]

Following the introduction of NEP, the Party was very careful not to dilute its ranks with workers who had lost their mettle. The Central Committee concluded in 1921 that "only those comrades who will bring a genuinely healthy spirit into the Party should be admitted. Let us bar the way to all others."[27]

The NEP-era siege mentality prompted the Bolshevik leadership to maintain that although the Party had to be working-class based, not all workers had to be in the Party.[28] The Eleventh Party Congress recommended that the shorter six-month probationary period be accorded only to those workers who had been employed in large-scale undertakings for a minimum of ten continuous years; the probationary period for other workers was extended and fixed at eighteen months.[29] Fearing a widening gap between the Bolshevik vanguard and the masses, Larin from the "workers' opposition" warned that the decision of the Eleventh Party Congress to dramatically restrict Party admissions "might turn us into a sect of mandarins." Responding in the name of the Central Committee majority, Zinoviev dismissed such "abstract truisms" about the alleged necessity of close contacts with the masses. "Our present task is not to increase our size but to roll up our sleeves and invest all our energy in improving our membership. We have to chase quality, not quantity."[30]

When a certain Neverovskii expressed a desire in late 1921 to become a member of the Leningrad State University Party's cell, his application was put aside and he was advised to reapply at a later date, "after you [have] performed enough social work." Despite his classification as a "worker," the discussion of his case was postponed indefinitely once the Twelfth Party Conference (August 1922) put a freeze on all Party admissions except for factory workers.[31]

In presenting the effects of admission restrictions on Party growth in 1923, the Central Committee reported that "enrollment involves now a much more careful screening requiring from the cell a more thorough familiarization with the newcomer."[32] In the mid-1920s, however, this choking of the pipeline was dramatically reversed. Desperate to "increase at all costs the proletarian core of the Party," the Thirteenth Party Conference (January 1924) decided to launch a massive recruitment campaign that became known as the "Lenin Levy."[33] Restrictive admissions regulations were temporarily suspended: candidates were still urged to try to "supply the statutory number of recommendations by established Party members," but the local officials were empowered to waive this requirement "if the candidates were adequately examined by the workers' general meeting." Thanks to a more permissive approach to admissions, the Party expanded by 40 percent from February 1 to August 1, 1924, accepting 203,000 new members, 190,000 among them (93.8 percent) "bench-workers."[34]

The Lenin Levy would not have been possible were it not for the change in the Party's perception of the strength and character of its proletarian class base. Popov, a Party publicist, wrote that "the massive influx of workers from the bench into the Party must be explained in terms of the increase in the scale of industrial production and the return of true workers to factories and mills." Zinoviev celebrated the fact that "the working class changed its face and began treating our Party differently. [. . .] Finally convinced that NEP does not amount to a new form of exploitation of the proletariat it recognized our Party as its own."[35]

The dramatic increase in the proletarian enrollment into the Party had another, no less important source: Lenin's death in January 1924. Lenin was a hero who dedicated his life to proletarian enlightenment. "He embodies the ideal of suffering for an idea of bleeding for the proletariat."[36] The total identification of Lenin with the working class was distinctly reflected in Bukharin's eulogizing: "Never again will we see again Lenin's enormous forehead, his splendid head radiating revolutionary energy in all directions, his living, penetrating, attentive eyes; his hard, firm hands; his strong figure bringing two epochs of human history together. The fulcrum of the proletariat's mind, the will and feelings are gone."[37] According to Vladimir Bonch-Bruevich, Lenin's personal secretary, the proletarian movement continued to be "led by Lenin after his physical death."[38] Lev Kamenev explained: "Aware of the wound inflicted on the Party by Vladimir Ilich's departure, thousands of pure proletarians surrounded the Party with a protective ring."[39]

With Lenin, the history of salvation arrived at its center, but it had not yet run its complete course. Now it became necessary to reverse the process, namely, to proceed from the one to the many, but in such a way that the many represented the one. Now the way led from Lenin to those who believed in him, who knew themselves to be saved through their faith in him.[40] With Lenin's martyrdom, the Party became the body of the one (Lenin). The Bolshevik press asserted: "Lenin is dead, but he lives in the soul of each of the members of the Party. Each member of the Party is a portion of Lenin. Our whole Communist family is the collective incarnation of Lenin."[41]

Through Lenin's final sacrifice the scales were to fall from workers' eyes and they were to populate his church. In calling for a massive Party recruitment campaign two days after Lenin's death, Stalin summed up the logic of the leader's replacement: "We, Communists, make up the army of the great proletarian strategist, Lenin. [. . .] Not just anyone is given the honor to be a member of our Party."[42]

The declarations made by students during the Lenin Levy reveal that Lenin's death and rebirth underwent a transformation at the hands of his followers: they came to serve as a flexible conversion metaphor.[43] Ponomarev, a student at Leningrad Mining Institute, tied the tragic events to a leap in his own consciousness: "The death of comrade Lenin and the following surge in worker participation in the life of the country brought home to me that my place is in the Party. Now I know that 'Whoever is not with us is against us!' " Another student, Gladkin, explained his request for Party admission similarly: "Lenin's death opened my eyes to the fact that the Soviet government and the Communist Party are the only supporters of the interests of the working class." What Leszek Kolakowski describes as the pyramid of substitutions which posits that "truth" + "proletarian consciousness" = "Marxism" = "Party ideology" = "Party" = "Party leader" —underpinned these declarations.[44]

Professing awareness that the Party stood for the proletariat, Gladkin focused on the link in the chain—"proletariat = Party"—in order to show that he was class-conscious. Once the bricks of this pyramid were rearranged—Gladkin is a proletarian, who gained class consciousness, who understood that the Party stood for his true self—the inevitable conclusion had to be that Gladkin should be accepted into the Party. Deploying the same rhetorical device, Karpunin addressed a higher layer in Kolakowski's pyramid, namely "Party = Party leader." In his declaration, this student wrote that "now that I have realized what a loss to the workers' republic the death of Ilich is, and since I am increasingly aware that the Party Ilich created is the only party that represents the will of the proletariat, I tender my application for Party membership." Tacitly but unmistakably, Karpunin was implying that his admission to the Party would, however incrementally, make up in part for Lenin's disappearance.

While Strel'nikov's declaration came very close to the same assertion, this student suggested not that he himself but rather the proletariat as a collective could fill the void that had opened with Lenin's death. Strel'nikov opened by saying that "At the institute I fully grasped what our great worker-peasant leaders, Marx and Lenin, taught us, which is that the Party is the only organization that has defended, now defends, and will defend in the future the interests of all the toilers of the entire world." Still, it was not until Lenin's death that his eyes were finally opened: "During the seventh year of its colossal enterprise, the Party has suffered an irremediable loss. Its great leader, comrade Lenin, has died. We, the workers and peasants, must try to fill this yawning gap through our collective energy. This is why I can no longer remain unattached to the Party."

It is now possible to piece together the narrative underpinning the declarations made at the time of the Lenin Levy. The death of Lenin vacated the space at the very top of the Party's pyramid. Since the removal of this keystone snapped all of the integuments holding the various layers of the pyramid together, its disappearance threatened the integrity of the entire pyramid. If the pyramid was to be saved, everybody in the Party had to climb up one step. The crucial transformation, or extension, of the socialist equation wrought during the Lenin Levy was from "class = Party" to "class = Party = Party's leader."

Yet by and large all these poetical exercises ended in trash heaps. No matter how hard they tried students were not allowed to replace Lenin, an honor accorded to none but "workers from the bench" (a new statistical category brought into existence in April 1923 by the Twelfth Party Congress). Whereas the time of the Lenin Levy saw a surge of student applications to the Party university organizations (fifty applications were registered in the Leningrad State University during the month of February 1924 alone; forty-three in the Mining Institute and forty in the Medical Institute), none of these applications was processed, let alone approved.[45]

A number of circulars coming from Moscow in the spring of 1924 stipulated that "applicants have to specify whether they are currently employed directly in production," leaving little doubt that even those students who were classified as "workers" by social position would be classified as "nonindustrial" (*nepromyshlennye*).[46] This discrimination had an immediate impact on the size of the university Party organizations. The data for the Leningrad Central Party district demonstrate that while local Party organizations grew significantly in the first half of 1924, their student component usually either shrank or remained unaltered.

Table 3. The Growth of the Central District Leningrad Party Organization (1923–24)

	November 1923		April 1924	
	Students	Total for the district	Students	Total for the district
Number of Party cells	20	217	19	230
Party members	1,713	8,212	1,503	8,360
Party candidates	216	973	246	4677
Total	2,176	9,185	1,749	13,037

Source: *Sbornik materialov Leningradskogo komiteta RKP,* vyp. 7 (Leningrad, 1924), p. 245; *Leninskii prizyv. Godichnye itogi* (Leningrad, 1925).

Tomsk academic Party cells were no more willing to accept new members in the spring of 1924 than their Leningrad counterparts. During this period, the Party cell at the Technological Institute hollowly boasted that "every week we inspect dozens of worker Party applications," while records show that virtually none of these applications were approved. While most of the applications came from students with proletarian social backgrounds (eleven workers, sixteen peasants, and only six non-proletarians), entries in the files of the institute's Party cell suggest that from January to May 1924 admissions were stopped almost completely. Clearly, neither proletarian social origins nor recent occupation in the factory sufficed to make a "worker-student" the equal of a "worker from the bench."

It was only toward the middle of 1924, when the Thirteenth Party Congress reopened the Party gates, that new admissions were recorded, among them five "workers," two "peasants" and nine "employees."[47] That the majority of the successful applicants were consigned to the "employees" column conveys a tacit admission that students could not be described as workers regardless of their social origins.

To the extent that the Lenin Levy had an effect, for example at the Tomsk Technological Institute, it was an indirect and delayed one. To be sure, the institute's annual statistical summation for 1924 claimed that "as a result of the enrollment campaign of the last year, the size of our Party cell quadruped, totaling now 250 members (200 members and 50 candidates)." What is conveniently forgotten, however, is that the rolls of the cell had lengthened mainly as a result of the registration of factory workers who arrived at the institute with Party cards already in hand.[48]

University Party organizations had to wait one more year before they could expand. If in 1924 university Party cells countrywide averaged 85 Communists, by 1926 this average leaped to about 150 to 200. Professing to accept the Central Committee decree, "On Party Work in the Universities" (January 1925), as well as the recommendations of the Moscow "Nation-wide Meeting of the Secretaries of University Party Cells" (February 1925), to the effect that the best among working-class students should be admitted, the Party cell at the Leningrad State University opened its doors. A stream of applications flew to the local Party bureau, with students pleading for a review of their requests now that the freeze on Party enrollment was removed. During the 1924–25 academic year alone the bureau examined 68 such cases and accepted 50 students.[49] But the integration of the new recruits into university cells continued to cause some anxieties: "often stagnant and philistine, their personal life stands in a glaring contradiction to the required discipline of social life," reported the district committee's instructor after reviewing the Lenin Levy contingent in the High Military Sport School (August 1924). The remedy was a "personal working through" (*personal'naia prorabotka*) of each and every young Communist by seasoned revolutionaries, its chief purpose being to explain that there has to be "no separation between personal and public life in the universe of a Party member."[50]

For workers, so Marxists firmly believed, entering the "Party of the proletariat" meant actualizing a built-in potential.[51] Workers could stray for awhile, losing themselves in their everyday struggle, or perhaps even be tempted by anarchist propaganda with its unsubstantiated promised of absolute freedom.[52] But when October came they recognized the Bolshevik government as their own. Viazhevich from the Leningrad Mining Institute explained his Party application from the mid-1920s thus: "I have realized in the process of my personal development that it would be criminal for a pure-blooded (*chistokrovnyi*) worker like myself to abstain from social activity."[53] But even those students who boasted a strong proletarian pedigree were busy fending off the Bolshevik assumption that they had lost their mettle in the university.

Gnesin, for example, barely made it through the questioning at the Technological Institute Party though no one disputed the fact that he was a stoker by profession (January 1926):

Q: Why have you procrastinated with your application?
A: Since I was uneducated, I went to the workers' faculty to refine myself a bit [*nemnogo ottesatsia*]. Only then did I feel ready to enter public activity.
Q: Is not the trade union enough for that?
A: The Party is a political organ, and I now feel I am up to the task politically.

A number of bureau members concluded that the applicant "demonstrates poor understanding of key issues" and that "he would benefit from doing some additional reading." It took the intervention of an unidentified benefactor to tip the scales in Gnesen's favor: "We are too strict with the applicant. The product of a workers' family [. . .] he has passed through the revolutionary crucible."[54]

Key to workers' conversion was the impact of the city and of its productionist environment on their psyche. Vostrov, a student from the Leningrad Engineering Institute, arranged his autobiography as a movement along the trajectory: city—working class—working class consciousness:

Since I lived in Turkestan, a backward place in comparison with Moscow and Petersburg, my impulse [to enter the Party] was initially not so strong. I was politically unprepared; my class consciousness was inarticulate. Petersburg, by contrast, is a politically progressive, revolutionary city. Classes are very distinct here, especially in my institute, where two and only two classes exist: the new students (workers and peasants) and the old students (children of the nobility and former gentry).[55]

The narratological strategy Vostrov adopted had another advantage— the time it took him to arrive in the city justified his procrastination in applying to the Party. Only with his move to the metropolis did Vostrov learn to identify himself as a worker. And here the university appeared in an unusual capacity; it had become a consciousness enhancing site—a metonym of both urbanity and industry.

The Party knew that many workers came from the countryside and that some of them still might have parents there. But it expected them to make a quick change, hatch from the shell of their old identity, and assume a robust industrial self. Interaction with the urban proletariat was the highlight of Korolev's conversion.[56] This son of the Smolensk province had not only his village rebelliousness to overcome. He was also freighted with the additional task of wrenching petit-bourgeois residues from his soul. In response to the questionnaire, Korolev described himself as a shepherd's son, a "peasant-worker": "When a liberal landowner offered to pay for Father's education Grandfather refused, preferring, as he put it, that "my son hand over to me a salary of three to five rubles per summer rather than studying God knows what in the city." This, of course, ultimately benefited our narrator, since an agricultural laborer, utterly bereft of property instinct, was the next best thing to a worker.

The autobiography's next section was tailored to convince the reader that Korolev's parents had always been proletarians. Restless and discontent in the country, Korolev's father migrated to the city, where he was employed as a factory worker, a shoemaker, and a conductor. Korolev's mother was "an orphan who worked first as a cook and later as a laundress." Since his parents had met in the city, the writer proudly reasoned that he was himself, as it were, the fruit of a proletarian union. Korolev piled up such details because he knew that the later part of his life was more problematic.

As hard as he tried to downplay the magnitude of his family's class transformation, not only had the Korolevs returned to the village, but they scorned the plough and metamorphosed into small-scale village exploiters. Still, the autobiographer tried to put a favorable spin on things:

> Having saved four hundred rubles in the sweat of their brows, my parents opened a dairy shop. But since the business went bad and the family never became rich, I was sent to a parish school that charged nothing and provided students with books free of charge. High tuition meant that I could not attend high school [. . .] so I went instead to a trade school in Smolensk, which was cheap and required no uniform.

To save his lower-class credentials, Korolev associated himself with the victims of the oppressive tsarist regime. "Although I began preparations for the *Realschule*, I was rejected. The director had decided that I was the unworthy son of the kitchen help [*kukharkin syn*]"—an expression that had become proverbial after Tolstoy, a minister of Alexander III, used it to refer disparagingly to the lower classes.

Next, the reader finds Korolev as an employee in the provincial administration. When he described himself as a tsarist clerk, the auto-biographer put a wedge between his identity and his occupation: "I dreaded the thought of staying in Zemstvo service forever. It was in this line of duty that I was able to observe all the beauties of our bureaucratic order." His irony indicated he had the correct class perspective. While he painted himself as that rare creature, a nonconformist in the imperial civil service, Korolev confessed that his radical self was not yet fully resurrected when the decisive events began:

The February Revolution caught me by surprise. I was working as a clerk in Tarnopol' at the time. Until 1917 my political virginity was intact. Familiar with no political program, the term socialism meant nothing to me except "riot-strikes"; that was what the lords (*gospoda*) my mother worked for taught me to think. When I saw how much of the Russian Army's precious property had been lost to the Germans in the Tarnopol' disaster—which had been blamed on "Bolshevik propaganda," [. . .] I bought into the accusations Kerenskii made against the Bolsheviks of treason and spying for the Germans.

Here Korolev's narrative attempted to match the speed of revolutionary changes taking place both outside and inside him with short, clear-cut sentences: "My interactions with workers led me to abandon my perception of the Bolsheviks as traitors. Communist literature helped by triggering an interest in the Bolshevik program." Korolev's conversion formula was unexceptionable: the workers' milieu revived the autobiographer's instincts as the Bolshevik press introduced the mediation of theory. Korolev was spontaneously united with his authentic identity: "All these changes in my mind took place without anyone's agitation or intervention."[57]

Another student-worker from Smolensk was Dzhus'. His background was checkered and complex, and the trajectory of his life had to be conveyed through a multi-staged poetical enterprise in the process of which the autobiographer assumed and then shed class masks.[58] With the first sentence Dzhus' confided to paper he betrayed a certain unease: "My father, a 'peasant,' was registered as a military clerk." Perhaps desperation better describes Dzhus''s emotions than unease. After all, his sole justification for claiming plebeian birth was the estate affiliation of his father, a totally irrelevant criterion even by the most lax of Party standards. It is no surprise that the autobiographer repressed all memory of his declassed childhood: "My recollection of my early days is poor. Vaguely I see before me some sort of basement full of military equipment and all sorts of other things." When he came to the more mature period of his life the autobiographer could hardly plead amnesia again: "Having failed to enter a gymnasium, I was provided with a position in the local bureaucracy by some who wished to help me." Despite what the reader was likely to recognize as petit-bourgeois upward mobility, the autobiographer insisted that "mingling with clerks and thoroughgoing bureaucrats, I constantly felt like a sheep among wolves."

"The year 1917 was upon us!" the text suddenly erupts with enthusiasm. Dzhus' now began to refer to himself as a "worker." This was a permissible slippage: the impact of the Revolution on social identities was so stark that everyone who took the Red side was transformed, in a sense, into a proletarian.

> The February Revolution thundered by and wrought havoc in Russian life. As the popular masses laid waste to bygone ideas and the old order of things, new influences and trends of thought were bound to crystallize and leave their mark. Alas, the mass of the clerks in whose midst I was thrust remained lackeys to the old order. Deaf to anything new, this riffraff criticized, sneered, and jeered at the revolutionaries and went about fabricating thousands upon thousands of supposedly factual [counterrevolutionary] anecdotes.

The autobiographer's soul was torn between two different socioeconomic classes with their respective frames of mind. "Naturally, in such surroundings my position was utterly unbearable. Still young and politically uneducated I could not oppose their opinions with my own."

There was only one remedy for this predicament—study. "I knew zero, and yet life required infinite knowledge. More than ever I was drawn toward the light." Dzhus''s consciousness expanded and he became a committed propagandist. "Simultaneously with academic work, I invested a lot of work in political effort to dispel the philistine illusions around me. Though at first only five of us had a clear-cut Bolshevik worldview within half a year we [. . .] had brought the rest of the students under our influence (*raspropagandirovali*)." A true worker after all, Dzhus' was worthy of a place in the brotherhood of the elect.

Some would see in the autobiographies outlined above little but a set of subjective representations reflecting the rapid urbanization Russia underwent between the 1890s and the 1920s as a native working class was created. Historians who treat autobiographical narratives as transparent traces of an objective past, however, completely overlook the mechanism through which interpretation produced reality.[59] Students did not voice in their autobiographies their preexisting working-class social being; rather, they used this medium to construct their subjectivity actively in accord with the Bolshevik ideal of a class-conscious worker-emancipator.[60]

The starting point of the autobiography had complex ramifications. We have seen that the social identity that they assumed provided authors with conventions that enabled them to tell the story of their voyage to the light in a particular, class-specific way. When possible, the autobiographers tried to put their background to good use, turning it into the cornerstone of their narratological strategy. Utilizing to the full the healthy dispositions with which their origins presented them, they attained universal consciousness. At the same time, however, every starting point, every social origin potentially posited serious hurdles on the road to political enlightenment. Every starting point could turn into a structural weakness that, under unfavorable circumstances, made Bolshevik conversion difficult if not impossible.[61] The peasant was always suspected of narrow-mindedness and religiosity, the member of the intelligentsia of weakness of heart and individualism. And, paradoxical as it may sound, we shall presently see that even a worker identity could at times backfire.

The proposition that affiliation with the working class could turn against the student is bewildering at first glance. Was the worker not in an ideal position to claim the title of Bolshevik? And if so, why should anyone worry about being classified as a worker? Yet the exalted position of the worker in the Soviet Union meant that students with worker backgrounds were expected to achieve high standards. While the potential payoffs were high, worker identity put high demands on its bearers.

The son of an "artisan-housepainter" and himself a sausage maker, Dvinskii, a student from Communist University, defined himself as a "worker," though this was perhaps a bit premature.[62] His application not only included the standard petition for membership in the Communist Party, it also involved a request for professional reclassification from artisan (a typical Jewish category) to worker (considered a supra-national group).

The autobiography opened by declaring the narrator's economic independence and by dating his occupation as a manual laborer from pre-adolescence to the present.

> From the age of eleven I learned the house-painting craft [. . .] and practiced it until the end of 1915. At that time family feuds forced me to leave home and live on my own earnings. I wandered from Minsk Province to Kiev and found a job in a sausage factory where I still work. In 1917 I was a member of an initiative group that got sausage workers' trade-unions started. When political discussions drove people into polarized camps, I, a youngster only fifteen years of age, vehemently defended the Bolshevik cause. Of course, I acted on instinct, but my behavior was characteristic of my milieu.

All this was part of Dvinskii's strategy to affirm that his proletarian sentiment was a natural, preconscious inclination bred by his native proletarian environment. Naturally, he also laid claim to a proper political consciousness: "At the same time [I aspired] to better understand the Bolshevik slogans of the time. I was also interested in the Bolshevik program." His activity during the Civil War appeared to be beyond reproach: "I assisted in the suppression of the [White and Green] bands and then the defeat of Denikin's offensive." In May 1920, Dvinskii joined the Bolshevik Party in Kiev. The last event was mentioned in passing to stress that it was a matter of course for the thoroughgoing worker that the narrator was.

As it turned out, though, this narrative was really the preamble to a very different chapter in Dvinskii's autobiography. The anxious exaggerations of the writer's proletarian virtues suggested a problem, but the source was not revealed until the reader was better prepared. In order to minimize the possibility of being perceived as a declassed worker-turned-bureaucrat, the narrator gave the impression that the brief episode of his separation from the factory had not dampened his proletarian spirit. "About that time I was detained. I escaped from prison but was obliged to hide. This made me uneasy. For a time, I had no connection with other workers." Traveling from place to place and suffering immensely from "alienation," Dvinskii finally managed to find himself a job at the Liudikovskii factory. "At long last, I successfully returned to production."

Though he was registered as an electro-technician in the factory, Dvinskii "worked in reality in a brigade, first as an apprentice and then

as an extramural electrician, laboring on an equal footing with other *artel'*
workers." To dispel the notion that this was yet another declassed episode,
Dvinskii reported that he had refused to honor his managerial responsibilities.

> Utterly consumed by the labor process, I worked hard to meet production
> goals. My personal example—we are talking about times preceding the
> introduction of premium in kind and collective labor responsibility—as
> well as my agitation for the enhancement of labor productivity, ensured
> that our work levels were high. In fact, some colleagues resented me
> for that. By way of conclusion, I wish to emphasize that production
> always attracted me. I always sought interaction with workers in mills
> and factories.

If only the appraisal of Dvinskii could be based on contribution to
productivity—as he clearly hoped—he might survive.

But what about politics? Although the autobiographer had just declared
that he had reached the end of his tale, only now did Dvinskii finally expose
the locus of his anxiety. Atypically, the autobiography was to be continued
beyond the conversion stage, in order to explain the protagonist's well-
documented participation in a workers' strike against Soviet power.[63]

This was no trivial issue—it reflected directly on Dvinskii's political
identity. On an unspecified date between 1920 and 1921, a strike had
broken out in the factory. It "erupted" (*podnialas'*), meaning it came out
of nowhere, and, surely, it was not organized by the factory activists among
whom the Communist Dvinskii was counted. "Our [electric] shop stopped
work only out of solidarity with the mechanical shop. When a Communist
who worked nearby—his name was comrade Blinofortov—urged workers
to resume production, explaining to them the economic condition of the
Republic, on the one hand, and calling the strike pointless, on the other,
workers softened little by little. Still, they refused to return to work."

A workers' strike mounted in defiance of the Bolshevik government
could not be blandly acceded to by a good Communist, and Dvinskii could
only claim that there was not much he could have done. "To make workers
return to work was too much of a responsibility to lay on the shoulders of
myself and comrade Blinofortov. We were totally dependent on the master
who, disregarding all exhortations, refused to work. Our labor system
depended on the cooperation of the entire *artel'*." The predicament led to
wild thoughts. "We could have hammered on the anvils, pretending that

work had recommenced. But that was unreasonable." Or was it? Dvinskii and Blinofortov conferred and decided to reject this course of action.

If Dvinskii had blundered, so the autobiography claimed, it was because the local Party organization had been useless. "I must make clear that at the time no Party cell operated in the factory. This, although no fewer than fifteen Communists worked there. The district committee was outside the factory walls and we were unable to get in touch with it." Back then, authorities understood Dvinskii's delicate situation: "That same day, when I swung by its office, I was admonished for not restoring production. But as soon as I explained what was going on, my conduct was immediately approved."

Because of his participation in the strike Dvinskii had been demoted in the Party ranks and only now was applying for full reinstatement. The autobiographer maintained that his demotion was an intrigue, a plot set up against him by "base individuals who did not hesitate to exploit the circumstances surrounding the strike when opportunity arose." At present, he reported, "these individuals have been hounded from their posts and purged from the Party. One of them was arrested; and another purged as a ballast though she claimed she was a worker!" The structure of the argument is by now familiar: Since the autobiographer's denouncer had been proven a class alien, then her intended victim must have been a good proletarian.

But a cloud continued to hover over Dvinskii"s proletarian self. Although the strike he joined ended after the lunch break—its span was apparently shorter than a day—his reputation was seriously blemished. "Unprepared workers" might be tempted to strike because of an ignorant confusion of the Soviet Power with the old masters, so local Bolsheviks reasoned. Dvinskii, by contrast, was a Communist, and as such, must have surely recognized that the workers' government was his own. Why then had he not opposed the strike more valiantly? Had he been a peasant-Communist, or an intelligentsia-Communist, his mistake would have been interpreted as a regression back to his former identity, but Dvinskii identified himself as a "worker" in the questionnaire. The higher the autobiographer climbed on the class ladder, the more difficult it was to live up to the Party's expectations.

CHAPTER 3

Peasant Enrollment

THE BOLSHEVIKS FEARED THAT THE COUNTRY in which they had carried out the "First Proletarian Revolution" was not sufficiently proletarian, and was not likely to become a classless society in the foreseeable future. Since the majority of the population in the Soviet Union of the 1920s had to be described as "peasants," some wondered whether "peasants" could be described as some sort of revolutionary allies.[1] "If the Russian working class could fulfill its tasks," Kamenev stated at the Twelfth Party Congress, "it was because it had found a path to the heart, brain, and historical sense of the bulk of the toiling mass. The trust of the peasants in the proletariat [. . .] sustained us in difficult moments."[2] Many social scientists argued that little distinguished workers who sold their labor in the cities from landless "agricultural laborers" (*batraki*) who did the same in the countryside. Their arguments produced a compound definition of "proletarians"—it seemed that some peasants, and not only industrial workers, deserved the honorable title. The landowning peasantry proved also to be a complex entity, one that included "poor peasants" (*bedniaki*), "middle peasants" (*seredniaki*), and "rich peasants" (*kulaki*).[3]

In complicated cases, the determination of a peasant's social position could be an arduous process. Only intimate familiarity with the economic conditions in the village of origin could provide definitive answers. Zal'ts from the Smolensk Institute claimed during the 1921 purge that he was born to a poor peasant family. "I studied in a village school but at the age of twelve my education was interrupted as I started helping father to run the household." Familiar motifs were in view: peasant origins, education crippled by the family's need of labor. Yet the committee received a denunciation portraying Zal'ts's father as a kulak. Zal'ts assured the cell that "father never used hired labor" and the purge committee found his explanations satisfactory. The young Zal'ts "volunteered into the Red Army" in October 1918 and was even co-opted into a committee of the poor, his defenders emphatically stated, and this certainly put the charges against him in a ridiculous light.[4]

Mikhailov from the Leningrad Communist University also stood the danger of being categorized as a kulak. But the student himself would have none of it. If he was to be believed, he was a son of a peasant, a peasant himself, and by extension, a toiler who had every right to the proletarian mantle. According to Mikhailov's autobiography, his parents were "middling peasants with a landplot enough to sustain one soul. Our village economy was run by my mother, brothers, and sisters." The land was scarce but "father had found subsidiary employment, as a smith and a forest guard." Hoping to "make him into somebody" (*vyvesti v liudi*) his family enrolled Mikhailov in Cherepovetsk professional school in the autumn of 1913. Four years later, profession in hand, Mikhailov came to Petersburg where he found a job as a welder in a dock.

The questions students put to Mikhailov were not registered in the protocol. His answers, however, suggest that he was grilled regarding his peasant background and his claim that he had almost become a worker was disbelieved.

- Before enrollment into the university I had connections with the village in the sense that I sometimes sent money home.
- Father has two cows and one horse. He did not use hired labor.
- Father's peasant economy was not confiscated by the Revolution. He paid his taxes.
- Because the attitudes of my father and sister are not revolutionary, I severed ties with them. But my brother was in the Komsomol, served in the Red Army, and is now conducting education work in the village.

Mikhailov managed to put some distance between himself and his retrograde family and students were eventually satisfied he was not a proprietor. This, however, did not mean he could automatically lay claims to the title of a peasant. The plurality of the registered opinion suggests how elaborate the classifying matrix was and how seriously it was taken by the discussants:

Rozov: Mikhailov is a "son of a middling-peasant" (6 votes);
Kotriachov: Mikhailov is a "son of a peasant from a well off to middling household" (11 votes);
Tonkii: Mikhailov is the "son of a peasant-employee";
Strintenchuk: Mikhailov belongs to the "bottom layer of technological intelligentsia";

Kotriashov: Mikhailov is a "worker who got ahead, moved forward, and received a diploma";

Nusulenko: One obtains qualifications of a worker through long practical work. This is why we cannot regard Mikhailov as a "worker."

The final decision went against Mikhailov, who was defined as a "member of the lower technological intelligentsia" and not a "peasant."[5]

Mikhailov's parents exploited the labor of others and could easily be regarded as kulaks and thus open enemies. But what about the middle strata in the village? Because these peasants did not exploit labor they were proletarians; because they owned means of production they were bourgeois.

How to define a peasant was a question long debated among Soviet statisticians during the years of NEP. From 1925 on, Communists whose main source of income was land tillage or cattle raising were relegated to the "peasant" category, provided they were not "hired laborers" but ran an independent economy of their own. Toilers in agricultural communes and collective farms were also classified as "peasants." Those Party members who "worked their own plots" were instructed to enter "land tiller" as their profession (unless they were engaged in a specific branch of economy and could describe themselves as "fisherman," "shepherd," etc.). While "agricultural laborer" (batrak) was defined as "hired laborer" (naemnyi rabochii), a peasant who worked his own plot or the plot of his father did not fit this category.

The period of "hired employment" was counted from the moment one began working regularly and deriving a substantial part of one's subsistence from one's salary. For example, a Party member who, when an urchin, was employed as a shepherd or an apprentice, could claim he was not a "peasant" but an "agricultural laborer," even if he had been supported by his parents. A hired laborer had to specify the exact number of years he spent as such and whether he was employed in agriculture or in industry. The intermissions that were longer than a year (unemployment, service in the Red Army) were not to be included in the count of "my years of hired employment."[6]

A straightforward analysis would suggest that the peasant's class affiliation depended on the amount of land in his possession and his propensity to exploit labor. But when the time dimension was brought in additional factors had to be considered, chief among them the tendency of the peasant to eventually transform into a proletarian or intelligentsia. Since "the peasantry" was a transient class category, a social cocoon that would be shed as Communism did away with the distinction between the city and the countryside, the class analyst was asking himself not only what the peasant was but also whom he tended to become.

Two basic strategies were open to the peasant-student autobiographers. They could either aspire to be promoted from the peasantry into the working class, arguing they had broken with the village and transcended their peasant identity; or, alternatively, they could adhere to the model of the good peasant, the worker's right hand, who deserves a place in the brotherhood of the elect.[7] During the early 1920s, when the Party opened its gates to nobody but production workers, the former strategy was widespread, as peasants sought to downplay their village origins.

The opening lines of the autobiography of Alashkin, an applicant to the Party cell at Leningrad Engineering Institute in 1923, are a case in point.

> I was born into a peasant family and educated in a village school. Then I found employment as a clerk in the local county Zemstvo department. The work of a scribe in the midst of a petit-bourgeois peasantry disgusted me. I made up my mind to go to Petersburg or Moscow to get acquainted with the life of the workers.[8]

Alashkin's rhetoric acknowledged the superiority of the industrial proletariat over the peasantry. So did Kostromitinov's; applying to the same Party cell, he was adamant that the local Party bureau limit his probation period to six months (the standard for workers), thereby reversing the Petrograd provincial committee's decision to relegate him to the peasantry.

In his autobiography, Kostromitinov granted that "my father, a Communist since May 1919, is a poor peasant."

> It should be kept in mind, however, that I am principally employed as a Morse telegraphist and I was employed as such during the Civil War on the eastern front. In accordance with the resolution of the Eleventh Party Congress, I should be considered, as far as my social position is concerned, a "worker." For a long time, I have been isolated from the village and, except for at times of extremely pressing need, I have had nothing to do with it.[9]

Things changed in the mid-1920s, and the polar opposition of "toilers" and "parasites" replaced "proletarians" (i.e., industrial laborers) and "nonproletarians." This semantic transformation paralleled an improvement in the Party's attitude toward the peasantry. While peasants remained inferior to workers, they now often found themselves on the positive side of the class divide.

Introduced on the first anniversary of Lenin's death, the Second Lenin Levy brought many peasants into the Party. Rescinding the Thirteenth Party Congress's (spring 1924) objective of raising the proportion of workers from the bench in the Party to 50 percent, the Fourteenth Party Conference (April 1925) forbade the imposition of class-based recruitment quotas and reduced the number of recommendations demanded from peasant applicants. The effects of these measures on the class composition of the Tomsk Technological Institute Party cell were clear.

Table 4. Alterations in the Social Position
of Tomsk Technological Institute Communists (1924–25)

Social position	December 1924	December 1925
Peasants and their children	43 (17.2%)	88 (32.7%)
Other social categories	207 (82.8%)	175 (67.3%)

Source: PATO, f.76, op.1, d.1176, p.123; PANO, f.2, op.1, d.461, l.127.

The growth of the peasant cohort in the institute was the result of two statistical adjustments: (1) the Central Committee decree that "teachers from peasant backgrounds who have not lost touch with the peasant environment" should be treated as a second category of Party candidates (i.e., as peasants); (2) the transformation of "medical assistants" from "employees" into "peasants."

But things got out of hand—peasants were flooding the Party. While only 11.1 percent of the 1924 Party inductees were peasants, in 1925 their share in admissions climbed to 29.5 percent. When it turned out that peasants were responsible for 39 percent of the fresh Party inductees in the first half of 1926, policy dramatically changed course once again. Party organizations were now instructed to see to it that peasants showed evidence of "active support of the Soviet government."[10]

Fluctuations in the numbers of peasant Communists at the Leningrad Agricultural Institute indicate how sensitive higher educational institutions were to these sorts of signals. If in 1925 the peasant cohort in this peasant-oriented institution registered a growth similar to the one in the Tomsk Technological Institute, following the new instructions from Moscow the trend was reversed in the second part of 1926 and the bias against the countryside firmly reestablished.

Table 5. Class Composition of the Party Cell
at the Leningrad Agricultural Institute (1924–26)

Social Position	Autumn 1924	Spring 1926	Autumn 1926
Peasants	95	192	156
Other social positions	64	156	254

Source: TsGA IPD, f.258, op.1, d.5, ll.40-41; d.42, l.47; d.46, ll.21, 24; d.114, ll.22, 45, 48.

Student autobiographies were no less sensitive a seismograph to the vicissitudes in Party admissions. Submitting his application to the Party in the midst of the "face to the countryside" drive attributed to the inclusivist Nikolai Bukharin, Parfenov, a student in the Leningrad Engineering Institute, enthusiastically proclaimed his peasant identity. "My father was one of the poorest peasants in his village," he stated. "Father's property consisted of peasant hut, one horse, and one cow. During the famine along the Volga we lost the horse as well."[11] Dispensing with the customary stress on his subsequent proletarianization, this author preferred a story of continuity in which he remained a poor peasant.

> Until 1914 I lived together with my parents in the village and helped the household as best I could. In the years 1911–1912 Stolypin's land program was implemented. Those who were unable to purchase an isolated plot [otrub] remained landless. My father lost his land and had to leave for Astrakhan' as a migrant laborer, taking the family with him.

Parfenov was eager to show that Stolypin's land reform had affected his household just as the Bolsheviks claimed—land consolidation and enclosure enriched the kulaks and drove poor peasants into the cities. He enunciated the following syllogism: If poor peasants were driven off the land and into the city—and that was the fate the Parfenovs faced—then the young protagonist must indeed have been a poor peasant.

For Parfenov, 1917 represented not a leap into an industrial future but a return to the bucolic garden of Eden. The autobiographer spoke of the longing he then felt to return to his home village and to "become a peasant again." Specifically, he wanted to reclaim the plot of land that Stolypin's measures had deprived him of. "The October Revolution returned the land to the peasants and distributed it equally among those who wished to till it." Parfenov identified with the Bolsheviks body and soul because they had terminated his marginal status and returned to him the pride of his peasant past. Since I recognize the Revolution as mine, Parfenov implied, the Revolution should consider a peasant like me its own.

Apparently, Parfenov's entire "return to the countryside" theme was little more than a heuristic device designed to establish the claim for a positive class identity. Aware he could be declassed for his prerevolutionary sojourn in the petit-bourgeois city districts, and hesitant, for reasons we do not know, to argue that the city had turned him into a worker, he chose to gamble on the identity of a poor peasant. Did he ever return to his beloved village? On this point the autobiography is mute. All Parfenov said was that "unfortunately," in his native village there was nothing left for him, "neither house nor home" (*ni kola ni dvora*).

Parfenov knew that the Bolshevik urbanism stemmed not from the veneration of the city as such but from the equation of city life with industrial labor. In the context of the discussion of student life in the professional and Party press, the city could be associated not only with healthy consciousness but also with degeneration. To emphasize the danger of urbanism, the Bolsheviks fell back on Populist images of the "healthy" and "natural" countryside that contrasted sharply with images of the decadent city. In grappling with the pluses and minuses of city life, someone like Parfenov could claim he preferred the naive but healthy countryside over the artificiality of the urban milieu of the intelligentsia.

Putting their wager on peasant identity, students wanted at all costs to remain in the proletarian cohort, not to be declassified as some sort of white-collar elements. Iuferev of Leningrad State University was trying to avoid being called a member of the intelligentsia. "Until now," he patiently explained, "it has not yet been determined whether I belong to the 'intelligentsia-employee' or the 'peasant' category, though some documents have already recognized me as a peasant."[12]

To buttress his claim, Iuferev laid out his autobiography: "My parents have never left the village and even today they till the land. Until 1923 I was a member of a typical poor peasant household. In a word, my life and work were always woven into the fabric of peasant life." While he admitted that his recent years had been spent in studies, the autobiographer insisted that this had not dampened his productionist ardor:

> Although I had a government stipend, I continued to work—manual labor is not alien to me. It is true that upon conclusion of my military service I taught at school. But even then I had to help out my brothers during the harvest because my father had died. My service career was short-lived and anyway I had spent most of my time working as a peasant. For all the reasons mentioned, I think that my natural place in the Party is with the peasant group.

At first the supplicant was told that "three recommendations were enough for his Party application" (the number required of a peasant), but the length of the probation period eventually assigned to him once he was admitted corresponded to what was required for employees.

During the 1924 Party purge at the Leningrad Communist University, Fedulaev was asked very specific questions about his occupation after leaving the village. Many believed he had degenerated into an employee and did not deserve proletarian education. Trying to introduce as much clarity into his class transformations as possible, Fedulaev explained that he was born to peasant parents, worked in agriculture for a year and a half, served in the army for fourteen months, and only then took some clerical jobs. A debate ensued:

> Potapov: Fedulaev is a "peasant"; he headed a peasant household
> for a year and a half and continued helping the household during
> his studies. One can be regarded an "employee" by social position
> only if he is living off a salary.
> Kozlov: True, Fedulaev's agricultural activity is somewhat short for
> his social position to be determined as "peasant" but his
> employment in the treasury in the capital is even shorter. The rest
> of the time he had been in the Red Army—a military service does
> not have any effect on one's social position. Thus we cannot talk
> about him being an "employee."
> Pachuliia: Fedulaev's social position should be put as "indeterminate."

Noting that the social position of this student is indeed "still unformed" Levenkin believed "It is best to inquire with Fedulaev himself what is his inclination." Fedulaev did not elaborate about his class attitudes but noted that "had I remained further in the Red Army my social position would have become peculiar, namely, a 'military employee.' " Finally it was decided that Fedulaev's social position is "undetermined, but connected to the peasantry."[13]

In the Bolsheviks' mind of the mid-1920s, a whole world separated "peasants" from "intelligentsia from the peasantry"—the former was a manual laborer, a producer, while the latter could easily be regarded a degenerate. Consider, for example, the interrogators' general alarm when Kuleev, an applicant to the Party cell at the Technological Institute, claimed to be a "toiling peasant" despite enjoying access to a privileged school before 1917. "What stipend did you used to receive and who used to give it to you?" Kuleev explained that "the zemstvo board categorized me 'needy' and issued me fifteen rubles." Neudakhin played the part of the devil's advocate: "Do we not remember what sort of people would get stipends in the old days!? It seems to me that this applicant had connections to the zemstvo; he is not a poor peasant, that's for sure." Kuleev's candidacy was left pending until further inquiries.[14]

Educational background could be a liability even to those peasant-students who were educated by the Soviet Power. Applying to the Leningrad Engineering Institute Party cell in 1924, Smirnov submitted a long autobiography in which he did all he could to distance himself from the intelligentsia:

Coming from a peasant family [. . .] I had to migrate and work as a wage laborer in the Northern Railway Company for no more than a piece of daily bread. This work was forced on me because there were three of us brothers in a nearly landless household. Only after the Revolution was I sent by the local provincial committee to study. Is this enough to make me a member of the intelligentsia? Let anyone prove this to me and I will not remain an additional moment in the workers' faculty, hanging on the neck of the state.

Smirnov's diatribe raised the following thorny dilemma: Should workers' faculties be regarded as proletarian institutions due to their class orientation, in which case Smirnov would have to be considered a peasant? Or should workers' faculties perhaps be considered a bastion of the intelligentsia since all educational venues were such? If so, when Smirnov promised to relinquish his student rights he thus proved he cherished proletarian identity above everything else. The web of tacit assumptions Smirnov wove into his text was remarkable in that it put him in a position where he apparently could not lose.[15]

A lot depended on storytelling. Many Party applicants contested the ways in which their biographies were interpreted and the criteria of peasantness applied to their own, concrete, cases.

Another who played the peasant card for all it was worth was Usol'tsev, a student at Tomsk Party School, who requested in 1927 to be transferred from the category of the "employees" to the category of the "peasants." The supplicant explained that the circuit committee, "guided by the observation that for the last three years I am engaged in office work, unfairly demanded from me two years of probation," effectively relegating him to the non-proletarian Party membership category:

> I do not work my land with my own hands only since 1923; until the present time I keep my own peasant economy. Perusing the list of Communists in my cell who were relegated to the third category I find that my case is not analogous to theirs. While I am occupied in production they carry out clerical jobs. If one takes account only of the number of years I spent in an office—and it seems the commission on the definition of social position had something else in mind—then I am indeed an "employee." But if one notes my continuous contact with peasant labor—and if I am not mistaken this was the commission's guiding principle—then I by no means fit the rubric of employees.

Constructing his autobiography around the theme of agricultural labor, Usol'tsev hoped to prove he was a peasant. "True, in the period 1920–1923 I worked in my village as a chancery worker and bookkeeper." But at the same time he took part in agricultural labor, "especially during harvest time. [. . .] My salary was negligible so that my main source of income had to be land tillage. Up to 1920 I was practically an agricultural laborer. We had no economy of our own. I and my mother lived with an uncle and worked in his household. This is my social lineage [*sotsial'naia rodoslovnaia*]." Concluding his plea by saying that it is simply false "to define someone who is tied to an agricultural household as an individual who occupies the role of the intelligentsia stratum in production" Usol'tsev sought, in vain as it turned out, to avoid the life trajectory that described him as a peasant who degenerated into a mental worker.[16]

Though it was better to be a "peasant" than someone "from the intelligentsia," peasants who applied for Party membership faced odds far worse than workers. As property owners, they were always suspected of being drawn to bourgeois parties. Any peasant would rather be called a member of the intelligentsia than a kulak, someone who has to be driven out of any Soviet institution, the sooner the better.

Korneev from the Smolensk Technological Institute was framed as a kulak based on his politics more than his economics. The protocol of the purge commission tells us that "Korneev had four *desiatinas* of land under the Old Regime," and that he now has double that amount. (In the 1920s, eight *desiastinas* of land placed a Smolensk household in the category of well-to-do). Korneev tried to dispel the suspicions against him: "I did not work the land." The family economy was so small that his help was not needed. But Grigo'ev insisted that he knew Korneev for years and that before the revolution "the latter used to speak like a kulak [. . .] and give the Bolsheviks a hard time." And Borisov added, "Korneev himself admitted to me that he voted for ballot No. 3 [the SRs] in the elections to the Constitutional Assembly. Clearly, he knew what is what!" Not an innocent peasant but a conscious exploiter, Korneev was thrown out of the Party.[17]

Highly controversial from the very beginning, the 1928 Party application that Ivanov submitted to Leningrad State University also highlighted the alleged link between kulak lifestyle and counterrevolutionary politics.[18] In his autobiography, Ivanov described his grandfather as a "peasant," both his parents as "workers," and himself as "by profession a carpenter." After "fighting with the Cheka detachments against banditry" and helping the Komsomol, Ivanov "desired to do more serious work in the Party ranks." The impediment was a letter of derailment from his native village of Bol'shaia Maklashkina in Smolensk Province to the effect that "the household of Ivanov's deceased father refused to pay back a twenty-seven ruble grain loan taken in 1923"—a fact that left no doubt the family was disloyal to Soviet power.

Skilled in the art of Bolshevik self-fashioning, Ivanov did not think of submitting readily. Having carefully examined all the material against him, he took his detractors on, point by point:

I am outraged by the behavior of the local soviet in my village. Since the soviet head was raised in a rich household, he refuses to lend an ear to the interests of the village poor [. . .] who burn in a crimson fire (*goriat v krasnom ogne*) [. . .] while building a brand new world! [. . .] Regarding the grain loan, I must say that here, in Leningrad, I learned from a conversation I had with Mikhail Ivanovich Kalinin, chairman of the last session of the Supreme Soviet, that poor peasants would be exempted from paying part of the sum and the rest of the payment would be postponed. I will write to the central authorities about how local agencies distort our policy. Nowadays, eleven years after the founding of "our" Proletarian Dictatorship, in the remote villages, the kulak is raising his head.

Having enjoyed the quid pro quo of smearing his critics, Ivanov turned to the substance of the charge leveled against him. It appears that he came from a background of extreme poverty: "My father was broke until his last days. He died in 1927 leaving behind a family of seven. I and my younger brother have to extract from our miserable stipends ten to fifteen rubles a month in order to help out the family budget."

But it was a dramatic rhetorical device, not an appeal for sympathy, that provided the core for Ivanov's defense:

- Did the proletarian state not promulgate decrees promising privileges to the poor peasantry?
- Do not the laws of the Soviet Power exist for us, the poor peasants?
- Does the revolutionary legal system aim to suppress the poor peasantry?
- Do any of the decrees of the Soviet Power read: "Strip the poor peasant to the bone"?

This case, then, was to be viewed from a political perspective. Styling himself as a Civil War hero, Ivanov invoked the superior legitimacy of War Communism over NEP. Writing at the time when the policy of "class reconciliation" was being dismantled, he suggested that only the petit-bourgeois in the Soviet apparatus, with their call on peasants "to enrich themselves" and their extortion of taxes from weak households like his own, would not honor the claims of such good peasants as himself.

The cell attempted to verify Ivanov's version of the story. Material on the applicant's household was requested and the local soviet authorities were given the opportunity to defend their case. In three months' time, a secret communication arrived at the Leningrad State University Party cell from Ivanov's village detailing the economic condition of the household:

The Ivanov family has a new hut, a barn in relatively good condition, one horse and one cow. There are enough working hands in the household. The standard of living of Ivanov's family is no worse than that of most other households in the village. Incidentally, photographs were found in the house that must have cost more than the sum needed to pay all the government tax arrears. [. . .] It seems that the family finds means for everything except paying its taxes.

Dismantling Ivanov's defense brick by brick, the new phase of the derailment turned to politics.

It is unworthy of a Communist to try to create an atmosphere of distrust toward local authorities. Ivanov's family has a reputation for pursuing its own utilitarian interests. "What have we fought for"—this is the motif that runs through Ivanov's application like a golden thread in embroidery. Yet, according to rumors which have yet to be ascertained, Ivanov was accused and tried during the Civil War.

If Ivanov filled his defense with images contrasting the corrupt countryside with the conscious center, the Smolensk Party organization portrayed him as a greedy peasant who was inciting the villagers against the Soviet Power. The resolution of the case is unknown, but the link made there between peasant wealth and animosity to revolutionary politics is made evident.

Difficult Conversions

The poetics of the Communist autobiography allowed some room for a rural, peasant paradise, precariously cohabiting with the more canonical industrial paradise. A toiling peasant who had internalized his role as the junior ally of the working class in the Proletarian Dictatorship had a legitimate place in the Bolshevik realm of the elect.[19] Of course, most peasants were supposed to move to the city; from there the road to conversion was short. Such narratives, however, essentially belonged to the genre of worker autobiography and have been discussed above. The road to Communism of the peasant who remained a peasant was always a checkered one, his "essence as a proprietor" supposedly inhibiting his ability to embrace the universalist message. The problem with the vision of the bucolic peasant was that the Party perceived the village as a dark place, rife with religious superstition.[20]

Priests and rituals were tabooed.[21] If peasant students wanted any chance to get enrolled they had to convince the cell that they were quick to abandon Christianity. In the autobiography Petrova presented before her fellow students in the Leningrad Communist University during the purge of 1924, she confessed to have been baptized. Equally true, she continued, "we had some icons at home until about 1912 or 1914. . . . But it was my grandmother who insisted on all that." Popova's father, a welder in a fire station, had been a Party member since 1902. Little wonder she "stopped believing in God at the age of twelve [. . .] and did not marry in church."[22]

Acknowledging the principles of peasant conversion, applicants detailed the hurdles inhibiting the transformation of a peasant into a Communist and how these were overcome: a peasant-author tended to describe him- or herself as poor and to justify political passivity early on by the "idiocy of rural life" (sel'skii kretinizm). He or she usually invested the local clergy with the role of the reactionary element, while the Marxist intelligentsia coming from the industrial center was assigned the role of the carrier of enlightenment. Service in the Red Army was a key step toward full conversion.

The autobiography of the Communist University student Vostrikov expressed these themes unequivocally. It was only shortly before his birth in the village of Aleksandrovka in Kustanaisk Province that his family managed to achieve some economic stability. By the age of eleven Vostrikov was already helping his father. When the family had no need of his labor, he studied in the village school, but his education was handicapped by his family's struggle with penury. Vostrikov patiently awaited his redeemer— who arrived in the form of his sister's husband, Prosolov. Since Prosolov brought the light to the village "only in May 1918," Vostrikov's failure to achieve any revolutionary exploits in 1917 was understandable. Having promised to teach the young and benighted peasant a thing or two, the purveyor of light invited him to go to Nizhnii-Novgorod. En route, however the train was blocked by the Czechoslovak mutineers. "Frankly, I could not comprehend everything at once. But I got the main point. Prosolov was the first to tell me who the Czechs were and why they were against the Red Guard and the Bolsheviks. He also explained to me about the union of youth [i.e., Komsomol]. At the time, my imagination was too limited to properly imagine something like that. Instead of clearing our way"—this important counter-factual was inserted by the autobiographer to show he knew which course events should have taken—"the Czechs occupied Cheliabinsk."

Prosolov may have been omniconscious but he was not omnipotent. Unable to break the Czech blockade, he had no choice but to rejoin Vostrikov in the city of Troitsk. This fortuitous chain of events set the narrator's enlightenment on the right track: "Sharing the same flat with Prosolov I became a witness to the secret conferences of the underground groups that frequently gathered in our flat. Our house was kept under surveillance and finally subjected to several searches." Unable to go on with their revolutionary labors, Vostrikov and his mentor fled to the countryside. But no change in environment could deter a revolutionary, and Prosolov organized a group of Communist sympathizers in Aleksandrovka, as the village was called. "Kolchak's government agents soon recognized our real political physiognomy—we named ourselves 'Bolsheviks'—and after a few shakeups, searches, and other such things we went underground."

The autobiography went on to dwell on how urban influences eroded "traditional" peasant narrow-mindedness. The entire rural district, shortly destined to rise against the Whites, had become politicized, so much so that even the autobiographer's father, an old peasant who had moved to within twenty miles of Aleksandrovka, joined Prosolov's secret organization. Surveillance and searches by the Whites intensified every day. Members of the underground were rounded up, Prosolov among them.

In March 1919, the so-called "Kustanaisk uprising" broke out. "Already before the uprising I had begun running small errands for the Bolshevik organization and during the uprising I was a go-between." But the uprising failed, the autobiographer and his sister were arrested, and their father was executed. Little wonder Vostrikov emerged from this experience a full-blown Bolshevik: "These circumstances revolutionized me to a considerable extent. When the Red Army came in fall 1919, I joined the Kustanaisk Cheka."

While the autobiographer laid claim to the consciousness of a devout Communist, the weighers of his soul were less sure: "Vostrikov is politically developed only within the narrow confines of the work he does." A typical peasant, he was thought to have a "weak Marxist preparation," a shortcoming that in turn explained "his unfortunately quite limited ability to orient himself within the general political situation." Hampered as he was by the backward particularism of the peasant mind, Vostrikov nonetheless managed to make it into the Party.

Experience in the Red Army often turned up in peasant applications in the guise of Communist baptism. Suspected of passivity during the Civil War, Beliakov from the Smolensk Technological Institute saved himself by showing that "since I lived in the countryside in 1917 or 1918, I was not fully informed of the Party platform. Only once I'd joined the Red Army did I hear something about Communism." The student who described himself moving away from the ignorance of the village was not challenged. But when the same Party cell discovered that the life trajectory of another peasant-student, Prokladov, took the opposite direction, the circle around him tightened and pressing questions were asked:[23]

Q: Why did you not serve in the Red Army?
A: I was kept busy as a chairman of the county's executive committee.
Q: Did you take technical military courses as a Communist?
A: I was a Communist in my heart, but without a Party card.
Q: When did you actually enter the Party?
A: In 1917, but since I lived in a village I had no Party card. [. . .] I was a sympathizer.

Prokladov's detractors maintained that "back in 1917 this student had not yet made up his mind about the Communist Party. Since he was worried about possible political shifts, Prokladov did not disclose his Party credentials in the village." The evidence pointed in an unmistakable direction—during the Revolution Prokladov had sat on the bench with the kulaks.

Ill-wishers testified that the Prokladovs owned thirty *desiatinas* of land purchased with the help of the Land Bank. Only kulaks had been recipients of such generous loans. Moreover, Prokladov's parents had owned a private brick-making enterprise that "could not be run without hired labor". Prokladov was found to be a "dubious" (*somnitel'nyi*) individual: "It was untrue that he had to return to the village in order to strengthen the household economy. He had no excuse to abandon the Party."

We have looked at a number of peasant autobiographies and it seems safe to say that their authors consistently presented themselves as uncouth, gut revolutionaries, driven to the light more by the merciless exploitation of the kulak or the noble landowner than by a refined theoretical knowledge.

The foregoing cases not only point to the direction the emancipating process had to take—from a poor village to the Red Army and then to Communism—but also provide us with the blueprint of its inversion, the narrative of decline—desertion from the Red Army, return to the village and enlistment with the White Army.

We have seen enough examples of peasant autobiographies to be familiar with the basic outline of the genre. I conclude this section with one especially rich autobiography of a tortured peasant. Indeed, the autobiography of Leven highlights the difficulties its author experienced in acquiring a Bolshevik outlook and leaves no doubt as to the difficulty contemporaries experienced in interpreting certain peasant life-trajectories.

Leven, a Moscow State University student who later became a Red professor in Leningrad, had many temptations to overcome. His had been a truly well-off, pious, and politically retrograde peasant household. At the outset Leven tells the reader that he came to this world in 1900 in the German village of Fiurtenau in Ukraine.[24] "When I was born, father was working as a carpenter in an agricultural equipment factory." The elder Leven worked as a carpenter for eight years until, in 1901, the Levens moved to Siberia.

The autobiographer himself lived off his own earnings "from the age of fifteen." For a while he seems to have wavered between peasant and intelligentsia identities. In a questionnaire of 1922 he identified himself as a "peasant" by social origins and a "member of the intelligentsia" by social position; asked whether he currently had any ties to the peasant economy, he left the space blank.

With politics things got even more complicated. It turned out that Leven had formally become a Bolshevik in Moscow on March 31, 1921. But he continued to be haunted by a brief period in the White Army during the final stages of the Civil War. A Party official of the day who had been acquainted with Leven's past would have explained this misstep in terms of a sectarian background. Such an interpretation would have contributed crucially to a very unflattering portrait. Faced with the threat of being unmasked as a counterrevolutionary, Leven began his autobiography with an extremely apologetic preamble: "My pre-Communist years have cast a certain shadow over my Party membership. But I have never concealed it. On the contrary, I have informed the Party about my White Army service both orally and in written form, going into the most minute details." The destruction of the documents by the Whites "further complicates my task of proving my statements true and makes it harder for the Party to check up on me."

Leven posed here the problem of how his sociopolitical soul could be "scrutinized." According to the standard Communist wisdom, class was the cause, consciousness and political action the outcome. But class identity was not easily established. Often the autobiographical argument had to be presented in an inverted sequence: from the narrator's political actions to his consciousness and then to his class self. Aware of the intricate workings of Communist reasoning, Leven first addressed his political vulnerability (service for the Whites), then turned to refute the view that his was a backward consciousness (sectarian religiosity), and only toward the very end of his self-presentation took on the problem of his potentially damaging socioeconomic background (wealthy peasant household).

In oddly pedantic fashion, Leven opened his main autobiographical text, to which he gave the title "Additional Explanations Regarding my Service in Kolchak's White Army," with a historical note. "Siberia was ruled by Kolchak for two full years—1918 and 1919," he informed the reader. "The February and the October revolutions were barely noticed in our region. The Kolchak regime had immediately supplanted the Tsarist regime there." Of course, Western Siberia had briefly been controlled by the Bolsheviks in 1918, but it was far better for Leven's case to portray the region as uninterruptedly reactionary. Not that Leven's native land was absolutely beyond redemption—as in other regions, the operation of historical forces was inexorably propelling Siberia along the road toward Communism. Siberia simply lagged a bit behind European Russia. By explaining that "sovietization was postponed in Siberia until 1920," Leven implied the corollary that his own conversion to Communism had to be deferred until that date as well. Leven and Siberia were both destined to become Communist sooner or later—that was never in question.

Having inserted eschatology into his sketch of Siberian history, the autobiographer turned to the difficult task of explaining how he had ended up in the White camp. First, the reader had to receive background information. Given that the lives of individuals tended, particularly in the revolutionary era, to fuse with the history of their class, the historical intermezzo that follows was not out of order: "The Kolchak government conducted an all-Siberian military draft. The first mobilization, extended to those born in 1898–99, was conducted in fall 1918. [. . .] It encountered many difficulties and provoked peasant uprisings everywhere."

At this point the dry historical narration yielded to orthodox Communist commentary: "Rebelling, the Siberian peasantry expressed its sharp hostility to the Kolchak government. The soviets were no longer popular only among the workers as broad segments of the peasantry lent their support." Much to Leven's regret, "Kolchak's forces were able to suppress the uprising." "Unfortunately, the diverse actions of the revolutionary masses lacked a unified, conscious leadership." Suggesting that its incapacity to act as a unified class was intrinsic to the peasantry in general and to the Siberian peasantry in particular, Leven echoed Marx's famous comparison of the peasantry with a sack of potatoes.

From macrohistory Leven shifted to microhistory. The sociopolitical context of the uprising was now clear, and he gradually narrowed the scope of analysis to the fate of his district during the Civil War, and ultimately to his own fate. "Only a few of the villages, those close to the cities, participated in the Slavgorod uprising. The villages of the Orlovsk district, which are about 40 to 70 kilometers from the city, did not rise up." At that time, Leven was at his parents' village of Nikolaipole. He had contracted typhus and "lay in the house, sick with fever" during the uprising. The absence of consciousness on the autobiographer's part was explained by a physical disease that had clouded his mind: "We only found out about the peasant uprising a day or two after it happened. In October my mother died."

Racked by a guilty conscience, less for his mother's death and more for his political passivity, Leven delved into a mix of lamentation and outrage in his depiction of the suppression of the uprising: "The Anenkov punitive expedition treated the rebellious peasants with great cruelty. Executions were summarily performed and there was neither interrogation nor trial. Peasant houses were robbed and set on fire." But Leven's immediate environment remained nearly unaffected: "Our villages were largely unscathed. All that happened was this: detachments passing by our village conducted a house search and took away valuables. But people were left alone." Why were the nearby villages unpunished? Clearly because they had not become politicized enough to present a threat to the Whites.

Though the great moment of proletarian revelation passed Leven by, the fault was not internal to him. Leven was simply constrained by superior forces, be they his retrograde milieu or his typhus-infested body. In any case, he was certainly not likely to join Kolchak's forces voluntarily.

In the spring of 1919 a mobilization of those born in 1900 and 1901 was announced. By that time, and by means of unbridled terror, Kolchak had cruelly consolidated his power. I had to comply. Only the crippled, the cult worshipers, and only sons were exempted. I could not take advantage of any of these privileges. A final possibility was a cash payment but I lacked the means.

The hapless, unwilling recruit was sent off to Irkutsk for drill and all that the reader learns of this period is that Leven did nothing willingly for the Whites. Conveniently, he "contracted dysentery and spent two months in a hospital." This timely reprieve let Leven's consciousness, which otherwise should have developed a strong resistance to Kolchak, off the hook.

On returning to the regiment, Leven learned that a group was needed to escort a draft transport to Barnaul. "I decided to feign a desire"—Leven was keen to suggest he was dissimulating when volunteering for a White military mission—"in order to get to Barnaul. The city is not far from my village— about 500 kilometers. I hoped I would not have to return to the regiment. On the way, we conspired to defect."

In June Leven reached home. "I hoped to hide at Korchigin's place," he went on, "but he had been drafted so that was out. Neither could I hide at home. On Kolchak's instructions, all the inhabitants of the village, and especially parents, were to be punishable for the presence of any deserters." All this by way of saying that the autobiographer had no choice but to return to the unit. His deeds spoke against him but Leven insisted that his soul was in the right place. "Prior to leaving my village, I managed to use personal contacts to get a certificate attesting that I was a cult worshiper." The autobiographer hoped that this certificate of religious obligation might relieve him from active duty.

Upon return to the White military unit in Irkutsk, Leven found out that "since they had assumed me to be dead, a church service had been conducted for the preservation of my soul." It is possible that this detail is to be interpreted to mean something like "As far as my contribution to the White cause goes, I was as good as dead." A request for release from active duty was denied, however, and Leven was sent to the front line at Omsk. He and a group of like-minded soldiers deserted en route, "taking the rifles and spades we had with us." The defection was premeditated and conscious. "The night before, we had filled out the leave blanks we had prepared in advance and had had appropriately stamped back in Irkutsk, switched to another train and traveled ahead of our unit. That was the end of my service in the White Army."

As he shifted from a realistic to a heroic narrative, the poetics Leven juggled were those of conversion. "Freezing and starving I and my fellow-defectors traveled on train roofs. In Anchinsk we ran into Kolchak himself with his entourage." Leven was moving forward. Kolchak was retreating. Two lines of historical development intersected at that moment. At this stage the autobiographer was beyond reproach. "Whenever my comrades grew depressed, I had to talk them out of returning to the regiment so close behind us."

Now a consummate Bolshevik, Leven continued with a matter-of-fact narrative. "On the way to Slavgorod, the Polish Whites seized our train from us. To avoid capture, we dispersed into the villages that were already under partisan control. When we were stopped by mounted partisans armed with hunting rifles, pikes, and pitchforks, we told them where we had come from, where we were headed, and why." The autobiographer glossed over the undecided, semi-anarchistic politics of the peasants in whose midst he found himself. His account only had room for Reds and Whites, and by deserting one group he must have been allying himself with the other.

We told the peasants that Kolchak was on the run; that of all Siberia he held only the railway line; that the regular Red Army detachments were making rapid advances; and that Siberia would shortly be under the control of the Soviet power. The partisans listened to us with great interest and enthusiasm, received us amicably, provided us with food, and helped us to continue our mounted journey home through the villages.

Ten days later, Leven was home. Along his journey, "awful sights had revealed themselves all over Siberia. Roads were covered with bodies of those frozen and starved to death, and the victims of typhus. At the stations, dead bodies were piled up in stacks like firewood." Somewhat belatedly, Leven had come to appreciate the calamity the Whites had brought to Siberia. At this point, the camera pulled back out and macrohistory replaced microhistory. The narrative took its cue from the standard Bolshevik histories of the Civil War, which describe how the young Soviet Republic withstood the combined attack of the imperialist legions and the native Russian elites. "For all intents and purposes, the front line disappeared. The Czechoslovaks, the Japanese, the English, the Italians, the Poles—all of them fled. They were accompanied by the Russian bourgeois who were trying to save their property."

Leven himself stayed in the village not too long, only until representatives of the village school in which he had worked the previous winter came to visit and urged him to return to teaching. In the spring of 1920, teachers' courses opened in Slavgorod and Leven enrolled.

Here the first circle of Leven's autobiography reached its conclusion. Every reader who had gotten this far would have been convinced that Leven was incapable of a counterrevolutionary act. Purely because of the bad luck of being in an area controlled by the Whites, Leven had been coerced by a superior force to act against his judgment. Besides, he had really done very little, having been ill most of the time.

Now that the reader was persuaded that by 1920 at the latest Leven's intellectual development was set along a Marxist route, Leven could address the checks put on his rise to revolutionary consciousness by his native sectarian milieu: "In German villages, many teachers were at the same time preachers. They had a reactionary disposition and agitated widely against [Soviet] teachers' courses, claiming they came from the Antichrist and so on, and those who took part would not be permitted to work." As a result, the courses were boycotted by the German teachers in the region. The fearless Leven became one of only two students who enrolled nonetheless. The other was Jan Jacob, who introduced Leven to "comrades" from the local German section and got him to attend "political discussions." This led, on August 8, 1920, to Leven's entry into the Party "on the recommendation of comrade Jan."

Concerns about establishing his origins in the mind of the Bolshevik audience are evident as Leven points out that the German section had recommended him to the Party only after "the section's delegates went to my village and studied my family to their satisfaction." In other words, it was generally acknowledged that Leven's family had transcended its background as Volga German resettlers. Furthermore, his growing detachment from his backward peasant milieu apparently did not go unnoticed: "Jan and I were the first in the German region to become Communists. We became well known in the area as a result, and even the small children heard about us. At that time, whenever we passed by a village people would go to the trouble of coming out and staring at me as if I was a wild bear." Leven boasted of having graduated in no time from teachers' school. He became a population poll inspector in the German region shortly thereafter, his efforts were appreciated, and he was next sent to study at the Central German Party school run by the Central Committee. "In Moscow I received a systematic political education for the first time in my life."

Securely locating himself in the theoretical citadel of Communism, Leven at last felt that he might permit a few disclosures that were a bit problematic—and these related to religion. In an unorthodox move, the text backtracked to the protagonist's adolescence. The clause that ushered in the flashback—"already from the age of fifteen I had been actively opposed to religion"—signaled a search for the roots of Communist consciousness:

> Although I was primarily driven by the anti-religious sentiment, my anti-religious activity was tied in my mind with a particular class line—hatred of the wealthy exploiters. I grew up and lived in a Mennonite sectarian village. Most people there, my parents included, were Baptists. A most powerful religious fanaticism was favored, linked with unimaginable hypocrisy. On Sundays, at church gatherings, the Methodist preachers pulled long faces and pretended to be otherworldly arch-saints. For the rest of the week they were the most shameless carousers. As a rule, the preachers were kulaks. On Sundays they taught good deeds and for the rest of the time they took advantage of whoever they could, however they could.

The reader who suspected that Leven might have been a believer was immediately dissuaded. "The preacher's hypocrisy aroused a deep hatred and protest in my bosom."

Yet, the autobiographer presented his protest as still emotional and unconscious at this stage. Leven's young mind could not but be somewhat adversely affected by the power of darkness. "Even though I passionately loved life and enlightenment, religious fanaticism blocked my way to a normal secular life and education. Books seldom fell into my hands. When they did I loved them madly, embraced them with all my soul, and even kissed their covers. Here is the source of my deep hatred of religion."

Since he resisted it so fiercely, religiosity, "itself a product of the kulak class that was so tightly woven into religion," could only be a temporary hindrance on Leven's path to true self-expression.

> At first, I ran away from the religious indoctrination my parents and outsiders tried to force on me. I attentively read the Bible and other holy texts, looking for contradictions and nonsense, which I used against my foes who, as a rule, did not read the Bible with any care.

Familiar with the enemy's way of thinking, Leven was ready for theological disputations.[25] In the winter of 1915–16, he experienced his "first tense showdown" on the religious front, one that earned him the reputation of being an "Antichrist."

> A famous wandering Baptist leader, going from village to village and house to house, was expected in my home. To avoid the encounter, I went away to a meeting of the village adolescents. There I learned many details about the lecherous personal life of this celebrated preacher. Fate determined that on my way home I ran straight into him. I tried to escape but he caught me by the sleeve and asked, "And how about your afterlife?" I laconically threw back at him: "Do not worry, your holiness. Mind your own soul. If someone like you makes it into heaven, I sure won't be left out." The preacher let me go right away. On the next day he declared from the church pulpit, in the presence of all the village, that he had called for the divine damnation of my soul.

Similar incidents narrated in Leven's autobiography do not need to be reproduced here since the thrust of the argument is clear: Leven's consciousness grew steadily through a constant battle with religion.

By his late teens, Leven was a vigilant antireligious militant:

> Frequently, when religious arguments would erupt, a crowd would form and the scene turned into a dispute. Attaining a certain dexterity in this sort of activity I began dismantling saints with great success, actively conducting antireligious agitation among the young. [. . .] This was our strategy: We would agree to attend a certain sermon. As a rule, the religious flock slept soundly in the church. But I listened carefully to every word the speaker said and then tore to pieces the heresies spread in the church once the sermon was over.

Leven was not just the recipient but also the carrier of light in the village, a young boy quite enthusiastic in his enlightenment endeavors: "Except for the children of kulaks and clergy, I succeeded in wrestling from the teeth of the Church almost all the adolescents my age. They later became Komsomol and Party members, entered [soviet] work, or went to study. The above may be described as my 'work for the public' for the years 1915 to 1920."

But then, as if he had gone too far, Leven partially retracted his claim. (After all, his true conversion would not happen for another five years, when he joined the Party.)

My anti-religious work, though it was along the correct class course, failed to elevate me to political maturity. I remained oblivious to the importance of politics and my focus on religion kept me on the sidelines of state issues. I was unable to arrive at the correct conclusions by myself, and at that time no one helped me. No one in the village received a newspaper and I never got hold of the right sort of books. The idea that antireligious work can have anything to do with the tsar never occurred to me.

Leven recounted an anecdote to convey the political apathy of the village: "After the February Revolution, the village elder told me that a command had been issued to remove the tsar's portraits. He instructed me to take down the portrait hanging in our school but not to damage it because 'we might soon have to hoist it again.' "

In describing the state of his consciousness during that period, the autobiographer had to be cautious. If he stressed its development, his time in the White Army would have become totally inexplicable, depriving the autobiographical narrative of any verisimilitude. If, on the other hand, he played the level of his adolescent consciousness down, he ran the risk of looking like a natural White supporter with a long retrograde spiritual history.

The text achieved a careful balance. Intuitively, Leven was on the right side, but why the right side was right he did not yet quite know. It took a while, but finally the situation cleared:

In the summer of 1918, studying at the normal course in Slavgorod, I had Frantz Frantzevich Fren as a peer. He was a Menshevik, a member of the Siberian Constitutional Assembly. Having received his education in Germany, he had gotten a taste of Marxism, albeit in an arch-reformist key. This Fren carried out a couple of illegal discussions with us, outdoors. He dwelt only on issues of worldview. I listened to him with the greatest interest although I learned nothing about politics. The experience in Kolchak's army gave me much more in that respect, and drew me into politics.

During the autobiographical flashback, the passive voice reappeared. But its time was up. With the opening of the Civil War, every Russian was forced into political action and Leven's tale of conversion could no longer be postponed. The time had come to retell the story of Leven's conversion from an experiential point of view.

The soldiers were generally very hostile to Kolchak. When once a priest told us we should die for the Orthodox religion and the fatherland, only pure luck allowed him to escape alive. We had been about to throw him out of a fourth floor window. [. . .] The organization of Kolchak's army provided us with rich material. In the barracks we were not allowed to read newspapers and the officers constantly told us that "a soldier has to stay out of politics." But we got hold of some issues and in the evening, seated on the plank beds and holding a candle, we read the news from the front. The discussions that ensued were marked by a clear sympathy with the Soviet Power.

Given that religion was an integral part of counterrevolutionary ideology, Leven did not hesitate to reiterate that he was immune to it. But his insistence on his resentment of all attempts to dupe the soldiers was an even more important way of inserting a wedge between himself and Kolchak.

Another anecdote conveyed the contempt Leven felt for the White officers. "Ordered to swear an oath of allegiance, many of us refused, citing various pretexts. My excuse was religious sensitivities. Before we were dispatched to the front, General Orlov read to us his parting words. When we were supposed to give a great 'Hur-r-a-a-a-h!' a group of us shouted 'Dur-r-a-a-a-k!' [idiot] instead. We shouted louder than the rest of the soldiers." At the end of his second account of his experience in the White Army, Leven concluded: "On my return from the army I started to understand some things." The focus on the inner state of understanding, rather than on the outward act of desertion, was in keeping with the main theme of this second autobiographical circle—the evolution of the protagonist's consciousness.

Having gone over his White Army past twice, and having examined the link between the peasantry and the White movement and then the peasantry and religiosity, the autobiographer was at last ready to take on the issue of his social background.

Finally I should say something on the subject of my social origins. My father was a peasant from 1901 to 1927. Our family economy while we lived in Orenburg Province was "weak, ill-empowered, middling." In addition to father and mother there were six of us children, all younger than twelve. Before marrying, my mother was a house servant and later a chambermaid in a wealthy Ukrainian German family. In 1901 we moved to Siberia. The government gave us twenty-five rubles and a sizable plot of land. The Ukrainian Germans gave us another seventy-five rubles. At first we were very poor. We lived in a dugout and later in an earthen-house. My father sowed only five to ten *desiatinas*.

With time, however, the Levens got richer. Considerably so. "Good harvests improved our condition and from 1913 to 1927 our family economy was considered middle." Leven reported that by 1919 the household had six horses and two to three cows. As many as twenty *desiatinas* of land were cultivated by the family—a considerable amount.

By labeling his father a "middle peasant" and stressing that "we used no hired labor," Leven hoped to lessen the impact of these numbers on the reader. But he did have to disclose that "at the time of our greatest economic prosperity, and for no more than two or three years, we had nearly thirty *desiatinas* of land," and this put him on the verge of being grouped with the village bourgeoisie. As at other perilous moments in his tale, there was a chance the entire scaffold of the narrative might collapse. To meet this danger, Leven embarked on a geographical excursus. In Siberia, he explained, "the land was in household tenure," that is, it was not communally held. "In our village each household had thirty-six *desiatinas* of arable land. The same went for my father." Under the three-field system, a third of the land was fallow at any given time. This left the Levens with only twenty-four *desiatinas* they could cultivate. "In any case, we tilled that much only for the few years I have mentioned."

The Leven household of the 1920s fell into the category of "having some indicators of exploitation." The land had not been divided among the children—this left the family economy wealthier but made Leven's part in the arrangement seem less significant. After all, he did move to the city very early on. No one was denying that Leven's sister eventually emigrated to Canada, that his father threshed the wheat of four to five neighboring households for payment in kind, or even that after the adult male children had departed Leven's household economy "hired" (read: exploited) laborers during the harvest. But then again, the Levens were not disenfranchised.

The structure of Leven's narrative could maintain its integrity only if he could convince his audience that he had never (quite) become a kulak. And so he closed with a fervent oath: The autobiography he had written was made up exclusively of "fact. What I have written are the details of my life story. [. . .] I can neither add not subtract a thing. This has been done in an effort to aid the Party in unveiling my past, and I hereby promise to make amends for my service in Kolchak's army by an unlimited dedication to Communism."

In writing his life account, Leven knew perfectly well there was nothing predetermined about peasants siding with the Bolsheviks and embracing proletarian collectivism. When Soviet sociologists looked west, all they saw were nationalist regimes based on peasant enthusiasm. And when Soviet historians turned to the annals of the French Revolution they noted that radical reforms suffocated for lack of village support. If in 1789 peasants stormed the manors and helped tear down the age-old rule of the nobility, in 1830 and in 1848 their children were content with the plots of land they had been bequeathed. They did not lift a finger to help the Parisian proletariat. Only interaction with native workers and Marxist proselytizers could overcome the peasant penchant for private property and insulated existence—and the autobiographers we examined structured their stories of spiritual awakening around those themes.

Indeed, even students from admittedly well-off peasant families were permitted to make themselves into good proletarians by showing they turned against their past and their families. But narrators had to make persuasive the distinction between their former, primitive religiosity and their present-day, enlightened thinking—and this was not a small task given the Bolshevik anti-peasant bias. The persuasiveness of the rhetoric of peasant autobiography depended on the writers' ability to fend off the suggestion of any linkage of the backwardness of the village with both the plague on the right and the plague on the left—retrograde conservatism or self-indulgent anarchism. Bolshevism was the only correct choice and it had to involve a risk to life. This is why the response to the Civil War—in which both the Reds and the Whites relied on peasant recruits and villages changed sides frequently—was the sticking point of the narratives we have examined.

CHAPTER 4
The Intelligentsia

IN PRINCIPLE, EVERY SOVIET CITIZEN could join the Communist movement. True, the Bolshevik party was the party of the proletariat, but
"proletarian" was a way of thinking, not a socioeconomic position into
which one was born. Every conscious individual who assumed the proletarian perspective on life could be accepted with open arms (and, inversely,
workers who were children of workers were barred entrance if their
consciousness was not ripe). This inclusiveness—provided the applicant
embraced the Party wholeheartedly and sincerely—made Communism into
a universalist creed, open not only to workers and peasants but also to
members of the petit-bourgeois intelligentsia.[1]

The autobiographical statement of Korenevskii from the Smolensk
Technological Institute, a navy officer who served during World War I in
the Baltic and in the Black Sea fleets from 1921, can be examined from this
angle. Korenevskii admitted that his background was scarcely proletarian
and that he "was not very much interested in politics before the Revolution."
But the year 1917 changed all that. "I developed an interest in learning Party
programs and in April became a Bolshevik in my soul [*v dushe*] and, one
might say, in my actions as well." Mistaking the Bolshevik party for a narrow
class institution, Korenevskii was convinced Party doors were shut before
him forever. "What stood in my way to Party enrollment—or so I used to
think—was my title as a former officer and the absence of comrades-in-arms
who would be Bolshevik idealists [*ideinye bol'sheviki*]. I looked around,
searched my way, and finally, in August 1919, found the right figure in the
face of a military commander, Serpen', who convinced me that the Party
welcomes any decent individual and that I would run into no grudge against
me as a former officer." His rejection anxiety alleviated, Korenevskii applied
to the Party in 1920. "Presently, I do all I can to help the toiling class," he
assured his readers, "although I have a major shortcoming—total absence
of rhetorical talents."[2] What was at stake here, first and foremost, was the
malleability of the soul, its openness to the light. Korenevskii's imperfect
class origins could be washed away. Politically, however, he had to be a
tabula rasa; if he had ever manifested a formed consciousness, it had to be
a Bolshevik one.

Judged from this perspective, the attitude toward applicants from the intelligentsia such as Korenevskii was ambivalent. On the one hand, the intelligentsia had a long-standing reputation as the class destined to bring light to the workers.[3] The "intelligentsia minority," its truly "conscientious part," had proved its loyalty to the working class by joining the Party before the Revolution, when dedication to the proletarian cause had been very dangerous. "When we deal with this segment of the intelligentsia," Party theoreticians stated, "we deal with people whose loyalty to Communism is beyond doubt."[4] On the other hand, the intelligentsia was suspected as a class traitor. During 1917, so the Bolshevik historians argued, this class got scared by the directness and violence of the revolutionary process. Terrified, it yoked itself to the defense of the old values—passivity, self-restraint, turning the other cheek.

From the early stages of his political career, Lenin believed that the intelligentsia was a pollutant, a group unfit for the new world:

The preponderance of the radical intelligentsia in the ranks of Social Democracy cultivates opportunist psychology. [. . .] In their very nature, such people are incapable of formulating questions in a steadfast, direct manner. Like snakes, they swerve between mutually exclusive points of view [*vietsia uzhom*], call their reservations "corrections" and "doubts," constantly profess their good intentions, innocent wishes, and so on.[5]

Immediately after the end of the Civil War, preparations were made for a comprehensive cleansing of the intelligentsia from the Party.[6] "Those who do not work with their hands have no place in our ranks," stated the official press in the autumn of 1921. "Comrades, bear in mind that it is this uncompromising interpretation of membership requirements that distinguishes us from the Mensheviks."[7] To be sure, a Bolshevik leader such as Rafail could label the propensity of some delegates to the Tenth Party Congress to see the origins of all their negatives in the intelligentsia that staffed the leading organs as "intelligentsia-cannibalism" (*intelligenstvoedstvo*). "Turning the Party rudder in the correct direction," he assured his audience, "we can easily digest all these tens of thousands of members of the intelligentsia who entered our Party."[8] "We do need the intelligentsia," Molotov agreed, "but we must check the intelligentsia very carefully."[9]

But Lenin, whose voice was more authoritative, urged the Party to get rid of the old intelligentsia, described by him as a bunch of "the dishonest and the shaky, the bureaucrats and the Mensheviks who had dyed their facade in new colors but who remained just the same in the depth of their souls." [10] Zinoviev argued that "even those members of the intelligentsia who accepted the Revolution had in fact accepted only NEP." [11] Indeed, the main question, as the Party ideologues saw it, was whether the intelligentsia would discard its ancient robes and transform itself into "new people" (*novye liudi*) or "assimilate the psychology of our comrades." [12]

The head of the Central Purge Commission, Sol'ts, translated what Lenin and Zinoviev had said into practical language. He issued a demand that "the purge commissions pay special attention to the Party members from the intelligentsia." [13] Taking advantage of their privileges as referees, "worker-purifiers" (*rabochii-chistil'shchiki*) tended to claim that the intelligentsia "came to us by mistake; the Communist Party is not the intelligentsia's party." [14] The purge commissions developed a special approach in dealing with members of the intelligentsia who clung to their old habits, "particularly the intelligentsia that joined our Party in 1921, or 1920, or 1919, that is, after the October Revolution. [. . .] We not only verified that such a person was not a careerist but a conscientious human being who works well in soviet institutions. We also checked to make sure that his spirit was sufficiently Bolshevik and revolutionary." [15] The official press recounted how, "when they come across a 'specialist' their vigilance intensifies and they ask one question after another." [16] A feuilleton entitled "The People's Judgment Day" threw the issue into sharp relief:

- The chair of the meeting summons the first Party member—a worker-peasant—to the table. Two, three words and his autobiography is exhausted. Any derailments? None.
- "Next!"
- An anxious Party functionary, a former chancery worker steps in. "Your autobiography, comrade." A long and boring story unfolds. One can see right away that this individual was never oppressed by capitalists, that this individuum hovers somewhere up in the sky.
- "Next!"
- A highly placed official wearing an intelligentsia face steps forward. Despite his higher education he had followed a wandering course without rudder or sail, had been with the Socialist Revolutionaries, with the Mensheviks, with the Bund. [. . .] As he tells his autobiography, this comrade seems contrived. Gradually workers shake themselves up and expose the physiognomy of a bureaucrat. [17]

The message to the purge commissions was unequivocal—subject intelligentsia autobiographies to merciless examination: "While mistakes committed by undeveloped workers may be forgiven, more should be expected from the learned." [18]

The detailed minutes of the 1921 purge kept at the Smolensk Technological Institute show that the baiting of the intelligentsia took place at the grassroots. The purge committee did its work in the presence of all the members of the cell as well as a number of "extramural workers representing the Smolensk proletariat." The meetings lasted for many hours, in one case from three in the afternoon to ten in the morning, as each member of the cell was called to the center stage to recount his autobiography aloud. Anyone present could comment on what he heard, advance derailments, and ask questions, the Party's "plenipotentiaries" (upolnomochennye)—Bolsheviks with underground experience and proletarian class origins delegated to the purge meetings by the county Party commissions—making their own inquires. [19]

About every fourth Party member in the institute belonged to the intelligentsia cohort which, as one would expect, suffered the brunt of the purge. Consider Mochelevkin's interrogation. Although this student claimed in his questionnaire that he was "of peasant origins," a brief interrogation showed otherwise. "You said your father was a land tiller. But did not the tsarist government prohibit Jews from working the land? Besides, you omitted the fact that your mother used to run a shop." [20]

When Mochelevkin confessed that "the February Revolution came to me as a surprise; in the beginning, I was unable to orient myself," an anonymous student recalled that he had been overheard to make such typically intelligentsia statements as, "The toppling of Kerenskii was premature and unnecessary." Besides, "when Mochelevkin delivered a speech at a political rally, soldiers wanted to beat him up for some reason"—a bizarre inclination on the part of a zealously pro-Bolshevik crowd, unless of course "the speaker objected to our withdrawal from the war."

Undoubtedly the most intriguing remark on this case was made when one of the detractors noted that "Mochelevkin liked to kiss ladies' hands." Miles apart from true working class conduct, such behavior "was quite typical of the intelligentsia." Ever on the alert for the slightest physical clues, this physiognomist believed that Mochelevkin's general demeanor, his grimaces, even the telltale floridness of his gestures, all betrayed an absence of proletarian masculinity.

Mochelevkin's effeminized portrait revealed the class–gender nexus integral to the official discourse. Bolshevik poetics symbolically grafted the intelligentsia onto the traditional and deprecated role of the female, assigning the active, masculine role to the proletariat. In this scheme, thinking itself became a feminine faculty whereas acting was strictly masculine. "Its feminine psyche," Trotsky believed, "the fact that it is trained to be contemplative, impressionable, and sensitive, undercuts the intelligentsia's physical power."[21] "Obsequious" and "weak," students of Mochelevkin's ilk were persistently described by the Bolsheviks as both malicious and effective, thanks to their ability to coax the strong but naive workers into turning their bodily strength against themselves, which kept them from demanding their rights. But now this strategy was unmasked, and Mochelevkin was defenseless.

Another detractor brought Mochelevkin's intelligentsia identity into particularly sharp focus when he called attention to the defendant's smoothness: "Mochelevkin is eloquent about things that the committee is not interested in, dodging what is really significant." As the following exchange suggests, not only had he shunned physical labor, but he had also lied in denying that others had done household chores for him:

Q: Your autobiography states that your means were strained. But have you not had servants?

A: No, my mother was the one who had servants, not I.

But apples could not have fallen that far from the tree. Mochelevkin could not prove that he had distanced himself from his family and made true sacrifices for the Revolution. Seen as bereft of will and rotten to the core, he was purged by an overwhelming majority.

Without a doubt, the apogee of the purge was the interrogation of the institute's rector, Razdobreev, a quintessential intelligentsia Bolshevik.[22] An older and better-educated Bolshevik, Razdobreev had completed his formal training long before 1917. With the coming of October he took the Red side and during the last stages of the Civil War he had served as the military commissar of the Smolensk Institute, a post he still occupied in 1921. Considering his social physiognomy, his successful career in tsarist Russia, and his late admission to the Party (April 1920), as well as the fact that "had been corrupted by long interaction with the petit-bourgeois milieu," Razdobreev's position was precarious.

The message that the Central Purge Commission sent regarding individuals such as Razdobreev was somewhat contradictory: "We have to be particularly demanding toward soviet employees and to the offspring of bourgeois intelligentsia," the Central Committee stated. At the same time, it went without saying that "each cell must find enough wit and tact to retain the truly conscientious and loyal people."[23] Overall, the anxieties associated with the dramatic liberalization of economic policies tipped the balance in the direction of exclusivism. "The main target of the purge," Shkiriatov explained, is not so much the "crook who wormed his way into our Party [. . .] but even a conscientious individual, if he has nothing in common with our Party. For when we take sharp turns—sometimes we have to swerve or go in full reverse—such elements can weaken us."[24]

Razdobreev's interrogation took almost an entire night. The bureau had done plenty of preparatory work on the case, soliciting and double-checking denunciations. As the process began, the rector responded to a list of questions presented to him in advance:

Q: Given that you are the son of a simple Cossack, how did you manage to pave your way to the tsarist Ministry of Transportation?

A: Through the recommendation of the railroad management I was accepted to an institute run by the ministry on an academic fellowship.

Q: Where did you get the money that allowed you to study abroad?

A: When I lived abroad, I was broke. [. . .] Father borrowed 900 rubles [for me]. He barely came up with the money to repay the loan.

Having established that Razdobreev was a social upstart, the interrogation moved to inquire about the evolution of his political consciousness:

Q: You say that your feelings about the Party platform were for a long time unsettled, but are not anymore? [. . .]

A: I did not want to join the Party earlier because Kolchak and Denikin were about to be defeated so I hoped to avoid the impression that I had become a Bolshevik only because the Soviet Power had the upper hand. But when the war with Poland began I did enroll.

Q: Was not the situation of the republic very sound in April [when you applied for Party membership]?

A: I insist that the republic was not safe then and that that was the reason for my enrollment.

Though Razdobreev claimed he lent his shoulder to the Reds at a moment of grave danger, his interrogators still suspected that he was motivated by his pursuit of a lucrative bureaucratic post.

Q: Having read Marx and Engels before, how could you waver for so long before joining the Party?

A: My interest in social issues goes back to 1905. I then participated in an Anarchist circle. In the institute I was doing scholarly work and met no one who could acquaint me with the Bolshevik program. Yes, I read Marx. But my impression was that his ideas could be the basis for any socialist party, not just the Bolsheviks. I wanted to understand [the basic ideas of socialism], so I read Marx.

The committee would focus on Razdobreev's interpretation of Marx, and he knew it was crucial that he distinguished himself from the old intelligentsia, whose reading tended to be quite Menshevik. Emphasizing that familiarity with Marxism did not automatically entail acquaintance with Bolshevism, Razdobreev conceded that the question of his 1905 consciousness was perhaps moot. But he was careful to make it clear that he was definitely and distinctly not Menshevik, or in any other way anti-Bolshevik.

Razdobreev's description of his past attitude as "underdeveloped" left room for his personal growth in subsequent years. This, however, was not the only interpretation available. "Razdobreev's belated enrollment in the Party calls for deep reflection," argued Zakharov, a member of the bureau. "He must have been politically developed, since he had already read the fathers of Marxism. Razdobreev joined the Party at a time when the Red Army had just achieved a great victory at the gates of Warsaw."

If Razdobreev, together with the rest of the chauvinist, petit-bourgeois intelligentsia, joined the Party not because he was committed to the idea of the universal revolution but because of his belief that the new regime was about to substitute "class war" for "national war," he may have stayed in the Bolshevik camp, according to his detractors, because he hoped NEP would restore capitalist order. Had Razdobreev accepted Bolshevism in general, including its War Communist episode? Or was he perhaps simply attracted by NEP?

> Q: Do you think the Party ever commits mistakes? Were the Bolsheviks right when they introduced *prodrazverstka* [tax proportional to the harvest practiced during the Civil War]?
>
> A: It would not have been bad to introduce *prodnalog* [a pre-set agricultural tax that enabled peasants to keep most of their product—one of the key innovations of NEP] right away and skip over the *prodrazverstka*.[25] This is the only issue over which I had disagreements with Communists.
>
> Q: What is your attitude toward specialists?
>
> A: Specialists are indispensable everywhere, and in our republic particularly so. If I thought otherwise I would not have taken the position of a rector.
>
> Q: Should specialists be financially supported?
>
> A: Yes, we have to secure their livelihood.
>
> Plenipotentiary: Listening to you one gets the impression that you base your sympathy for Communism on the NEP. But what if our economic policy changes?
>
> A: It cannot change because it was meant to last for some years. If the Party, sensibly and reasonably, will alter its policy, I think I will be able to comprehend such a step, come to terms with it, and endorse it. It is essentially temporary, but the New Economic Policy is necessary and appropriate right now. The Party ideal will have to be resurrected some time in the future. The dictatorship of the proletariat can wither away only gradually.

Citing Lenin to the effect that "NEP has to be embraced seriously, and for a long time," Razdobreev professed temperance. His enthusiasm for NEP, however, was open to the objection that what might be desirable for the intelligentsia could be a step backward for the proletariat. To prove he was in all respects a Bolshevik, Razdobreev had to show that he was not one of the intelligentsia softies who harbored qualms regarding the use of force, for example, during the merciless suppression of the Kronstadt rebellion. This was especially important since the purge committee had noticed that despite his role as military commissar Razdobreev had not participated during that crisis. He did not go to the military barracks when a military emergency was announced during the Kronstadt uprising because, he claimed, "I was needed at my workplace."

As the flood of questions from the floor subsided, the bureau revealed the damaging material against Razdobreev that it had collected. Its affidavit included twenty-three complaints of minor misconduct and three more-substantial denunciations, including charges of embezzlement, high-handedness, and possession of a bourgeois proprietary instinct—all typical intelligentsia failings. It was asserted that Razdobreev had humiliated his subordinates. Razdobreev countered: "I did not use the institute's manpower for my personal needs. Neither is it in my character to desire to be called 'master' [*barin*]. The old nanny who calls me such is no longer young and cannot be untaught. There is no crime in that." Other accusations alleged that Razdobreev had used the institute's car "as if it was his property," that he had constructed a fence around his summer house with the help of Red Army manpower, and that his maids had thrown away part of his meat ration muttering that "even dogs would not eat it." Here Razdobreev's response was brief and dismissive: "In general, workers dislike Communists and administrators. But I did not teach my staff to say such things."

But the charges were accumulating, and Razdobreev was beginning to look like a grandee. Another wave of allegations followed:

> You could not possibly have produced a one-to-eighteen potato harvest when the average in this area is one to eight. While you and your collaborators get fat on the potatoes you embezzle, workers are starving on the Volga. What do you say to this? [. . .] And why does not everyone receive the same ration? Why should some be mighty and some be mice (*krali i karliki*)?

Razdobreev defended himself point by point: "I see no crime in the land returning so much. Believe me, the Volga famine was much on my mind when I dug potatoes. Whether I will donate my potatoes for relief is as yet uncertain."

Because Bolshevism did not distinguish between political and economic crimes—GPU, for example, regarded "economic sabotage" and "political sedition" as equally counterrevolutionary—the following diatribe, launched by a student named Grigorev, offered a unified model of Razdobreev's class and political outlook.

The abnormal size of Razdobreev's harvest indicates where fertilizers were used and where they were not. [. . .] Potatoes were dug by Red Army soldiers; they had not contracted to do this work, but had been ordered to do it and were indignant at such exploitation. [. . .] Razdobreev says workers on the state farm do not approve of Communists. How could it be otherwise? Once they have seen the example a prominent Communist like him sets they start thinking in a non-Communist way.

This was a line of damaging prosecution. Using the language of class war, Grigorev portrayed the rector as an enemy of the working class, precisely the type of element who sets workers against their own party. How else, if they see in the Bolshevik ranks arrogant exploiters who continue treating them as the dregs of society and who believe that workers are too obtuse to see the tricks played on them? The remainder of the speech was a condemnation of petit-bourgeois possessiveness, unfortunately brought back into favor by NEP:

Razdobreev is a specialist to the bone, a sweet-talker who wriggled out of trouble before and might succeed again today. I will not deny that as a specialist Razdobreev is priceless. But as a Communist he is good for nothing and has to be thrown out. The Party is not a shelter for specialists! I am not against providing specialists with an allowance, but this allowance is not a license to "take as much as you can." Why should other trustworthy comrades of old standing suffer worse material conditions? The scion of a petit-bourgeois family, Razdobreev has never been and will never become a part of the worker-peasants masses. Razdobreev adores the New Economic Policy and likes to say, "This is mine." He may be a worthy member of the petite bourgeoisie but he is not a worthy member of the Party.

Grigorev persevered, insisting that Razdobreev's intelligentsia instinct had led him to "surround himself with cronies who took shelter behind him and wove themselves cozy nests. This is how the tiny little Mensheviks infiltrate our ranks." The "Menshevik bond" Grigorev was talking about did not need to be understood in terms of a specific set of political convictions. Rather, it stemmed from the general "physiognomy" of Razdobreev's company, "which was sprightly, philistine, and exploiting." Grigorev relied here on the Bolshevik press, which advanced the notion of "the-good-for-nothing philistine intelligentsia that exists in every Party cell."[26]

Even as the attacks became less concrete, they became more dramatic and, possibly, devastating. Grigorev squeezed Razdobreev into a coffin, Zakharov nailed it. "His theoretical position was always in agreement with the Party—but in practical terms he was aloof and alienated himself from the grassroots—in no way had Razdobreev proved his loyalty to the Revolution."

At this point, Ioffe, the first to speak in favor of the defendant after a long interval, interjected that ideological endorsement must be worth something: "Razdobreev supports the Party platform, does he not? Believe me, an old Bolshevik; it is wrong to put on the same plane the work of a specialist and the work of an unskilled worker. Shepherd and specialist do not reap the same." But Zakharov dismissed this attempt to defend the embattled rector:

I still insist that Razdobreev lacks a healthy proletarian instinct because he was raised and now revolves in a milieu that is alien to the proletariat and to our Party. Everything suggests that our institute is not a Communist, but a White organization. Razdobreev neither enlisted in the special detachment, nor did he volunteer to participate in Saturday work [subbotniki]. To be sure, Razdobreev has pieces of paper to justify anything he does. This only further proves he is not a staunch Communist, for had he been one he would have pleaded guilty and begged us for forgiveness."

Refraining from a head-on critique of NEP, Bolshevik zealots limited themselves to showing that now that alien economic forces had been released it was all the more important to defend proletarian purity. If Razdobreev had to be tolerated as an administrator, there was no need to put up with him in the Party. "I respect Razdobreev a great deal as a practical man," one of his detractors stated. "It is impossible to exaggerate his contribution to the institute since 1918. Yet, a Party tribunal is another matter. [. . .] He is a man of another camp and another set of convictions."

The time had come for the moderates to attempt a rebuttal. Slesar' reminded the cell that Party specialists deserved special consideration: "Razdobreev's peccadilloes are no grounds for expulsion. Razdobreev does not interact with the masses because his work has to be conducted in the office. [. . .] Our responsible workers do not and cannot live on a ration of the same size we live on. Everyone should receive not only "according to his needs" but also "according to his talents." Slesar''s combination of the egalitarian "to everyone according to his needs" and the meritocratic "to everyone according to his talents" betrayed contradictory feelings regarding the class meaning of the New Economic Policy. Apparently Slesar' had said the right thing, however contradictory, because Zakharov promptly backed down: "I will summarize that Razdobreev is a bad Bolshevik but a good specialist. Our Party still needs him. In my view, we should not drum him out but expel him for a month with the right of readmission subject to a probation period." Another speaker proposed that "since Razdobreev has never been on probation, he should be downgraded to Party candidate." These compromises, however, were ruled out by the plenipotentiary on procedural grounds: "Communists are reduced to the status of Party candidates only if they make unintentional mistakes and are able to improve their conduct. A rector of the institute cannot go in this category. Probation is not a 'penalty battalion' "! If Razdobreev was to be retained, "somebody had to touch on his political work in the institute."

This was the cue for Korolev, the Party secretary, to speak.

Had everyone had Razdobreev's discipline, things would have been excellent. Razdobreev came to all the meetings of the cell and regularly carried out the bureau's assignments. He reported on the Eighth Congress of Soviets, on the events in Kronstadt, and on the *prodnalog*. [...] His scholarly work explains why he has not done more politically. [...] The main charge against Razdobreev seems to be that "his soul does not seem to be Communist." The impressions of a few comrades, their idea of how things "seem," are not sufficient grounds to have someone's political character assassinated. [...] We should not forget that in facing the present forum and having to justify himself in front of a hundred individuals, Razdobreev has already been sufficiently punished.

According to Korolev, the intelligentsia could not be measured by the same yardstick applied to workers. Razdobreev could not be a Bolshevik by instinct; but—and this was a no less important indication that his heart was in the right place—Razdobreev was loyal and committed. Korolev's concluding speech saved the rector—only nine votes were cast for his expulsion.

In terms of the Bolshevik discourse, Razdobreev represented the upper intelligentsia, comprised of old-time bureaucrats and specialists. But the intelligentsia could also appear in the shape of a "declassed" mob; thrust into a disorienting class alignment, it might turn to the anarchism of the extreme

Left or, just as likely, to the Black Hundred sentiment of the extreme Right. According to Party ideologues, impoverished intelligentsia swerved toward "infantile radicalism," "nihilism," and anarchism, that "quintessential intelligentsia deviation."[27]

Despite the crackdown on anarchism after the Kronstadt rebellion, in the early 1920s the Party was lenient toward the arch leftists from the intelligentsia provided they distilled their radicalism into pure Bolshevism. Of Podzniakov, students said that "in his youth he identified authority and the upper classes with Jewishness." Podzniakov's negative features, however, were "impressed on him" by his petit-bourgeois, intelligentsia milieu. "Although Podzniakov had gone through a street school of anti-Semitism," his defenders explained, "this mood is long since a mere ghost from his past." In view of his "exploits in defense of the Revolution" Podzniakov was retained.[28]

Redkov, on the other hand, who had seemed to be facing similar difficulties, was unanimously purged. In 1918 Redkov took part in the dispersal of the Bel'ts' soviet by "waving around a 'Smith' revolver," a denunciation maintained. The accused tried to explain: "When I heard that in Moscow and Petrograd power had collapsed I confronted the local soviets, in keeping with the slogan "To hell with all that constrains us!" [. . .] Since I believed that the Bolsheviks said one thing and did another I was anxious that the October Revolution might not fully realize its goals, that the commissar would simply replace the tsar as our new ruler. Now," Redkov assured the cell, "I endorse the Bolshevik tactics. During the Kronstadt events I even got out my Nogan—I have liked revolvers since I was a child—thinking I would need it against the mutineers." Having heard all that, the cell concluded that "in all likelihood Redkov is not a real Bolshevik. A Kadet, a Menshevik, or an Anarchist,"—what else could a declassed member of the intelligentsia be?—"he might turn his revolver against us at any moment."[29]

Nikiforov, also from the Smolensk Technological Institute, was candid about his syndicalist past.[30] "Before the October Revolution," his autobiography stated, "destiny brought me to an Anarchist circle where I became acquainted with the literature of this party. My soul and my mind felt at home there." Nikiforov confessed that his Anarchist pranks and daredevil feats were all tokens of childish exuberance:

Only a gymnasium student, I already started quarreling with my fellow pupils. I also rebelled against the administration, which brought down retaliation upon me. Since mine is a rambunctious character, I always pursued my goals openly and disregarded all obstacles. Direct and candid, I trusted the people I loved and rebelled against grandeur.

At this stage, Nikiforov was full of impulsive spontaneity, not true revolutionary consciousness. Left alone during the war, "unemployed and forced to take desperate measures to survive," he "withdrew into himself."

During the Revolution, Nikiforov embraced the revolutionary cause with all his heart. His autobiography makes it clear that resolute Bolshevik action left a deep impression on the protagonist: "When the October Revolution erupted, the whirlwind of events turned society upside down. The strong will of the Bolsheviks overcame the feeble will of Kerensky. The open and merciless struggle against the bourgeoisie made of me a Bolshevik supporter and, slightly familiar with the history of socialism as I was, I embraced Communism—the only way for humans to live together."

This, however, did not mean that Nikiforov had fully converted. The autobiographer confessed to having thought that "if evaluated from the universal perspective, Communism is a temporary state of things," which would one day yield to anarchism. Little of that mattered in 1917—the distinction between anarchism and Bolshevism was, as far as Nikiforov was concerned, purely academic.

Asked to expand on his autobiography, Nikiforov elaborated on his early political stand:

> I did not like Kerensky because he talked too much. The Bolsheviks I respected but I was scarcely familiar with their program. While the history of socialism was known to me in broad outlines I knew nothing of the evolution of this party. I belonged to an anarchist-syndicalist group—"Communism is the shortest way toward anarchism," that was my argument. [. . .] Only later did I realize that Communism was unavoidable. I joined the Bolshevik party because at the front, in the battle, specific party affiliation was secondary.

In July 1918 Nikiforov volunteered for the Red Army. Deployed to Smolensk during the last stage of the Civil War, he joined the Party in April 1920 and became the secretary of the military committee.

Nikiforov's confessors in the Smolensk Institute were in a quandary: on the one hand, the defendant had clearly been committed to the victory of the Reds in the Civil War; on the other, his lingering theoretical weaknesses could well be a dangerous vestige of anarchism. When he was quizzed as to why he had joined the Party, Nikiforov explained that "I wanted to support the Bolsheviks in their struggle against capitalism, so that reaction would be eradicated. I realized that, as far as political parties went, the Bolsheviks were the furthest to the left." In principle, Nikiforov was against "parties"; forced by political exigencies to choose one, he had made the correct choice. In a sense, the Communist Party was in his eyes not the absolute good but the least of all evils.

Nikiforov knew that his hesitation to accept organizational discipline and a hierarchical chain of command could be held against him. Earlier in the year he had even clashed with the bureau: he had initially refused to submit an autobiography and escaped purge only by a hair. Now he stated that "the Party is strong because of its discipline. Even if expelled, I will not abandon my convictions. A Party card does not prove that somebody is a Communist." Again and again Nikiforov stated his hope that everybody would calm down and realize that he had weaned himself of anarchism. But he had gone too far in downplaying the significance of Party affiliation, one of the worst breaches of Party discipline a Bolshevik could imagine. A sympathetic listener described the defendant as "a bitter proletarian [. . .] who has no problem throwing the truth in one's face, one in whom the spirit of 'rebellion'—not 'anarchy'—is dwelling." "Nikiforov is full of defiance," another speaker stated, "but we should not blame him for this. True, he refused to work in student organizations, but this was because he thought they were bureaucratic." Nikiforov was ultimately retained on the strength of the following argument: "Take Razdobreev: doubtlessly a specialist, he carries the title of Communist. If we accept someone who is to the right of us, why should a person who is to the left of us have no place in our party?"

The above proceedings bring to the surface many catchwords, nuances, and shades of meaning that were linked to the notion of the "intelligentsia" in the official discourse.[31] Granting that some members of this class united with it body and soul, the Bolsheviks of the early 1920s maintained that, as a whole, the intelligentsia was the nemesis of the proletariat. Party members from the intelligentsia brought with them petit-bourgeois economics (an exaggerated enthusiasm for NEP, or, inversely, a total incomprehension of its importance), petit-bourgeois politics (rightist Menshevism or its near opposite, leftist Anarchism), and petit-bourgeois self-fashioning ("slyness" [lukavstvo] and "narcissism" [samovliubchivost']). Tailored to fit a stock pattern of a class whose very essence was lies and dissimulation, intelligentsia Bolsheviks were described as individuals who pretended they shared the Party's goals but who remained, in reality, "spineless" (*bezkhrebetnye*) and "without principles" (*bezprintsipnye*). Believing that intelligentsia Bolsheviks were by and large sophists, clerks, and glossators who turned every healthy impulse into abstract formulas, utopian blueprints, and much "learned dust" (*mudrstvovanie*), the Party purists poured buckets of scorn upon this "arid and cerebral cohort."[32]

Restrictions of Intelligentsia Admissions

Very soon after the 1921 purge the Party unfolded a complementary series of measures hampering intelligentsia admissions. The Eleventh Party Congress tightened the statutory screws that kept the intelligentsia out of the brotherhood of the elect.[33] As nonproletarians, members of this class had to find five recommenders and, in the rare cases they were accepted, spend two years on probation as "Party candidates." As a result of the purge and admission constrictions the portion of the Party made up of intelligentsia dropped by 3.6 percent from 1921 to 1923.[34]

This anti-intelligentsia campaign affected higher education most directly. Take Petrograd, for example: from September 1922 to February 1923, only 4 Party applications were submitted to academic Party cells in the Volodarsk district. (This can be compared with 88 applications submitted in the factories during the same time). In the same time period in Vasil'evsk Island district where most of Petrograd universities were located, only 3 Party applicants from the intelligentsia became Party candidates (in comparison to 76 workers and 33 peasants).[35]

The Party cell of the Leningrad Engineering Institute reported that "we have received almost no student applications in this time period." No tears were shed, however. "Most of our students come from the intelligentsia anyway. There is no suitable material here."[36] While the number of applications rose during the following year, the district committee instructed the cell to regard all these applicants as mental laborers. "Though we have no formal grounds to block the enrollment of the intelligentsia into the Party," the cell candidly reported, "we will take all possible measures to do so."[37]

If we consider the sheer volume of Party admissions, "intelligentsia oriented" academic institutions compared poorly with the technical, "proletarian oriented" institutes, to say nothing of the workers' faculties.[38]

A comparison between the Party cells at the two main academic institutions in Tomsk, Tomsk State University and Tomsk Technological Institute, suggests that the latter's cell "attracted proletarian students," while the proletarianization of the former left a lot to be desired.

**Table 6: Social Position of Bolsheviks Enrolled
into Tomsk Academic Institutions (1923)**

Social Position	Tomsk Technological Institute	Tomsk State University
Intelligentsia	17 (35%)	26 (72%)
Workers and peasants	32 (65%)	10 (28%)

Source: GANO, f.1053, op.1, d.682, l.23.

Plagued by the "preponderance" (*zasilie*) of the intelligentsia, the university fell out of favor with the Tomsk Party leadership. During the 1923–24 academic year, its Party cell was evenly divided between proletarian and intelligentsia members (38 intelligentsia Party members and 38 Party members from the working class and the peasantry).[39] But even this breakdown would not have been possible had it not been for the classificatory ingenuity of the local Party bureau.

The work of statisticians was in fact crucial in the constitution of the Bolshevik subject thanks to their role in assigning class identity. The data lists at their disposal were divided into two categories, "social origins" (*sotsial'noe proiskhozhdenie*) and "main profession" (*glavnaia professiia*), and how these were combined into the most important "social position" (*sotsial'noe polozhenie*) category was effectively at their discretion. Determined to bestow acceptable class feathers upon as many students as possible, the statistician grew outright creative at times. "Peasants" and "workers" remained on his lists as such even when the students in question assumed intelligentsia responsibilities: a "hereditary worker" such as Galichanin remained a "worker" by social position although he had served as a clerk on the state agricultural farm; a daughter of a peasant, like comrade Derevianina, dodged the intelligentsia column despite the fact that she had been a teacher in primary school. "Peasants by social origin" such as Sleznev, Chernov, and Zolotorev retained their proletarian status as well, though the Tomsk Party organization stipulated that medical assistants like them "are no good in class terms and should be considered, strictly speaking, as employees." When the university statistician conferred an intelligentsia social position it was usually the lesser of two evils. Baskovich and Khiletskaia, two "merchant daughters," were thereby spared the ignominy of being thrust into the category of "class aliens" and gained a modicum of acceptability.[40]

Once the Lenin Levy was over and the freeze on admission to university cells was abolished, the Technological Institute's Party cell grew by leaps and bounds. Admitting "pureblooded workers" into its ranks, it passed the two hundred benchmark in 1925. "Teeming with intelligentsia," the university, by contrast, had to discourage students from applying to the Party: as a result, between March and June 1925, only seven applications were submitted.[41] When a modest growth did occur in the 1925–26 winter trimester it, much to the cell's chagrin, further enlarged the nonproletarian cohort.

Table 7: Social Position of Bolsheviks at Tomsk State University
(1925–26)

Students' Social Position	November 1925	April 1926
Workers and peasants	33 (77%)	33 (60%)
Intelligentsia	10 (23%)	22 (40%)
Total	43 (100%)	55 (100%)

Source: PATO, f.115, op.2, d.3, ll.6-16; d.4, l.41; d.7, l.55; d.8, ll.26-35, 146.

Rather apologetically, the cell's spokesman argued that class statistics "are misleading" and that the "bald intelligentsia figures give a false impression. In reality, at least every second intelligentsia student comes from a semi-proletarian family." The local statistician continued doing all he could to improve students' class profile: while he counted only 22 students as non-proletarians, the cell's personnel files contained 9 "chancery workers," 9 "medical assistants," 3 "doctors," 7 "schoolteachers," 1 "agricultural expert," and 1 "Party functionary"—all of them excellent candidates for the intelligentsia column.[42]

Eager to act in concert with the statistician's agenda, students played down the intellectual component of their lives. Ostankin, a student at the

Leningrad Agricultural Institute, stated in his autobiography that he was born to a worker family. The young boy wanted to follow in his father's footsteps and he "would have become [. . .] a manual laborer, if not for the complete absence of factories in our vicinity. Thus the only alternative I had was either to remain at home or to study."[43]

Suspicions were aroused by the many telltale intelligentsia traits displayed by "the unskilled worker Mal'kov." Bolsheviks at the Tomsk Technological Institute grilled the student in 1925:[44]

Q: Before you entered the institute, what did you do?
A: I studied in a *Realschule*. [. . .]
Q: What rank did you reach in Kolchak's army?
A: I was a private.
Q: When were you drafted into the Red Army?
A: In Marinsk, in 1920. [. . .] I became an assistant to the communication officer.

"What kind of Red Army service is that if he sat in Tomsk and was in no battles?" Mal'gin exclaimed. This lack of commitment was typical of the intelligentsia. "As far as I know," Zaikin commented, "guys with education were officers in the White Army."

"We need facts," not supposition, Borisov rebutted. But nothing could dispel Prikhod'ko's unease: "only the privileged attended *Realschule* before the revolution. Something about Mal'kov is just not right." "Mal'kov's past is vague." Zaikin agreed. "We should not attribute too much importance to his political erudition. When necessary the intelligentsia can master theory better than any of us."

Popov called for more leniency: "Remember that if we accept him we accept him not as a full Party member but as a candidate. It is up to us to make sure that Mal'kov will make a good expert. If we reject him we will demonstrate our attitude to such a category of persons." Boiling down to the desirability of accepting the intelligentsia into the Party, the case remained pending.[45]

Education was not inevitably construed as a degenerating experience.[46] The 1923 autobiography of Tydman, born in Vitebsk to a family of railroad employees and at the time of his application a student at the Leningrad Engineering Institute, forcefully argued that his studies had helped him to penetrate the meaning of class relations.[47] Tydman, like Mal'kov, had attended a *Realschule*, but his studies had somehow pointed his youthful consciousness in the right direction: "I was converted to the revolutionary cause by the October uprising of 1905, which became engraved in my memory. At that time, workers seized power for a short while in our small but revolutionary town." Even university studies did not cloud Tydman's consciousness: "In 1912 I entered the economics faculty of the Moscow Commercial Institute. There I attended lectures by almost the entire Social Democratic Central Committee: Manuilov (political economy); Novgorodtsev (philosophy and history of political theory); Kizevetter (Russian history) and Bulgakov (history of economic theory)." Believing they gave him the basic tools of social analysis, the autobiographer presented his Kadet professors as Social Democrats! In any case, "familiarity with the right literature and with Bolshevik students—who held several demonstrations and strikes—vaccinated me against a pure bourgeois ideology."

All of this evidence of revolutionary activism was supposed to erase any suspicion that Tydman was a member of the old intelligentsia. A Red Army commissar, the autobiographer turned out to be a paragon of Bolshevik virtues: "NEP disenchanted me. I found it very difficult to come to terms with this new atmosphere after I had been purified by the flames of War Communism. At the sight of thriving speculation and drunkenness I was as miserable as the dog who has to tolerate a cat right inside his doghouse." Aware that NEP was widely regarded as an attempt to reconcile the intelligentsia to Bolshevik power and that identification with War Communism was characteristic of workers, Tydman was broadly hinting that he deserved to be classified as a proletarian.

The problem with Mal'kov and Tydman was that they were beneficiaries of the tsarist educational system. If students with such backgrounds could only hope for consideration, Party applicants educated already under the Soviet regime could on occasion actively oppose the discrimination against the intelligentsia. Realizing he had been grouped with nonproletarian applicants, Trifonov, a student at Leningrad State University, was dismayed:

> To my considerable surprise, I was facing a terrible dilemma: should I apply to the Party as a member of the intelligentsia or abstain from applying altogether. I reject the first option on principle and protest against the second as unfair. I feel compelled to declare that a policy that does not distinguish between the old, conservative intelligentsia and the new, toiling intelligentsia, is misbegotten down to its roots.

Was the new intelligentsia not educated by the Soviet Power itself? [. . .] The very possibility of a comparison between me [and the old intelligentsia] is an insult to my spirit. Comrades, tell me what I have in common with members of the hereditary intelligentsia, who were educated in the old times![48]

To prove his point, Trifonov quoted from his autobiography: "I attended high school in 1919–1921, and served in the Red Army during that same period. Had it not been for the Revolution, I would not have seen the university anymore than I can see my own ears."

A "peasant-proletarian" and by no means weak or effete, Trifonov felt that any talk about his degeneration "is tantamount to a bad joke. I was sent to study not by mommy and daddy but straight from the plough!" All this was to no avail: his Party application, coinciding with the Lenin Levy, was flatly rejected (February 1924). Trifonov was instructed to start working in a factory and reapply later.

By and large, one's intelligentsia background could be overlooked only if one had accomplished meritorious deeds when political passions raged. Consider the brief interrogation of Cherniakov:

Q: When did your active political life begin?
A: I became a revolutionary in 1921 after my father was killed.
   I have been working in the Cheka ever since.

And a similar exchange with Trofimov, also from the mid-1920s:

Q: How did your political consciousness develop?
A: My father participated in the February uprising. I helped to distribute Bolshevik leaflets and arms. I am now applying to the Party merely in order to formalize my commitment to the Soviet Power.

Both of these intelligentsia students at Tomsk State University were accepted into the Party with honors as professional revolutionaries.[49]

In 1926–27, the status of the intelligentsia within the Party improved significantly. Rechristening it the "toiling intelligentsia" (*trudiashchaiasia intelligentsia*), class analysts put the intelligentsia on the same level as other "laboring classes."[50] According to the terms of the August 1925 Central

Committee circular, the "intelligentsia" was merged with the "employees," a category that included "administrators," "professionals," and "workers in culture and enlightenment."[51] Furthermore, the category "others," referring to declassed elements such as "artisans," "housekeepers," and "students who had no profession before they entered the Party," took on some of the worst connotations formerly associated with the intelligentsia category.[52]

Fluctuations in the Leningrad State University's Party membership vividly display this short-lived tolerance of the intelligentsia. Depleted by a recent purge, the Leningrad State University Party cell numbered only 162 members in early 1925. However, during the 1925–26 academic year it tripled its size, in large part due to the admission of "employees" and "others"; by 1927, the non-proletarian cohort comprised almost 40 percent of the cell:

Table 8: Social Composition of the Leningrad State University Party Organization in 1927

	Party Members	Party Candidates	Komsomol Members
Workers	190 (48.5%)	65 (37.4%)	394 (34.6%)
Peasants	51 (13.0%)	27 (15.5%)	365 (31.9%)
Employees	89 (22.7%)	55 (31.6%)	318 (27.9%)
Others	62 (15.8%)	27 (15.5%)	64 (05.6%)
Total	392 (100.%)	174 (100%)	1,141 (100%)

Source: TsGA IPD, f.984, op.1, d.148, l.148.

So dire had the situation become that in order to keep university Party cells from being completely overrun by nonproletarians the Vasil'evsk Island District Committee (under whose jurisdiction the LSU cell was) refused to approve any more student memberships. This led to unhappiness in the "enormous" local Komsomol organization, which was the pool from which applicants were drawn, and, after a general meeting of the university Party organization, an appeal was made to the highest Party organs "to reverse this decision."[53] Eventually a memorandum, drafted on December 7, 1927, by the Leningrad Regional Party Committee, proposed guidelines that would ensure the induction of at least some students into the Party but "solely in the third membership category."[54]

As the 1920s were drawing to a close, battles over the class categorization of student Bolsheviks were growing in intensity and sophistication. Statistics was a key turf for administrative machinations. Fearing "finagling in classification," in March 1928 the Central Committee instructed all Party organizations to review the class affiliations of their membership.[55] As subsequent events in Tomsk make clear, however, this command was thwarted and revisions in bookkeeping backfired. Instead of unmasking the masquerading Party intelligentsia, the commission that was working toward the implementation of the Central Committee's directive leaped at the opportunity to further improve local students' identities:

Table 9: Alteration in the Social Position ascribed to Tomsk Students (1928)

(Cases in which a student's social position remained the same were not included in the table)

From	To	Technological Institute	State University Workers' Faculty
Other	student	21	–
Other	employee	19	–
Other	worker	13	–
Employee	worker	9	3
Other	peasant	19	1
Worker	employee	2	–
Employee	peasant	2	1
Peasant	worker	1	10
Employee	student	1	–
Peasant	employee	–	1
Worker	peasant	–	1

Source: PATO, f.76, op.1, d.483, ll.132–133; 138–142.

Very few workers or peasants were "unmasked" as members of the intelligentsia; conversely, many who had been identified as "employees" and "others" saw a marked improvement in their status.

Due to the flexibility built into the system, classes were made and unmade after abrupt Bolshevik policy changes. The social categorizations used by the Party apparatus were progressively refined: following the appearance of "workers from the bench" and "peasants from the plough" in 1923–24, the "toiling intelligentsia" was called into existence a year later only to be amalgamated with the "employees." Rather than having the status of an objective given, "intelligentsia" appears to have been a flexible discursive artifact, made and unmade depending on the vagaries of Party politics. But the fact that fluctuations in the status of the intelligentsia emanated from policy shifts at the apex of the system does not mean that class was not a question of discourse. In describing the discourse that classified and described the intelligentsia, my point is not that the meaning of class categories was the result of a free exchange of opinion, but that the center never had, nor could it have had, full control over how class vocabulary was used. The leaders of the local Party cells, the statisticians therein, and the grassroots themselves had real latitude in identifying who belonged to the intelligentsia and which individual intelligentsia students deserved Party admission.

Intelligentsia Conversions

The Party's increasing emphasis on identifying those with proletarian spirit led to enhanced attention to storytelling as the best means of determining class identity. The distinction between social origins and social position gained in importance, and in many late 1920s documents the question "What were your class origins?" was replaced by the question "What sort of milieu did you grow up in (*sreda gde vyros*)?"[56] Since one's "formative milieu" was much more amenable to narrativization than one's "socioeconomic background," the element of self-fashioning in the creation of an intelligentsia subject grew in importance.

The autobiography was of tremendous help here. Offering its writers a variety of strategies regarding the narrative presentation of their life experience, this genre allowed intelligentsia Bolsheviks to inject proletarian spirit into a nonproletarian frame. Bolsheviks believed that typical members of the intelligentsia came from the urban petite-bourgeoisie (*meshchanstvo*). Their sins were usually committed close to the beginning of their lives. Given that their origins were impure, the corresponding life story had to describe a fairly unilinear self-improvement, a steady and uninterrupted movement toward universalist consciousness. It was as if the volume of their sins placed members of the intelligentsia in a disadvantage in comparison with workers; any further corruption of their soul would have made Party enrollment highly unlikely.

Thus the influences that formed the intelligentsia consciousness were usually presented as progressing from good to better. Interaction with the proletarian milieu and revolutionary activity drove protagonists toward the comprehension of class relations, gradually relieving them of their petit-bourgeois character traits. Alternatively, intelligentsia autobiographies could be composed according to the conversion-crisis model, describing a story of miraculous transformation. Such an intelligentsia narrator tended to claim that deep within his or her soul a proletarian ember lay hidden, glowing beneath the cinders. Once blown into a flame, it kindled a conflagration that destroyed such intelligentsia vices as opportunism, utilitarianism, and the tendency to make corrupt bargains with the enemies of the proletariat. The playwright Aleksandr Afinogenov described in the 1930s how he discovered his true revolutionary identity underneath his intelligentsia self:

I killed the self inside me—and then a miracle happened: no longer hoping for anything and having already prepared myself for this death, I understood and suddenly saw the beginning of something altogether new, a new "self," far removed from previous troubles and vanity, a "self" that arose out of the mist of all the best that had ever been in me and that had faded, vanished, evaporated. And now it turns out that it hasn't faded or evaporated, it hasn't died completely but has laid its foundation of a new—if still very weak and small—beginning, in which the new master of my body speaks to me.[57]

Here the renunciation of the intelligentsia self was simultaneously a discovery of a lost proletarian identity.

The autobiographical genre was perfectly suited to flesh out the subtleties of intelligentsia conversion. Composed in 1925, the autobiography of a Leningrad State University student named Andronov presented the arduous process through which a petit-bourgeois individualist evolved into a conscious proletarian.[58] In full accord with the genre, Andronov supplemented factual biographical details with a detailed account of how they had shaped his soul. He needed to set down a narrative because only that literary form enabled him to emphasize duly the changes in his spiritual outlook.

The autobiography opened with Andronov's confession that his family background was less than perfect:

I was born in 1903. My father was an employee of the Old Regime, the assistant director of a railway station. [. . .] I did not know him and he played no role in my life. He died when I was four years of age. My mother says he was a drunkard and a loser, that he beat me with no mercy and took bribes. Starting with the terminal illness of my father, I lived among strangers, since mother had no time or means to raise me. [. . .] She lived in Vitebsk, but kept a shop in Petersburg. [. . .] I lived with my grandmother and with family acquaintances.

At this stage, Andronov and the emancipatory cause were worlds apart. But the reader was urged to be patient—the autobiographer was young, and so was the Revolution.

Before he began his studies at the Vitebsk Gymnasium, Andronov rejoined his mother. The text had to confront the nature of her economic activity, to which the protagonist was exposed:

At first we were very poor, no one knew my mother, hardly any orders came in. Then things improved, mother expanded her business, took female apprentices, and opened one other shop, which she staffed with her helpers. Mother's business, she herself, and the surrounding atmosphere at the time, I recall, were typically artisan. Yet they were not marked by a tendency toward capitalist enrichment (*obrastanie*), but rather, the opposite tendency of proletarianization.

The autobiographer's analysis of his family's economic activity had nothing to do with his contemporary self-understanding. Instead, the economy of the household was assessed from the hindsight of the mature Andronov who had absorbed Karl Marx's theory. It was from this perspective that the family's "tendency of economic development" was carefully evaluated:

Mother's family became impoverished and scattered. Grandmother's shop was falling apart. Mother's sister became a maid in Petersburg. One of my mother's brothers became a vagabond. The other worked in a factory. During the Revolution he was a Communist, occupied important posts, and died at the civilian front. Further development of capitalism would surely have plunged my mother, too, into the ranks of the proletariat.

Good Marxist that he was, Andronov knew that the influence of his mother's economic life on his thinking had to be examined: "The unique conditions of her craft—piecework according to concrete orders—both facilitated my mother's proletarianization and hampered it. It also brought the family into contact with female customers, which naturally bred in us a petit-bourgeois consciousness." Why would the writer have chosen to emphasize the retrograde aspects of his urban background? Presumably, he hoped to make his own progressive orientation all the more remarkable for having resisted the temptations of the surroundings into which he was thrust. Contact with the intelligentsia could be beneficial. In this regard, Andronov mentioned the time he spent living with a highly educated family that took care of him shortly after his father died: "As I recall, I spent a particularly long stretch of time in the rich intelligentsia family of an engineer. This environment must have left an imprint on me." Unlike the artisans with whom he had rubbed shoulders earlier, these members of the intelligentsia at least cared to develop their consciousness somewhat.

Soon Andronov was sent to the gymnasium. This was a missed blessing. Studies tended to intensify the petit-bourgeois individualism of the protagonist:

> Mother saw to it that I received a proper education, hoping that I would "become somebody" (*vyidu v liudi*). In the gymnasium I was in the same class with the children of petty-clerks, village priests, and Jews who taunted me as a "tailor's son." This led me to have a certain contempt for human beings [. . .] and to distance myself from social life. [. . .] In general, the gymnasium gave me very few positive values and only encouraged individualism, renunciation of society, and the desire to live only in order to study. I still have much of this individualism entrenched in me even now but I want with all my heart to exorcise it.

The autobiographer described his Vitebsk period (1919–1921) as a "period of major work on my personal development and widening of my intellectual horizons." The protagonist read literary works extensively, wrote and earned money by tutoring. He met "all kinds of people and argued about urgent issues, among them Communism." Skillfully, the autobiographer sketched a portrait of himself as a member of the Russian, pre-Marxist, traditional intelligentsia. At this stage of his life he was consumed by heated intellectual debates: "My convictions were very close to those of the

Tolstoyans; I somehow managed to combine them with the philosophy of imitators of symbolism. The image of myself talking a lot about nonresistance recurs. No one could budge me from my position, although sometimes I was able to change the opinions of my opponents." With a good dose of irony, Andronov resuscitated his long-overcome, arrogant intelligentsia self, a self convinced he had arrived at the eternal truth.

Under such circumstances, who could be surprised that Andronov had missed the importance of 1917? In the questionnaire Andronov admitted flat out that "I took no active part in the Revolution." What else was to be expected from the pacifist intelligentsia that loved to talk endlessly but do little? "The Revolution erupted. I saw it, talked about it a great deal, but failed to understand its meaning. [. . .] I read no political literature and the Communists around me were incapable of presenting an articulated Marxist system. Doubts abounded but no one could show me a Communist path to their resolution." As a true member of the intelligentsia, Andronov could experience events only intellectually. There was not even the smallest bit of proletarian instinct in his soul. Having not yet surrendered his hope that the bourgeoisie could be shorn of its exploitativeness, he continued to believe in a class compromise.

In 1921, Andronov entered the Petrograd Herzen Pedagogical Institute. Upon arrival in the old capital, he dove into the activities of the local literary circles. For example, the autobiographer took a leading part in the republication of Nekrasov's collected works. Nekrasov's elegies to the poor peasant had made him one of the Bolshevik's favorite writers of the nineteenth century. His work on this publishing event managed to gain the writer a position somewhere along the line between Tolstoyism and Bolshevism. Eventually, Andronov realized that he had to join forces with the Revolution and sever his contacts with the literary world, "which smacks of intellectualism and the cult of individuality." He transferred to Leningrad State University and volunteered to teach a course on the economics of the Soviet Union at the Institute of Technology and Electronics. Andronov proudly stated that having no formal education in these matters he had been able to master them on his own. Clearly, not all of the intelligentsia's attributes were liabilities.

During those years Andronov attended many student gatherings. The healthy proletarian environment left its mark on his soul: "Not a trace remained of my Tolstoyism. The creed of nonresistance became as distasteful to my mind as the ignoble Menshevik sweet talk." While the "malevolent social tone" of his effeminate, infantile intelligentsia milieu turned many away from the light, Andronov was happy to report he was redeemed by the vibrant atmosphere at the workers' faculty: "Though I clung to old philosophical tenets, I had begun to think about Communism and the historical importance of our Revolution." As the aesthete became the activist, Andronov was clearly on the right track. "Gradually I became a fellow traveler, though with one important difference: fellow travelers know everything and yet remain fellow travelers, no more and no less, whereas I knew then only little and was politically completely illiterate." The outline of a proletarian self-consciousness was already visible at the end of the narrator's road. The fellow travelers, who had to remain a part of the old intelligentsia, went as far along their particular eschatological journey as they could, but they were forbidden from seeing the promised land. Though for the time being he was hardly more advanced in his thinking, Andronov had the impetus to continue on.

It was the mastery of proletarian theory that made Andronov's conversion imminent. "I forced myself to read Marx thoroughly. These readings brought about my first mental upheaval. The shaky philosophical constructions that I had embraced fell like a house of cards." The moment of conversion itself, however, still lay ahead. "If theoretical doubts disappeared, personal ones remained. The essence of my vocation, books and ideas I was imbibing—all these had so deformed (*iskoverkali*) me that little remained of my initial proletarian base except an unconscious hunch that the downtrodden on earth had a moral right." Though the autobiographer confessed he was still somewhat polluted by "my environment," and that "very little of my self abstained from wallowing in the intelligentsia's morass (*intelligenshchina*)," the abundance of pejoratives in his prose indicated the approaching apotheosis of Andronov's proletarian self.

Lenin's death completed Andronov's transcendence of his intelligentsia identity. "The crucial thing that allowed me to overcome my doubts was this departure. The Revolution became a necessity not only in my mind but in my heart as well." In the Communist economy of pure souls, Andronov's soul would fill the vacuum left by the death of the most saintly of all Communists. His conversion already behind him, Andronov did not rush to the Party as a typical hanger-on would do. Beset by nagging fears that he might be unworthy, he devoted the following year to self-examination, as he attempted to determine whether he could become a loyal Communist. In his quest for his true self, the autobiographer read extensively and worked with working-class students. His willingness to compare himself with the salt of the proletarian university helped him to conduct a final examination of his "class inclinations."

Once he was satisfied that he was ready, Andronov swore to remain dedicated to the Revolution even if the Party turned him down. He expressed bitter regret that the chance to join the Party underground had been denied him forever, since that would have constituted the very best proof of his inner good. Yet, Andronov intoned, his intelligentsia past was worth something if the Party put it to the proper use. The autobiographer concluded that the intelligentsia could donate its knowledge to the proletariat. "I am not dross in need of a lot of refinement. The Party can expect me to contribute to its goal from my first steps. My time is not yet completely lost although a lot of time has been wasted. At present I feel I am still young enough."

Life had no meaning unless Andronov was enrolled. He concluded his autobiography with a thinly disguised ultimatum: "The thought that I stand outside the Party pains me. It is very important for my future development that I not remain a 'loner.' I realize that I do not yet stand shoulder to shoulder with the proletariat and this knowledge depresses me and brings me down. It is pointless to go on living this way!" Even death was less frightening than a relapse into an old intelligentsia consciousness.

Intelligentsia autobiographers paid much more attention to the phenomenological aspects of their conversion than worker or peasant autobiographers. Incessantly self-reflective, they documented every movement of their soul, revealed every inner spring of their intentions, and described every inch of their personal growth in cerebral terms. Cut off from active life, the nonproletarians had to keep their narratives logical because rational deliberation and theoretical insight were the only impetus that was accepted as a force that could convince them to embrace the Party.

Numerous Party applicants claimed to have refashioned themselves as members of the new intelligentsia. The autobiography of Kasintsev, a student at the Leningrad State University and a professional musician, is interesting in this regard.[59] Recapitulating those parts of intelligentsia autobiography that dealt with the transformation of declassed urban dwellers into conscious proletarians, he made a powerful case for being able to contribute not necessarily as someone reborn into the working class but as a proud member of the new intelligentsia.

Kasintsev claimed he had come "from a poor workers' milieu." His mother was a peasant, "completely illiterate to this very day." His father, "while still a barely literate urchin, was apprenticed to a carpenter." When he had witnessed the cruelty the exploiter inflicted upon the exploited, Kasintsev's father became a champion of the working class. "He took the revolutionary nickname 'Artar,' and made a red shirt from his favorite cloth." The post-1905 reaction, however, soon deflated this radicalism and Kasintsev had to admit that his father then crossed the lines and became a foreman. In a word, the autobiographer's background was shoddy. But not all was lost: rent into bourgeois and proletarian halves, a petit-bourgeois soul could evolve in a positive direction if circumstances were propitious. When Kasintsev began his studies in the Vladikavkaz high school, his wealthy classmates identified him as their social opposite: "I would constantly hear insults like 'muzhik,' 'paper boy,' and so on thrown in my direction." Long years of experience in the struggle against Denikin bands completed Kasintsev's conversion, "and the experience left me devoted heart and soul to the Soviet Power."

But it is the autobiography's concluding section, where Kasintsev comes close to speaking of the tutelage of the working class, that is the most interesting:

Advancing hand-in-hand with the people and fighting to defend their interests, I wished for only one thing, to be an honest human being, a friend and a servant of the Russian people. In 1922, the urge seized me to become an engineer, for the good of the people. [. . .] I now write to relieve and cleanse my soul, and my aim is to earn the trust of the workers [. . .] and prove that we, the new generation of the intelligentsia, do not strive to separate ourselves from the working class but on the contrary seek to be close to it, to be its friend. I look forward to a new way of living, working with the working class, so that no barriers will exist between us.

The use of "we/them" suggests that the autobiographer distinguished himself, a member of the new intelligentsia, from the working class proper. At the same time, the allusion to the fall of all barriers between the workers and the intelligentsia attests to Kasintsev's hope that in the classless future the gap between work and thought will at last disappear. "Down with bureaucratism!" he inveighed. "Let the engineer be distinguished from the worker by occupation alone, not by ideology. Once we have travelled a hard, thorny path, the day will come when the worker perceives the expert not as a softie (*beloruchka*) but as a friend." When, in the passage cited at the beginning of this paragraph, Kasintsev switched to the present tense, this indicated that he was describing the contemporary transitory period in which certain divisions between the working class and the intelligentsia were preserved. Shifting tenses yet again and adopting the future tense, the author replaced the division between "me" (Kasintsev, a member of the intelligentsia) and "them" (the working class) with the promise of a new "we"—the unified revolutionary Subject. Since the tasks of the Party and the new intelligentsia were basically identical—to enlighten workers and bring about the worker–intelligentsia synthesis—Kasintsev's place, the autobiography tacitly concluded, was with the Party.

No matter how bright and erudite, members of the intelligentsia always doubted their relevance. Knowledge was not a value in itself; detached from life it was obscurantist and irrelevant. Truth could not be assessed on a strictly theoretical level, though this was certainly important; it had to explain real events and make sense to the proletariat. This is why many intelligentsia autobiographies combine descriptions of intellectual discoveries with proof that these discoveries were relevant to the revolutionary struggle. Consider a segment from the autobiography of Osinskii, a prominent Bolshevik economist who was already a member of an intelligentsia circle as a student in the gymnasium:

> Although our circle evolved toward Marxism quite slowly it had a politically radical and materialist bent almost from the very beginning. [. . .] In the winter of 1904–05 our activity took a political direction and we began putting out a daily newspaper, making presentations and arranging discussions. Finally the time had come to decide what our political orientation was to be (*politicheski samoopredelitsia*). For this purpose—and such behavior is quite characteristic of the theoretical deviations that occurred over the course of our spiritual development—we decided to review [. . .] the history of the revolutionary movement in Russia.

When he chose the Decembrists as his subject he was overcome by a need to "oppose strenuously everything 'fashionable.'" Such an inclination to assert the originality of one's mind was—Osinskii saw this clearly from the vantage point of the mid-1920s—"the psychological plague of the intelligentsia." The autobiographer had tried to give the Decembrist movement a non-Marxist interpretation, mainly out of spite. "I set out on the road of baseless liberalism and this allowed [his instructors] Lebedev and Kerzhentsev to demolish my argument. Once I had carefully thought through the reasons for my "defeat" I arrived at the conclusion that old Marx knew what he was talking about."

The intelligentsia's purely intellectual insight was not enough. It was not until the stormy months of late 1905 that his Marxism was "tangibly reinforced." After the uprising had been put down Osinskii went to Germany to study political economy. He no longer tarried in unwholesome ideological byways: "I divided my time between the study of Plekhanov and Lenin." Having finally acted on his beliefs, Osinskii returned to Russia and, in the autumn of 1907 "became a conscious Party member."[60]

The pitfalls the intelligentsia met along the way to enlightenment feature prominently in the autobiography of Reisner, a prominent Bolshevik professor of sociology. The beginning was modest: "intelligentsia romanticism—a jumble of unscientific ideas—doomed my young mind to years of slogging through an intellectual morass." As Reisner describes how he plunged into "mysticism" and "Tolstoyanism," and then underwent the "strong influence of Dostoevsky" his self-sarcasm is quite evident. But soon enough he came to hate classicism and reject science as intellectual preoccupations relevant only to a pretentious, obscurantist, and totally detached intelligentsia, and the young graduate of the Petersburg gymnasium went to study at Warsaw University and then in Kiev. "A careful investigation of political schools" brought the autobiographer to the gloomy conclusion that contemporary scholarship was unable to decide "between two equally binding and logical systems of thought that were glaringly, irreconcilably antithetical. [. . .] Political science appeared to be an accumulation of equally binding 'verities' (*pravdy*) and 'truths' (*istiny*), each flatly contradicting the other." It was then that Reisner was presented with the task "to which he was to dedicate his life—finding an objective law that would explain why various worldviews have come into existence and why they have to be mutually exclusive."[61] While in Europe in 1903 he finally saw that "the dialectical, contradictory character of political systems could not be explained in their own terms, only in terms of their social underpinnings."[62]

No theory, not even Marxism, could be fully absorbed without practice. Utilizing his legal expertise to defend Social Democrats accused of crimes of state enabled Reisner to connect with the historical process.[63] Once he discovered the proletariat, this member of the intelligentsia found his true audience. Although the prerevolutionary university auditoriums were full when Reisner lectured, his explanations of the social determination of human psychology fell on deaf ears. Only when he made his way to workers' auditoriums to disseminate scholarly socialist propaganda did his listeners seem attentive and receptive.[64] Autobiographers such as Reisner, who taught young Bolshevik students, concluded that "higher education must be inspired by the life going on around it: theory must be subjected to practice."[65]

Even as it set about inculcating the proletariat with Marxist theory, the new intelligentsia was losing much of its identity in the process. For the "purity" of the voice of the new intelligentsia depended, in the last analysis, on its ability to speak with the voice of the proletariat. By instilling a universalist consciousness in their working-class audiences, Osinskii and Reisner, themselves unequivocally offspring of the intelligentsia, came to identify with their protégés. To the extent that universalism was an intrinsically proletarian quality, those revolutionary intelligentsia who acquired it through great mental labor somehow became proletarians. Of course, this dynamic worked both ways: with the obliteration of his exclusive identification with manual labor the proletarian likewise lost his authentic self. As they became aware of their proletarian identity and grew to be conscious of their revolutionary duties, politically mature workers became, in a sense, members of the intelligentsia.

One Self-Doubting *Intelligent*

To be worthy of the Party, intelligentsia students had to show that they had overcome what were regarded as their most intrinsic traits—selfishness, high-mindedness, and anti-sociality. This became all the more urgent when the applicant's intelligentsia individualism had taken a political form and had been expressed through identification with one of the infantile, ultra-leftist currents that tried to outdo Bolsheviks in their radicalism. The autobiography of Buntar', a student at Leningrad State University, brought into sharp relief such a connection between intelligentsia identity and unbridled sentiment.[66]

Born in 1902 in a village called Iarunino in Tver Province, the autobiographer had, despite his poor peasant origins, become an employee. "The loss of class roots occurred very early in life," he confessed. The early death of his father and his mother's subsequent move to Petersburg, where she found employment as a servant, had had a declassing effect on the children: the autobiographer's youngest sister became a chambermaid, while the young Buntar' was placed in a petit-bourgeois primary school. Having abandoned agricultural work and failed to enter the capital's industrial labor force, Buntar' lost his social compass and embraced the dissolute pastimes of urban riffraff. "After I graduated from school, a teacher with anarchist inclinations helped me enroll in college. I consumed some of the Social Democratic literature that filled her bookshelves."

In 1915, the autobiographer came across a particularly impressive inflammatory leaflet that prompted him to join a local anarchist organization. In fact, the name "Buntar'," which means "rebel" in Russian, was clearly a pseudonym of the sort favored by defiant anarchists. Buntar' played a major role in the occupation of Durnovo's summer house as well as the capture of the palace of the Duke of Leikhtenberg—two major anarchist actions accomplished during that revolutionary year. Somehow—he does not tell us quite how—Buntar' evolved from a wild and militant anarchist into a dedicated Bolshevik. During the Civil War many anarchists had decided to "sell their swords" and side with the Reds.[67]

By 1920, Buntar's opinions too had definitely "drifted away from anarchism." The local Party cell went so far as to enroll him in its ranks without any probation period—a rare honor indeed that can be explained by the autobiographer's committed service in the ranks of the Red Army. But his past returned to haunt him, and during the purge of 1921 he was expelled from the Party. The protocol of the proceedings of the Petersburg Control Commission, which oversaw his reinstatement request, indicates that "Buntar's purge was motivated by the sympathy he showed for the Anarchist party before the February Revolution." Worse yet, Buntar' had reportedly refused to cooperate with the Cheka in suppressing anarchist organizations despite explicit orders to do so. "Even at the present [June 1922], the supplicant is sympathetic to anarchist idealists (anarkhisty ideinogo tolka)."

The matter of his expulsion obliged Buntar' to disclose to the Leningrad State University Party cell a set of highly revealing autobiographical reflections. Only toward the very end of his second autobiographical letter did he directly confront the accusation that he was an Anarchist sympathizer: "As far as my old views go, I renounced them a long time ago. Can anyone seriously believe that an Anarchist would command Red Army battalions? [. . .] True, I did display a certain weakness in Tver when prominent anarchists were arrested. All I ask, however, is that the Party use me without bringing pressure to bear on those parts of my constitution that remain weak."

The remainder of Buntar's text was dedicated to reflections on the role of the new intelligentsia in the Party, an issue that had a direct bearing on the autobiographer since he preferred academic studies to a military career:

> You refused to allow me to remain in the worker's party, basing that decision [. . .] solely on the fact that I am not a "worker" but a "member of the intelligentsia." The Party, you argued, draws its strength exclusively from workers from the bench. First, let me tell you that I by no means regard myself to be a member of the intelligentsia in the full sense of the word. My course of university studies is not yet completed, so how can I be classified as a "mental laborer"? Shouldn't you wait until I graduate and start actually working in a white-collar profession? Second, if I am purged from the Party and, following that, from the university, will I not have to work in a factory like any other worker? [. . .] In my view, this makes me not a "mental laborer" but an "educated unskilled worker" (*intelligentnyi chernorabochii*).

Had he been an old-fashioned member of the intelligentsia, Buntar' averred, he could have remained a chancery worker in the Red Army. The sole reason for his demobilization was a "lack of desire to become a military specialist in times of peace."

Next, Buntar' turned to the general meaning of the term "intelligentsia": "Setting aside for a moment the definition of a member of the intelligentsia that is based on one's relation to production, one has to admit that, from the point of view of proletarian ethics, mental development (*umstvennoe razvitie*) should be considered not a burden but, quite to the contrary, an asset. The workers' revolution cannot win until every single worker becomes sufficiently developed to be able to supervise the production process." A wholesale attack on the intelligentsia and its spiritual values, Buntar' reminded the reader, had a name in the Bolshevik parlance—it was *makhaevshchina*, a syndicalist heresy condemned by the Party in every possible language.[68]

According to Buntar', a workers' intelligentsia had to be built in order to secure proletarian victory in the struggle over minds:

> During the transitional period [. . .] the intelligentsia that thinks and feels with the Party is particularly valuable, especially when it comes from the lower echelons of society. It is not inferior but complementary to workers from the bench. [. . .] The Party has to be on the alert for the

possible effects of economic hardship on the working class: when under duress, a worker may easily succumb to all kinds of deviations. At the moment of economic distress, only an imaginative enlightenment, and not some propaganda loaded with clichés, is capable of reanimating the workers and of forcing them to think as workers should.

Buntar's underlying assumption was that each class had characteristic patterns of thought, but at times individual members of a class could be swayed by alien modes of thinking. Without assistance from the new intelligentsia, workers who were in trouble could succumb to petit-bourgeois temptations. The autobiographer believed that only an alert and genuine revolutionary intelligentsia could unmask the false prophets who tried to lure the workers away from the right path:

A worker who is relatively poorly developed—and we should keep in mind that fully developed Bolshevik workers are still rare—is generally vulnerable to all sorts of criticism advanced by the seditious Mensheviks who worm their way into the factory. If that danger is to be staved off, the presence in the factory of intelligentsia with working-class roots is crucial. Saving the GPU plenty of effort, such intelligentsia can create the conditions for widening the freedom of speech, without which it will be impossible to rekindle workers' political thought.

Since many workers were not yet conscious enough to have the upper hand in political debates with the Mensheviks, so Buntar's argument went, political freedoms had unfortunately to be suppressed.[69] But this situation was bound to change with the growth of the true workers' intelligentsia.

Almost imperceptibly, Buntar's autobiography metamorphosed into an extended apologia for the intelligentsia. A vanguard of the proletariat, it alone could lead workers to a classless society. Buntar' was adamant that those who had purged him from the Party had inadvertently blasted the buds of the new intelligentsia:

The Party cannot and does not rely solely on workers from the bench. Its anti-intelligentsia policies are aimed only at the worthless intelligentsia, the intelligentsia that is alien to the proletariat. To confuse me with that kind of intelligentsia [. . .] is to offend my pride. Insult is added to injury when I am identified with the hordes of individuals who grope for loopholes so as to worm their way into the Party. We seek not loopholes but legitimate ways to become Party members.

Pleading that he was not an old intelligentsia interloper but a member of the new intelligentsia that fully belonged to the Soviet political order, Buntar' sought to turn the weaknesses of intelligentsia identity into a source of strength. The conclusion of his autobiography—"in my view, the doors of the Party should be open to each and every member of the intelligentsia who thinks like a worker"—might have served as the motto of those who believed in the transcendence of class distinctions in the brotherhood of the elect.

The autobiographies we have just examined might as easily be described as treatises in class theory. But this was entirely appropriate. One of the founding principles of the Bolshevik illiberal self was that society instilled in an individual his or her sense of identity. In presenting themselves, authors never limited their narrative to the contents of their private lives but, by dwelling at length and with considerable sophistication on the past and the present of the Party, elucidated their own place in the proletarian movement. Our autobiographers were well aware that after the Revolution the relationship between the intelligentsia and the working class had been reformulated from relations in which the intelligentsia played the guiding role to a class alliance under the guidance of the working class. Kasintsev, Reisner, and even Buntar', albeit a bit less enthusiastically, all acknowledged that in the pupil–teacher relationship, the two sides had switched positions. "The intelligentsia has been adopted by the proletariat," Party spokesmen explained.[70] "It is now the Party that sets the rules. The intelligentsia," Lunacharskii explained, "is not the manager but the servant."[71]

But Lunacharskii could also be cited by members of the intelligentsia who wanted to substantiate their claims for Party membership. When asked, "should we create a new intelligentsia? Can we not jump directly into a period devoid of intelligentsia?" Lunacharskii answered that "We take the Dictatorship of the Proletariat seriously, though it is temporary, do we not? Why should we not treat the intelligentsia with equal seriousness, transient category though it is?"[72] Explaining that "No form will be complete until the construction of Communism is complete," Lenin himself had warned that "the antithesis between mental and physical labor [...] cannot on any account immediately be removed by the mere conversion of the means of production into public property, [or] by the mere expropriation of capitalists."[73]

The inclusiveness of the Bolshevik brotherhood ensured that alien social origins were never insuperable. The Soviet Constitution of 1918 established the category of the disenfranchised (*lishentsy*): formerly privileged states and occupations such as nobles, merchants, and tsarist gendarmes were relegated to the ranks of the exploiters and deprived of citizen rights.[74] Despite the discrimination against these categories, the offspring of antisocial elements could claim a Party card if they were able to prove they had severed ties with their parents. If a youngster broke with the retrograde thinking of his parents he could claim to become a full participant in the Soviet social order. "Our family fully degenerated (*razlozhilas'*), Sashanova, a student at the Leningrad Communist University, stated in 1924. She had nothing to do with her father's business and "was not in touch with any of my relatives since 1917."[75] The parents of the above mentioned Mal'kov, to give another example, were artisans in the Altai, and "perhaps they own things." But Mal'kov insisted he could not add to what he already wrote in his autobiography: "It is difficult for me to state in a responsible way how my parents are. [. . .] I have had practically no contact with my father since 1921."[76]

The most horrible class identities could be whitewashed. Even the son of a gendarme could become a Party member, as was the case with Galenchenko, who was accepted by the Smolensk Institute cell in May 1920. "[It is] already eleven years since my father left that occupation," Galenchenko explained. "True, I get along with my father but this is so because he is a kind man with Tolstoyian convictions." Pointing out that Galenchenko was one of the first in the region to join the Bolsheviks, students concluded they "should not brand Galenchenko because of what his father used to do."[77]

In principle, conversion was open to all. Universalist consciousness was the ultimate standard of Bolshevik identity, not class origins or occupation. And the new intelligentsia had plenty of this universalism. Lenin scolded those who delegitimized its members on the grounds that they were petit bourgeois: "If social origins are fetishized, workers, having been small landowners in the past, would have to be relegated to the petit bourgeoisie as well! " Individuals related to members of the intelligentsia were not barred from becoming "proletarians in spirit" (*proletarii dukhom*). In the words of an anonymous Marxist pamphleteer, Marx and Engels, unhampered by their nonproletarian origins, "were the best among the intelligentsia, capable of renouncing individualism, plumbing the depths of human suffering, and sacrificing themselves for the proletariat."[78]

Autobiographies of the Politically Suspect

Lenient on the class aliens, the Party apparatus was much more demanding on those who were guilty of thought-crimes, and supporting contending socialist parties, such as the Socialist Revolutionaries, the Mensheviks, or the Bundists, to name only the most prominent ones, could not be viewed otherwise.[79] Very different criteria were brought to bear on a seemingly similar misdemeanor—refusal to enlist with the Bolsheviks. The motive, more than the act, was what counted: being "unaffiliated" (*bezpartiinyi*) was making a naive mistake, while a "former" (*byvshii*) liberal or phony socialist was deliberately rejecting the revolutionary call.

"Former affiliates" found it much more difficult to compose a credible narrative of their movement from darkness to light. Their autobiographical task seriously complicated, they had to tell and retell their life stories with a particularly strong emphasis on their past political blindness. One-time Bolshevik rivals focused on politics and left out everything else that was considered neutral or trivial. Careful not to become dispassionate compilations of individual thoughts and actions, their autobiographies were united by the idea of ex post factum political judgment. Instead of charting all the peaks and troughs of his past, the "former affiliate" described only those events which enhanced his ability to distinguish between the Mensheviks (or the SRs, or the Kadets) with whom he erroneously sided and the Bolsheviks. Whatever precipitated his political awakening was right, whatever obstructed it was wrong.

The autobiographers claimed at length that they had shed their old political self and embraced the Bolshevik truth. When the tensions in the political situation reached a boiling point, they suddenly realized their terrible mistake and experienced a leap in their soul. If in case of the worker or peasant autobiographies the author could present a natural, incremental process of enlightenment, here the break with the past had to be as sharp as possible. The author referred to the experience of such a dramatic conversion by expressions such as "transition" (*perekhod*) or "remolding" (*perekovka*) or "spiritual break" (*dushevnyi perelom*). Witnessing the events of 1917, a typical autobiography would announce, "I realized the treason of the petit-bourgeois parties and embraced the Bolshevik position as the only one truly representing the interests of the working class."

In writing their autobiographies, applicants with tainted political pasts did everything in their power to persuade distrustful Party authorities that they truly regretted their past mistakes. Expressions of sorrow, contrition and willingness to atone were key to their narratives. The former affiliates claimed estrangement from their past political affiliation. When they sat down to compose their autobiographies, they found it difficult to understand how they could have had anything to do with reactionary organizations. Barely recognizing themselves as Kadets or SRs, they used the first person singular for the passages describing their past political activity only hesitantly.

And yet, no matter how insistently they affirmed their new political selves, former affiliates had to assume full responsibility for their deeply mistaken political history. They could not blame environment or family for their individual political choice. Each convert from a petit-bourgeois party had a duty to announce his or her faults openly and in public, recognize the temptation that landed him or her in the wrong camp, and bear witness against him- or herself. Whether they presented their life stories in written form or read them aloud during a Party meeting, applicants with tainted pasts entered a tense dialogue with their audience of judges. Here autobiographical interrogation was especially intense as the audience was determined to find out whether the applicant was truly conscious of his or her mistakes and truly sincere about conversion.

Attempts to cover up one's former affiliation with a non-Bolshevik party were, once uncovered, generally fatal. Asked directly in the questionnaire whether he had "any record in other parties," Siniukhaev, a student at the Leningrad Engineering Institute entered, "None."[80] Rather than discuss his political past, Siniukhaev's autobiography dwelt on such standard topics as the protagonist's social origins—"my mother was the daughter of a poor landowner"—and education—"I graduated in 1898 from the faculty of history in Petersburg University." Siniukhaev stressed how much he wanted to become a Party member: "I wish to comply with the Thirteenth Party Congress call for teachers to assist the Soviet Union's struggle to improve the lot of the toilers of the world," he wrote, and was already with one foot in the Party.[81]

But then came the letters of derailment. "I deem it my duty to inform the cell that during the years 1905–07 Siniukhaev was the representative of the rightist Constitutional-Monarchist Party on Vasil'evsk Island," one letter stated. Another anonymous denouncer linked Siniukhaev's Kadet identity to the political indecisiveness considered typical of that party: "As my teacher in the workers' faculty, Siniukhaev has always struck me as a phony who goes along with current trends," the inference being that the applicant frequently leapt from one political bandwagon to another. Siniukhaev's Party application was turned down.[82]

How desirable it was to enroll "former members of petit-bourgeois parties" was a question that had animated official debates since 1917. During the Civil War, the Central Committee welcomed political conversions. Either because their party of origin was put outside the law or because they came to the conclusion that the Reds were the lesser of two evils, a good number of Mensheviks and SRs took Bolshevik Party cards at that time. In 1920, "former members of socialist parties" comprised 6 percent of the Party.[83]

Only in rare cases could affiliation with a non-Bolshevik party be preferable to an uncommitted, nonpolitical existence. Former members of parties that voluntarily dissolved into Bolshevism when the battles against the Whites were still raging—Menshevik Internationalists, Maximalists (radical SRs), and Revolutionary Communists—enjoyed certain privileges.[84] Membership in these parties was construed not as opposition to Bolshevism but as a sign foreshadowing it. The closer the platform and tactics of the mother party had been to the Bolshevik stance, the higher the applicant's chances were to retain some, or all, of his "length of service for the Party."[85]

Merging with the Bolsheviks during trying times—late 1919— the Menshevik Internationalists, for example, proved their loyalty to Communism beyond any doubt. Consequently, a Bolshevik circular from December 30 of that year stated that "their admission into our ranks can be carried out through a simple substitution of old Internationalist party cards with new, Bolshevik party cards." The Internationalists who wished to become Bolsheviks had to do so by February 1, 1920—only a prompt Party enrollment proved they were truly a bone from the flesh of Bolshevism. Beyond that date they could apply for membership "only on a general basis," as the last thing the Party apparatus wanted was to give vacillating Internationalists political insurance.

The terms of admission of Maximalists—an extremist branch of the Socialist Revolutionaries that decided to fuse with the Bolsheviks in April 1920—were less advantageous. Although Maximalists too could become Party members more or less automatically, only their post–October 1917 stretch in their party of origin counted toward length of service for the Party. The reason for this restriction was the official view that Maximalists adopted true proletarian positions only during the years of the Civil War; prior to the Bolshevik seizure of power, they were believed to be closer to the Socialist Revolutionaries.

Lastly, there were the Revolutionary Communists—a radical fringe that seceded from the Left SRs after the failed July 1918 uprising and, after a brief independent existence, fused with the Party in September 1920. The official press praised the Revolutionary Communists for complying with the resolution of the Third International that two Communist parties must not coexist in the same country. The Bolshevik Central Committee requested the creation of Revolutionary Communist troikas; these would transfer all materials on the personnel of this party to the Bolshevik regional organizations. It was the responsibility of the troikas to submit membership lists, numbers of party cards, and detailed autobiographies for each Revolutionary Communist. Compromising evidence against Revolutionary Communists had to be included, as well as lists of individuals purged from the Revolutionary Communist cells in the past.[86]

Converts from the recently disbanded Jewish parties presented a special problem. A majority of young Jews had taken the side of the Reds during the Civil War and Communist propagandists knew that full well. And yet they could not ignore the fact that scions of Jewish political organizations often had their own, narrow expectations of the Soviet Power. The Party apparatus found itself in a quandary: on the one hand, it welcomed no particularist worldview, no nationalist sentiment, Jewish or otherwise. On the other hand Stalin, the leading authority on the nationality question, promised to be forgiving toward national minorities who answered tsarist prosecution with misguided nationalist agendas of their own.

Overall, the Bolshevik leadership treated Party applications coming from Jewish revolutionaries with sympathy. Properly told, the autobiographies the latter composed were effective in describing a story of a spiritual growth, a transition from Jewish particularism to supranational, proletarian universalism. The 1924 autobiography of Leznikov from the Leningrad Communist University, for example, portrays a conscientious student always concerned with the lives of his proletarian brethren. True, the protagonist, a young Jew with a Jewish elementary school education, waited to apply for Party membership until the final stages of the Civil War, but his political consciousness began moving in the right direction as soon as revolutionary events erupted.

When World War I began, Leznikov, like many other Jewish youth, was drafted into the tsarist army. He saw some action and was seriously wounded in May 1916. "The Revolution caught me convalescing in Moscow," he states in his autobiography. The period of recuperation excused the absence of the autobiographical segments describing Lezninkov's activity during the February and October Revolutions—gravely ill, he saw none of these events firsthand. The Party cast a blind eye at these omissions—young soldiers who were recovering from serious injuries were not to be equated with petit-bourgeois vacillators who wanted to enroll into the Party only if the Bolshevik victory was secure. Be that as it may, injuries transformed Leznikov's soul and he recovered his conscience. "I was first introduced to [Lenin's] ideas in a military hospital in June 1917." Upon recovery, the autobiographer was performing only good Bolshevik deeds: helping the Red Army in times of war and disseminating Marxist teaching in times of peace.[87]

But what about an ex-Bundist? Was such a well-meaning revolutionary also eligible for smooth Party enrollment? Leznikov was innocent of political affiliation before his Party application, but Bundists crossed swords with the Bolshevik leadership on more than one occasion. Despite constant feuding with Lenin before the Revolution, the Bund was widely regarded as a forerunner of Bolshevism in the early 1920s. The absence of a chauvinist bent and a deep commitment to Marxist theory usually made applicants coming from its ranks trustworthy enough.

The autobiography of Sashanova from the Leningrad Communist University, for example, told the story of a young Jew who joined the Bund in 1917; she conducted educational work at the union of housemaids as a member of this party. After the schism in the Bund she entered the Komfarband, a Jewish revolutionary organization that soon united with the Ukrainian Communist Party in the face of the advancing White forces. Sashanova considered herself a Bolshevik from August 1919 when she joined the anti-Denikin underground, "coordinating secret apartments, working with the press"; her flattering autobiographical self-presentation was endorsed by her peers.[88]

Or consider the biography, or one may say, the hagiography of the Nakhimsons, a Latvian Jewish family that was held up as a model during student evenings of reminiscences precisely because it bridged Jewish and all-national revolutionary activity. It was as if the Nakhimsons believed in a division of labor: they contributed to the Bund, active among the artisans, but also to the Jewish Social Democratic Party that focused on the intelligentsia. The anonymous hagiographer presented both parties as Bolshevik in spirit—their independent existence was a mere tactic designed to address the different attitudes among the population and to find specific keys to the conversion of each and every Jew.

"The old Nakhimson couple" could not be described as mere "sympathizers" to the Bolshevik cause during the 1905 Revolution. Their revolutionary commitment had run too deep. "This is especially true of Mikhaila Iul'ianova, a person with a delicate spiritual organization who gave her soul to the movement." Mikhaila's husband was also a proto-Bolshevik. He set up the propagandists' headquarters in the family apartment and contributed mightily to the growth of the Jewish revolutionary consciousness. When their son, Salia Nakhimson, grew up, history was already at a more advanced stage. October was at the door and the zealous youngster was eager to move beyond the parochial activity of his parents. "Work in the Bund did not satisfy Salia. While he could not lead a circle of Jewish artisans due to insufficient knowledge of the Jewish language, the circles of the [Russian speaking] Jewish intelligentsia did not interest him"—this intelligentsia was not exciting raw material for a revolutionary propagandist. After a long and torturous journey, Salia Nakhimson saw his dream come true: he was assigned propaganda tasks in the Red Army. For that, he paid with his life: he was killed by the Whites in 1918.[89]

Was there really almost no difference between a Bundist and a Bolshevik? Could all Bund inductees be turned into loyal Party members, or would they keep a soft spot for their national heritage? Doubts grew as the decade progressed. When the Bolshevik organization in Belorussia conducted a campaign against "remnants of Bundism" in 1925, Krinitskii, a local Party secretary, was asked "Was not the Bund a forerunner of Bolshevism?" Krinitskii maintained there was no simple answer to this question: "Each of us must examine himself: is not a retrogression to the old ideology possible? [But in general I must say that] it is absolutely impermissible to act toward a Communist who was in another party as if he were a second-class Communist."[90]

If the Bund occasionally misunderstood Lenin's strategies of drawing workers into the Revolution, other Jewish parties challenged the official view of the national question directly. If most organizations of the Bund fused with the Bolshevik party, the smaller Jewish political factions strove to preserve independent party organizations and pushed for Jewish cultural autonomy or even for emigration to Palestine.[91] Past affiliation with those parties seriously complicated attempts to obtain a Party card.[92]

Grusman, a student in the Leningrad State University, spilled lots of ink explaining the roots of his attraction to the social-democratic Zionist party of Poalei Tsion.[93] "From 1917 to 1919," his autobiography stated, "I participated in self-education groups in Harbin that went through [. . .] the history of the workers' movement. In these circles the first foundations of my Marxist worldview were laid." Although Grusman was totally absorbed by questions of the Jewish worker movement, he drew wrong conclusions. "The year 1920 was the year of my entrance into the RSDRP Poalei Tsion party—later known as the party of Jewish Worker-Communists." Was this a consciously anti-Bolshevik political choice? No. "My limited theoretical training in Marxism prevented me from understanding what the true path for the economic rejuvenation of the Jewish toiling masses is." Geography also had something to do with it. "I embarked on the wrong path while in the Far East"—then outside Bolshevik control.

When finally he moved to Siberia and enrolled into the Irkutsk State University, Grusman's eyes opened: "Two years of life in the RSFSR and access to higher education proved to me very clearly that Poalei Tsion could not solve the challenges facing [. . .] the Jewish toilers. Every day I witnessed how the Bolshevik policy furnishes proof of the thesis that only a successful revolutionary struggle of the working class as a whole can bring resolution to the national question." Timing his conversion very carefully, the autobiographer is keen to show the immediate effects of Soviet propaganda on the identity of young Jewish students: "While the first signs of self-transformation appeared already late in 1921, things ripened toward the end of 1922 when, together with a number of friends, I departed from the Jewish RSDRP and applied to become a Party member."[94]

Such smooth transition from one political identity to another was the exception, not the rule. Not that the Bolsheviks did not encourage wayward revolutionaries to realize they had made wrong political choices. But affiliation with SRs or Mensheviks was, in Bolshevik eyes, an unlikely prelude to conversion. Methodically discriminating against the ideologically suspect, the Bolshevik leadership was not shy about its unease with former members of these parties. As Smilga warned at the Tenth Party Congress (1921), "we all know that during the Revolution our main political rivals went bankrupt. But we also know they did not disappear, did not, as it were, evaporate into thin air." The only change wrought by the Bolshevik victory was that "the struggle against the Mensheviks and the SRs is now taking place within our Party itself."

Smilga told the story of an incomplete spiritual transformation: "Although the vast majority of these comrades came to us with the genuine intention of becoming true Party members, a relocation of membership from one party to another does not ensure that the past is left behind completely."[95] Seeing the close relations that sometimes developed between the Bolsheviks and ex-Mensheviks as a "sign of trouble," Lenin insisted during the 1921 Party purge that "no more that one percent of the Mensheviks who came to us after the beginning of 1918 should be left in the Party."[96] Converts among former SRs were treated no less harshly: "SR fossils easy to spot in Bolshevik organizations had to be mercilessly expelled."[97]

Over the following years, this paranoia deepened. Matvei Shkiriatov reported to the Eleventh Party Congress (1922) that "we have tried to determine to what extent Mensheviks and SRs have truly renounced their prejudices." His answer was not comforting: the members of the dissolved parties could easily become a Trojan horse.[98] Dmitrii Manuil'skii was also skeptical regarding the Bolshevik melting pot: "We have absorbed other political groups but have not necessarily managed to digest them completely." Moscow warned provincial Party organizations that many former Social Democrats "did not wrench the petit-bourgeois 'ancient Adam' out of their souls."[99] The key question was whether the switch of allegiance by so many Mensheviks and SRs was ideologically motivated or just an adjustment to circumstances. Zinoviev expressed profound skepticism in this regard. "If not for the political monopoly we established, people rushing to join us would have sided with [. . .] some breed of petit-bourgeois socialism—they are, as yet, only half-conscious or wholly lacking consciousness."[100]

Apparently these were compelling arguments, and the Central Committee designated former socialists an "exceptionally dangerous category." If not carefully watched, they could infect the Bolsheviks with the pestilential "petit-bourgeois psychology."[101] The Central Committee introduced strict measures into the 1922 Party Regulations to curtail the induction of former Mensheviks and SRs. They had to obtain five recommendations from comrades who had been Party members for at least five years. They also had to spend two years on probation and then had to keep their fingers crossed that the Provincial Party Committee would ratify their admission.[102]

A Party applicant could overcome his unsavory political past if he proved it was indeed a matter of the past and did not reflect his present state of mind in any way. Should Kuznetsov, a student in the Siberian Communist University in 1923, be accepted into the Party despite his six-month stint as a secretary of an SR organization in Petropavlovsk some fifteen years earlier?[103] While recommenders praised Kuznetsov as a workers' son "free of any corrupt inclinations," the Omsk provincial committee appended a cautionary note to the effect that "Kuznetsov's Socialist Revolutionary peasant ideology has not yet been fully eradicated." The candidate was accepted, but to prevent him from backsliding to his old consciousness the Communist University was advised that "Kuznetsov be put to work in an area densely populated by workers."

If they wanted a chance to be inducted into the Party ranks, former SRs had to claim they had turned to Bolshevism immediately after their errors were clarified to them, whether by official agitators or by the general course of historical events. Zvers, the rector of the Leningrad Workers' University, stated in her autobiography: "True, I enrolled in April 1918 in the Left SR organization. But when the SRs organized a mutiny in Moscow in July 1918 I left their ranks. Thus I was in a Left SR organization for only four months."[104]

Leonov, a Left SR from 1917 until 1918, was accepted into Party ranks once he proved that he had sided with this radicalized political movement only as long as the Bolsheviks themselves cooperated with them.[105] "Recall that after the dispersal of the Constitutional Assembly, the Left SRs worked hand in hand with the ruling party. Was the first Soviet government not a coalition of the Bolsheviks with the Left SRs? Smol'nyi [the Bolshevik headquarters in Petrograd] sent me [a Socialist Revolutionary] to Orel as an emissary to organize soviets in the city." Following the Left SR mutiny against Lenin, the autobiographer departed from their ranks "via the press." In 1919, when Iudenich was besieging Leningrad, "I was already fighting in a Bolshevik detachment."[106]

The "formers" described their realization that petit-bourgeois politics was a reaction in a revolutionary disguise, and detailed how they had embraced the Bolshevik cause as the only one serving the international proletariat. Offering them a narrative of their spiritual awakening, a questionnaire authorized by the Siberian Party bureau in 1924 asked: "When did you begin sympathizing with the SRs or the Mensheviks and when did you actually enroll into that party?" "What issues were the main contributors to your disillusionment with the SRs or the Mensheviks?" "Who influences you in the Bolshevik direction," and so on. The apparatus explained that the information regarding the "motives that drive workers to leave the Menshevik and SR parties will facilitate our agitation in the proletarian quarters and enable us to expedite the process of liquidation of the Menshevik and SR parties."[107]

Possibly worse than the SRs, the Mensheviks were an intimate enemy, dangerous precisely because they spoke words some workers mistakenly recognized as their own.[108] The temptations Menshevik organizations set in the workers' path allegedly made them an especially direct threat to the Revolution. Doing all they could to exploit workers' lack of consciousness, activists of this party set about distributing their leaflets and brochures in the factories and mills. Presenting themselves as true Marxists, they disseminated disguised petit-bourgeois ideology. Temptation seemed to be the heart of the problem. Mistaking an alien political vocabulary for their own, naive workers jeopardized their own emancipation.

Any leaning toward Menshevism was likely to close all doors.[109] Aware that El'man, who expressed his wish to become a Party member in 1923, had been a supporter of the "liquidationists" at the prerevolutionary Social Democratic congresses, the Petrograd Party district committee made detailed inquires with the Agricultural Institute where he used to study. "As a student," the institute archivist wrote back, "El'man took no part in political work. Although his general educational level was high, he kept quiet during meetings [. . .] hoping to project an image of loyalty." A crypto-derailment, this reply sufficed to block El'man's enrollment.[110]

It was incumbent upon the Party applicant who erred in his first choice of allegiance to erase traces of any past cooperation between the Mensheviks and the Bolsheviks and to blow the smallest clashes between the two parties into important ideological disputations. In his apologia for supporting the moderates in his adolescence, Lopatnikov from the Leningrad State University unfolded a masterful narratological strategy.

"While in the sixth form at the gymnasium," so his story began, "I was invited to attend the meeting of a socialist circle, about sixty men strong. Captivated, I formally joined the circle on December 6, 1916." Such chronological precision may have been unnecessary, but it proved that this was a very important event, enshrined in Lopatnikov's personal history.

At every biographical juncture the narrator had one and only one choice to make—the choice between the forces of good and the forces of evil—and this choice always took a concrete political shape. In the 1890s, for example, he had to decide between Social Democrats and Social Revolutionaries, in 1900 between Leninists and the pseudo-social democratic "economists," and in 1917 between Mensheviks and Bolsheviks. Lopatnikov's response to the challenge was mixed: "The February Revolution heightened my commitment to the revolutionary cause. I began working in the city militia. To deal with the food shortage, I proposed the idea of organizing city [consumption] cooperatives." Whatever political faction Lopatnikov eventually joined—as an employee of the city duma rather than the soviet, he must have been fairly conciliatory in his political views—this faction was not a Bolshevik forerunner.

Lenin had been a mystery to Lopatnikov, and he, highlighting February and not October, made the startling admission that the Bolshevik seizure of power "caught me by surprise. I had nothing to do with the Bolshevik uprising." This was all the more stunning since he had been in Petrograd in October 1917. Here was a man who had been revolutionized during the World War. How could he have been completely unprepared for this proletarian apotheosis? The attentive readers of Lopatnikov's story now recalled that the political circle that changed his life was described as "socialist"; needless to say, he would have described it as Bolshevik if only he could have. As late as 1917 Lopatnikov was still politically naive; his autobiography suggested that it was the Soviet educational policy that finally opened his eyes. This was not because tuition fees were waived during the Civil War years but "because the policy of proletarianization opened the gates of the university to folks like me."

There are several reasons to doubt Lopatnikov's claim to have been a hereditary worker: five recommendation letters were appended to his application (as required of a nonproletarian applicant) and his father was described as an employee (he was an accountant). In the hope of circumventing these obstacles, the autobiographer wrote that "my grandfather was a worker," employed in the Putilov mills, widely hailed as the "cradle of the Revolution," and added that "I myself worked as a hired laborer from the age of eighteen." We can deduce why he made his shaky case so vigorously: Lopatnikov realized that the slightest admission of an urban intelligentsia background would make him look like a typical Menshevik.

Shortly after Lopatnikov enrolled in the university he was "drafted into the Red Army on the basis of the decree by the Trade and Defense Soviet (November 25, 1919)." Clearly, his military experience was Lopatnikov's strongest suit, and in the ensuing section he argued that he had embraced Bolshevism as a result of that experience and was entrusted with "secret work"—anathema for the fence-sitting socialists and thus a telltale sign of true conversion.[111]

Examination of the way former SRs and Mensheviks were questioned, and consideration of the unwritten rules governing the interactions between the antagonists, should explain how old political sins were compared to each other. What methods of investigation were employed to unearth the applicant's past state of consciousness? How much interpretative leeway did students have in assessing each other's political commitments during momentous events in revolutionary history? Disputations relied on comrades' ability to legitimize their judgments through recourse to the official Party line. If eloquence and persuasion did influence the outcome of debates, success could not be won without a firm grasp of the history of the "petit-bourgeois" party organizations as told by official historians.

A skillful defense depended on the student's full mastery of the Bolshevik narrative in the present as well as claims of political unawareness in the past. The main defense strategy open to those who had flirted with rival parties, however briefly, was to insist that they had gone astray only because they had failed to grasp political differences in time. They had imagined that by signing up with the Social Revolutionaries or the Mensheviks they would advance the revolutionary cause. Only later did they discover their mistake. Such apologies did not always succeed, but alternatives were scarce.

How, for example, could Boldyrev have been tempted by the Social Revolutionaries after February 1917? This question occupied his fellow students at the Leningrad Communist University for quite some time. Worse, this veteran of "four Civil War fronts" remained loyal to the Social Revolutionaries even after Lenin seized power: having just arrived in Petersburg in April 1918, Boldyrev officially enrolled in a Social Revolutionary youth group. That June, he found work in the Aleksandrov factory, where he remained employed until September, at which time all local Social Revolutionaries, including him, were arrested. The protagonist spent a month and a half behind bars but was never tried. Apparently the young Bolshevik regime did not find him especially dangerous.

The counterrevolutionary crusade against the workers' state and the outbreak of hostilities across the country had a salubrious effect on the consciousness of many. Boldyrev's political mind quickly approached the desired condition. Though he went to attend a Social Revolutionary congress (entirely legal) upon his release from jail in December, the autobiographer no longer identified with the party program. "I made a speech at the congress arguing that "one should not spend too much time criticizing the Bolsheviks. It is also important not to forget to promote the revolutionary cause, and this is what the Bolsheviks are now doing." These comments were shouted down, and after he had been ejected from this meeting Boldyrev took to lambasting the SR at various public rallies. "From April 1, 1919, the district committee numbered me among the Bolsheviks."

Was Boldyrev's path to the light as smooth as his autobiography indicated? Students who interrogated him in 1924 could not understand how his mother, a "seasoned Bolshevik" who chaired a soviet in 1917, could have failed to influence him. "How could she not have prevented him from siding with the SRs?"

Boldyrev tried to explain: His mother was helpless because "I simply did not have a clear political physiognomy at the time." But a fellow student, Comrade Zorina, rejected this explanation: "It is impossible that Boldyrev, who was nineteen, had no idea what signing up with the SRs meant! Had he really understood nothing [he would have followed his mother blindly.] And her influence would have drawn him to the Bolsheviks." In Zorina's reading, Boldyrev must have been a steadfast Social Revolutionary who consciously objected to his mother's political views.

Blom, who worked with the Boldyrevs in the Nevskii district, rushed to the rescue. "Our friend acted on impulse," he insisted. "Boldyrev is extremely hotheaded—this is his nature. When he saw that everyone was joining the SRs, he did too, especially since he was involved with the Left SRs for so long. [. . .] Many local workers did the same. But as soon as they figured out the political orientation of their party they left." Nor was Boldyrev's mother the mature Bolshevik Zorina made her out to be. Blom testified, "When she returned from exile, she was not a fully temperate Social Democrat. Only in late 1917 did she commit firmly to the Bolsheviks.."

At the end of the day, a benevolent reading of Boldyrev's autobiography prevailed: the majority was convinced that he took a roundabout road but grew disillusioned with the Social Revolutionaries and eventually found the truth.

While someone who had once been on the rolls of a wrong party faced a difficult task in applying for Bolshevik membership, the odds were not insurmountable. In composing a life story that would justify him, a repentant SR or Menshevik had a set of apologies at his disposal. He could argue that he was influenced by his family members who already made political commitments, or that he was initiated to politics in the past only partially and did not understand the differences between the parties well enough. Such rhetorical devices allowed the repentant applicant to suggest that his lapse had been ephemeral—his consciousness resurged once he observed the unfolding of the Civil War.

The transition from a general Marxist disposition to Bolshevism proper could be quite complicated and prolonged. Involving issues of ideology and deep knowledge of Marxism, such a spiritual journey invited a particularly close scrutiny. The Party judges examined the mindset and intentions of such individuals under a magnifying glass. Was Nasulenko, another student at Leningrad's Communist University, a member of the indeterminate Social Democratic mass who joined the Bolsheviks as soon as they came into their political mind and took flight as an independent political formation? Or was he a Menshevik who donned Bolshevik colors when it suited his personal ambition?[112]

In the words of his personal evaluation, "Nasulenko enjoys great prestige in the university," and as a local propagandist "he has revealed himself to be temperate and disciplined." Still, a number of students noted during the 1924 purge that "something Menshevik, irresolute, and conciliatory surfaced in him from time to time." One student suggested, "We should be especially strict with Nasulenko because he has been around." He always has "his beloved middle path," another student agreed. "We are speaking about his psychology here."

Under the circumstances, Nasulenko's autobiography underwent careful scrutiny. Born in 1885 to a worker father and a peasant mother, he recalled that "we were in grave financial need." When he was fourteen, Nasulenko's education was interrupted—the family needed money. "I went to Petersburg and became an apprentice in machine shops, where I remained for two years." Next he worked as a locksmith's assistant in a shop that built carriages. "All together, I worked as a manual laborer for five years." Finally, the narrator reached the political part of his life: "I enrolled in underground circles in 1904 and got acquainted with the revolutionary movement and the Social Democratic party." During the 1905 Revolution, "I participated in strikes that won a one-hour reduction in the work day." Nasulenko distributed pamphlets and was even arrested (he is vague here and says, without further explanation, "My arrests did not have a juridical significance"). By this date he had been a Social Democrat "but never a Menshevik."[113]

If Nasulenko had been so near to Lenin so early in his life, why did he not lay claim to the esteemed status of Old Bolshevik? Though he claimed he could point to a few survivors who remembered him from 1905, he "did not really know how to go about all this."

Nasulenko appeared evasive. "In the autobiography he did not dwell directly on important aspects of his past," his questioners pointed out. "What about his departure from the revolutionary movement before 1919? The autobiography is vague [zatushevannaia] and the context is unclear." "I can see only pluses here; the minuses are hidden," Voronov complained.

Others said, "We asked Nasulenko to tell us about any despondency he experienced [during the period of reaction, 1907–12], but he speaks of nothing but his revolutionary activity." The cell demanded that Nasulenko ransack his memory and write his autobiography anew, "shedding more light on pivotal points."[114]

But even as he told it anew, Nasulenko clung to his story. His revised autobiography reaffirmed "all the information he had previously supplied." Students who remained dissatisfied—and they were many—grilled him for hours about his party affiliation during the first Russian revolution, determined to prove that he had embellished his past. Korobko, for example, claimed that Nasulenko sided with the conciliators at the time "and therefore must have been a Menshevik." Bogachev was even more specific: "He must have been a Menshevik-Internationalist."

Denying all petit-bourgeois connections, Nasulenko described himself instead as a "rank-and-file activist." He added, "My organization had a Bolshevik coloring." This was clearly a retroactive judgment, as the following remark showed: "I found out about Bolsheviks and Mensheviks [only] in 1907." How, his questioners wondered, could he have missed the Second Party Congress (1903) and the Lenin–Martov split? "The connection with the center was very weak," Nasulenko explained. "All I knew about the revolutionary movement came from [newspaper] articles and essays."

This excuse aroused even more suspicion. "Was he ever a Bolshevik?" students wondered aloud. "Or was he influenced by liquidationism?" (This referred to alleged discussions among the Mensheviks about giving up all underground activity.) "It's impossible that he knew so little about the party he supposedly belonged to for three years," Voronov stated. And Strizhchuk pointed out further evasions in Nasulenko's autobiography. "While history books tell us that Party organizations in the south were already active in 1902, Nasulenko is mute about the [Bolshevik] literature [he presumably received]. Nor has he said a word about any other links with headquarters." The dream he had of enlightening the masses by working as a schoolteacher "was supposed to help the peasantry and not the working class."

Could it be that Nasulenko was a political charlatan, a Marxist one day and a populist the next? By no means, Nasulenko retorted with all the resolve he could muster: "The SRs did not influence me at all. I made no attempt to reach out to their organizations."

The time had come for Nasulenko's benefactors to speak. Naiman took issue with students for "approaching Nasulenko with the hindsight of 1924 Communists." Anachronistic judgment was enough to condemn anyone. "Comrades, true Bolsheviks could not exist in the provinces in 1904. All we had then was an undifferentiated Party mass. The additional designation attached to Nasulenko here, "internationalist," is based on a misunderstanding: there is a great difference between Mensheviks before and after 1917." The former, he explained, had not yet decided whether to join Lenin, whereas the latter had already made an unforgivable error in rejecting his leadership. A pre-1917 Social Democrat could be forgiven if he repented; a Social Democrat who defied Lenin was utterly hopeless. Nasulenko, said Naiman, might possibly be of the first type, but certainly not of the second.

Khodaseev built on this defense. In his view, "Nasulenko did not officially take part in the Social Democratic movement in 1904–05—he had simply been drawn into the movement as a worker." His arrest should be seen not as tsarist censure of an important revolutionary but as part of "routine police persecution." This less-individualized reconstruction of Nasulenko's past consciousness, according to which he had been victimized not for his actual thoughts or actions but for his line of employment, turned out to help. According to Khodaseev, Nasulenko had just been part of the crowd throughout the first Russian revolution, never fully aware of his political duties. Once he left the factory he also abandoned his proletarian outlook. This was not treason—hardly a committed revolutionary in 1905, he could not have been an apostate.

As speaker after speaker belittled his prerevolutionary political development, Nasulenko started to breathe easily. Kostylev presented Nasulenko as a Social Democrat in his heart but not in his mind. "Because of his sensitivity [*chustvitel'nost'*] he enrolled in the Party, but his aspirations were not yet fully developed. It would be wrong to speak of Party-mindedness [at that time]." Had Nasulenko been a Party member in the fullest sense of the term, "his deviations would have been criminal"—but this was simply not the case. According to Kostylev, the real trouble with Nasulenko's self-presentation was his stubbornness, his unwillingness to expose his weaknesses. "He should not cover up his vacillations with revolutionism. [. . .] The only way to clear things up is to speak directly and not evasively." But even this weakness, so common in uncouth and callow workers, may have helped his case.

Taking his cues from his defenders, Nasulenko presented himself as a naive and inexperienced toiler who prized social justice but had only a rudimentary understanding of the Revolution's true driving forces.

In 1904 I was an unsophisticated boy, eighteen years old, uneducated. My Party activity was unconscious. [. . .] I was carried away by the developments around me. Our chief [vozhak] [. . .] and the rest of us set ourselves modest tasks: strikes and strikes alone. The conditions were difficult and surveillance kept us from doing much. Reprisals were a scary prospect—if one fell into the hands of the gendarmes one was lost. [. . .] Since I was working in an artisan's shop staffed by inexperienced workers, my activities were hindered. [. . .] Our organization—no more than thirty or forty people—operated intermittently. [. . .] Membership dues were only paid intermittently and we did not have a safe house [iavka].

After Stolypin's constitutional coup of 1907, Nasulenko abandoned revolutionary activity altogether. Pinning his hopes on a diploma, he spent the next three or four years studying to become a teacher. Clearly, pounced his detractors, "Nasulenko made a sharp turn away from the working class." Maron found this part of the autobiography particularly "confounding." He said, "It is unclear why Nasulenko's prerevolutionary Party activity was interrupted. He tells us that in 1904–07 he was serious, but after 1907 he was a 'Communist without a party.' " Zhezlov pulled no punches: "We have to view Nasulenko's participation in the Social Democratic party as an attempt to get ahead in life." Khoduseev was a bit softer: "The reaction pushed Nasulenko into petty cultural activity [kul'turnichestvo]). [. . .] As a result, he shared the general fate of the intelligentsia." Even Khoduseev, though, had to admit that Nasulenko had gone "further that others along that road."

Nasulenko confessed that immediately before 1917 his contacts with the Bolsheviks were strictly "personal." Though he lost touch with the underground following the extirpation of his local organization, he insisted that he had "never ceased speaking out." Here is how he justified his retreat:

I was never a traitor and never did I sink into "liquidationist" moods, as we use that term today. There were no revolutionary organizations in Novo-Mikhailovsk—it was a philistine city. My culturalist bent was simply an expression of my thirst for knowledge. Though I hate arcane bookishness [pis'movodstvo] [. . .] I could not continue doing manual labor because of the three operations I had.

It took a while for Nasulenko to return to his revolutionary self. At the time of the February Revolution, he was working as a clerk in Khar'kov and the events took him completely by surprise. When the Bolsheviks seized power, he was with Lenin only in the most general terms. "In October I participated in the broad movement." For two years there was no evidence of renewed commitment: from April to December 1917 Nasulenko worked as an accountant, and from December 1917 until 1919 he was in school. Not even the most dramatic events of the Civil War waged all around him interrupted his philistine routine.

Students were "taken aback" by Nasulenko's apathy in 1917. One student did not understand how someone could remain indifferent to the flurry of insurrectionist agitation coming from all corners. "We must bear in mind that the Novomoskovsk suburb of Ekaterinoslav [where Nasulenko spent most of the year] was extremely revolutionary: a number of political organizations were formed there. Everybody knows what kinds of proclamations were hanging [on the walls]. Somehow, all Nasulenko managed to see were the sort of revolutionary brochures read not by workers but by the intelligentsia." Another was similarly dismayed: "In 1917 the Party was going strong, but for some reason Nasulenko knows nothing about this. What does he do as a member of the Novomoskovsk soviet? He goes off to study in a specialized school! What is this if not running away in the heat of the struggle?"

Nasulenko stood up to defend his revolutionary record. "It is not true that I was indifferent. I opposed Kerenskii, and comrades from work can corroborate that. [. . .] As soon as a Party committee was organized in Novomoskovsk, I joined." During Grigoriev's infamous mutiny, Nasulenko was among the organizers of a defense detachment. His constant movement from place to place "was a result of revolutionary activity," not of any aversion to the theater of operations. In the face of the German advances in 1918, he had to leave for Poltava to dodge execution. But the narrator did not even think of abandoning the cause and he cited his election to the Party's provincial committee to prove the Party trusted him.

Quite satisfied, Mikhailov wanted to leave Nasulenko in peace. "When they speak out against Nasulenko," he stated in an emotional speech, "some comrades just go too far. There is a bit of romanticism in their judgments. True, one can hardly think of Nasulenko as a struggling hero, but we should not push him into the hands of the purgers either."

"No one is about to present Nasulenko as a hero," scoffed Maron rebuffed. "He's the one who characterized himself as a conscious revolutionary."

Seeking a compromise, Savinov maintained that everything became clear if Nasulenko's road to Bolshevism was interpreted as that of a member of the intelligentsia and not that of a worker: "An ordinary member of the intelligentsia was always critical of the [tsarist] regime, and Nasulenko was no exception. There is nothing strange in him joining the Party in 1919 rather than 1917." In 1917 the intelligentsia was not ready for Lenin. Most important was that he was never an Anarchist, a Menshevik, a Social Revolutionary, or any other zealous opponent of Bolshevism.

The majority of the students felt that the prerevolutionary Nasulenko had not fully grasped the political landscape. He may have sometimes been an ignorant fool, but he was never an adversary. And in due course his proletarian roots had asserted themselves: as Khuduseev said, "His worker origins made him part of a stream that naturally spilled into the Party." Although the circle concluded that Nasulenko should be sent back to work in production, he walked away with his Party card.

No one was denied Party membership because he or she was objectively in the wrong. Not only were students interested in material facts pertaining to autobiographies only to the extent these could be used as signs illuminating motives; punishment was tailored to correspond to intention, not to consequence. Nasulenko was eventually pardoned because the makeshift disciplinary court that judged him was convinced that he had committed his offenses "unconsciously."

The induction into the Party was a one-way ticket, a rite of passage that was supposed to make an individual infallible. Past sins were confessed and absolved, future wrongdoing impossible, for how could someone who was omniconscious reject the truth? The Party line was their line, Party decisions were their decisions. The only apology open to Bolshevik apostates was to argue that it was their body that pushed them into sin and that they were therefore not fully accountable for their actions. Whatever error appeared was a result of an infirmity or madness, not of a wicked will. In their autobiographies, applicants with serious political blemishes claimed that their mistakes were made out of political naiveté and ignorance, not out of premeditated wickedness. No matter how blemished their past, they were not irredeemable.

Bykov, a student at the Engineering Institute in Leningrad, claimed that he dropped out of the Party in 1922 "only because of my feeble health."[115] It was not unusual to blame one's body for one's mistakes. Explaining his own defection, his peer, Gel'man, argued along similar lines four years later:

I contracted an infection of the spinal cord and was paralyzed for a long period of time in the lower part of my body. Having spent nearly half a year in bed and having lost almost all hope for a cure I mechanically departed from Party ranks. When I regained my health, I volunteered into the Red Army and joined the Party.[116]

Zaitsev brought the corporal apologetics to near perfection. Having abstained from the 1919 re-registration, this student from the Leningrad State University was scratched off Party rolls. In the autobiography he prepared to support his 1923 readmission application, Zaitsev justified himself with medical language: "A physical illness led to psychological abnormalities that impinged on my attitude toward Party responsibilities. 'A healthy mind in a healthy body' [*mens sana in corpore sano*—a Roman proverb very popular among the Bolsheviks]. This is not an empty phrase: as soon as I recovered I felt a new attraction toward intensive public work." Since Zaitsev was reinstated it appears that the cell accepted that the return of his physical vigor would be accompanied by the reappearance of a sense of the working-class brotherhood.[117]

Even criminals could sometimes get away with using this line of defense. A blacksmith's helper and a student at the Tomsk State University workers' faculty, Sirota was accused of shooting a girl, just because "she mocked me when I asked her out." Comrades described this wayward Bolshevik as a "hooligan" but Sirota skillfully justified himself with the claim that he was a "neurasthenic" who had been in a stage of "agitation."[118] The Party purge commission accepted the claim that his hot-blooded temper pushed Sirota into crime, not his mind, and returned him his Party card.[119] The case of Tipeev from the Leningrad Communist University will be our final example here. Summoned to the control commission of the Leningrad Central District in October 1923, this young member of the Bashkir Turkic minority was accused of shooting his wife. Tipeev blamed everything on "frequent family quarrels: I do not get along with my wife, a daughter of a mullah, because we do not have matching ideologies. [. . .] Besides, I suffer from a nervous illness." Taking into account the fact that "Tipeev's sickly condition was corroborated by medical documents" the control commission limited itself to a reprimand. The student was warned "not to repeat such extreme actions in the future."[120]

The above examples shed light on the theory of action that undergirds Bolshevik autobiography. Party ideologues maintained that human behavior could be explained in two radically different ways: as causally determined or as an expression of free will. A naive individual could do terrible things against the Party and still be forgiven. We have already met students born to alien classes, hiding from the Revolution in the village, even fighting with the Whites—and yet, eventually, enrolled. But woe to the one who challenged the Party willfully, fully aware of what one was doing. Since Bolshevism demanded the active choice of good, it had to allow for the possibility of the active choice of evil. What the Party shepherds enjoined was having a will, "a faculty placed under the full command of the subject." [121] It was this faculty that moved individuals into the realm of freedom, enabling them to accept or reject the message of the Party.

When a comrade became self-conscious, the will immediately split against itself. The will to embrace the proletarian call activated another will, the will to reject the Revolution, so that the one will was never quite without the other. If there was no counter-will within him, a Bolshevik would not have needed a will at all, becoming a Bolshevik not consciously but automatically. But the Party was supposed to grow when enough Leninist disciples chose to embrace it, actively and enthusiastically—not when a blind and mindless historical process had run its course. If Marxist theory seldom treated the will as an autonomous mental faculty, this was due to a considerable degree of interdependence between "will" and "consciousness." Since every instance of volition was necessarily preceded by a theoretical apprehension—it was assumed that one cannot will what one does not know—there was no way of determining whether one had a good or a wicked will before one had read enough Marx and Lenin and attained full consciousness. In Bolshevism, which retained some of Saint Paul's shifting of the accent from doing to believing, from the outward actor living in a world of laws to an inward subject whose will can only be scrutinized by God, the will retained its role as the principle of individuation. [122]

However swift and superficial the rituals of admissions and purges were, comrades were always examined individually because only the individual could possess ethical faculties. The injunctions to write and rewrite one's autobiography remain a mystery unless we take seriously the contemporary concern with the will. Comrades had to speak about themselves because only they were genuinely privy to their inner truth—a source of endless curiosity from the members of the various admission and purge commissions.

CONCLUSION

WE WILL NOT UNDERSTAND THE BOLSHEVIK revolution if we examine the questions of power and meaning as separate from each other. Power relations always leave a linguistic trace, and this was especially so in the Bolshevik discourse that legitimized itself through world-transforming ideology. Moreover ideological disputations were always also a seat where power was contested. Alerting historians to the symbolic universe that underlines action, sociologists, anthropologists, and literary theorists present the subject as an interpreting creature, one determined to construct his or her own meanings.[1] To be sure, these interests remain a necessary explanatory term—certain readings of their autobiographies served their authors while other readings served their detractors—as long as it is understood that such interests are always already structured by discourse.[2]

Insofar as historians must rely on sources (almost exclusively written materials) they remain in the domain of a textual universe. Instead of establishing a critical distance from my sources, I have sought a measure of complicity with them, trying to show how the autobiographical discourse operated. Because the question of the self was in flux, I took seriously the self-understanding of the Bolshevik autobiography as something that encompasses radical discontinuities and ruptures. Students' self-presentations constantly changed not because they were exceptionally opportunistic but because at moments of historical crisis the revolutionary discourse called on them to retell their life stories, adding new insights into where they came from and where they were heading.

It is clear that the Soviet discourse of the 1920s cannot be described as a completely solid monolith and that the individuals who inhabited it cannot be seen as completely conformist. Yet while traces of resistance can be found in all walks of Soviet life, it is nearly impossible to find individuals resisting in the name of values external to Bolshevism. Indeed, we have met a number of students who challenged the apparatus and demanded a different interpretation of the Party regulations, or a return to what they believed were pristine revolutionary values—purity, equality, revolutionary consciousness. Buntar', the unrestrained anarchist, Razdobreev, the intelligentsia softy, Dvinskii, the untrustworthy worker, and many others refused to be marginalized. But they were willing to reject a position of individual autonomy not only because they needed something to eat and to wear but, and perhaps primarily, because their lives as solitary individuals were abhorrent to them. By disciplining their words, Soviet students honored the rules. In return, the official discourse empowered them to demand the recognition of their participation in the revolutionary society in the making through admission to the Party.

Autobiographies served not only to reassert the Bolshevik identity of their authors but also to guide the multitude still in darkness. According to Marx's famous scenario, the proletariat was to develop from an implicit, unreflective mode of existence as an objectively given economic category, a "class in itself," to its explicit and self-conscious state as a revolutionary subject, a "class for itself." In the Bolshevik autobiographical writing the attainment of adequate self-understanding was tantamount to the acquisition of "consciousness"—a crucial word in the Bolshevik lexicon.

While the meaning of "consciousness" in the autobiographies under study was multifaceted, it is clear that in the Bolshevik usage "consciousness" did not have the highly individualistic overtones sometimes attached to that term in liberal discourse. In Bolshevik autobiographies, the Christian, ethical, and subjective meaning of consciousness, based on the notion of consciousness as "conscience," a trial of the interior self, was fused with the other sense of consciousness which, after Descartes, came to denote an awareness of something objective outside of the self. Reviving the original duality of the Latin *conscientia*, which had both an ethical and an epistemological sense, the Bolshevik "consciousness" combined the sense of knowledge of the external world with the sense of a moral imperative residing in the internal soul. While the Party believed that a Bolshevik became aware of the world only when he purified his consciousness, the inverse also held: the Bolshevik's comprehension of his own soul was the fruit of his insight into the ways of the world. Self and the world, the subjective and the objective, were two aspects of the same reality. The boundary separating the subjective and the objective was porous—the "objective world" was nothing but the reification of laboring humanity.[3]

So long as the Bolshevik autobiographer was a proletarian the universal epic of human emancipation converged in his writings with the individual life story. But how could these two genres coexist? Was there not a necessary contradiction between the autobiographer's self, crippled by a limited perspective on life, and the objective truth so dear to scientific Marxism? In other words, how could Bolshevik autobiography somehow remain true to science? Bogdanov asked himself whether his idiosyncratic voice could be removed from his autobiographical essay of 1925:

> I used to dream that, toward the end of my life's journey, I would write a book describing everything I experienced objectively. My self was to be absent from this narrative and I would include only the socially real and the socially significant. Later I realized that this fantasy emerged from two mistakes: first, it is wrong to think that one can remove one's self from a narrative; second, it is wrong to think that objectivism demands anything of the sort. To be sure, one can refrain from mentioning oneself. But the only result of such restraint would be needless difficulties, artificiality, and falsehood. Certainly one can limit one's discussion to recording what one saw and how one understood what one saw; what one saw was seen with one's own eyes and what one understood was understood in accordance with one's own way of comprehending things. Neither one nor the other can be done away with, even if one meticulously crosses out "I" wherever it occurs in the narrative.

According to Bogdanov, the memoirist was not precluded from being an impartial observer and scientific interpreter. "Doubtless, he has a point of view and operates according to his own methods. But in what sense are these his own? Insofar as he belongs to a collective—a class or a social group [. . .]—his personality is only that small point where various social forces meet, one of the zillion points where these forces intersect—and insofar as his point of view and mode of apprehension belong to these forces, embodying and expressing them, it would be more accurate to say that his personality belongs to these forces than the other way around." When, then, can an autobiographer's point of view be described as scientific? "When it is inspired by the most progressive collective armed with the widest experience." Bogdanov believed that the autobiography he had written expressed the perspective of the class that oversaw the operations of science. He had no doubt that his personal, inner truth and the truth of this class— the proletariat—were one and the same.[4]

Having recognized himself in the story of Communist emancipation, a Bolshevik autobiographer shifted the center of gravity of his personal identity. What became fundamental to his self-description was not his concrete, individual being, but his contribution, no matter how small, to universal emancipation. Every person who applied for admission to the Party had to embrace the idea that the Party embodied the truth about one's own self and that one's life was meaningless outside it.

This emphasis on collectivism and objective truth meant that Bolshevism had to reject the liberal ethos of individualism, with its validation of open-ended personal growth. A Party autobiography was very different from a liberal autobiography precisely because it had a predetermined goal—the light of Communism. Since the Bolshevik self was openly and deliberately set up in opposition to the liberal self, the latter merits a brief examination. The liberal conception of the self, as Karl Weintraub demonstrates, "is apposite to a belief in society as a highly differentiated social mass." Liberalism highly values the features that distinguish one individual from another—presenting them not as accidental variations from the norm but as a precious aspect of human existence. "For when a man concludes that his very self represents one unique and unrepeatable form of being human, it becomes the perceived task in life to 'fulfill,' to actualize this very specific individuality." Man, Weintraub goes on to say, will commit a terrible crime against the human cosmos "if he neglects to fulfill his individuality or if he falsifies it, for if he does, he impoverishes humanity in leaving one of its variants forever unexpressed."[5]

Such liberal values were of course anathema to any decent Bolshevik. Nothing could be more remote from the system of values he held dear. "Will I really be different from the others?" was an oft-repeated anguished cry. "The mere idea of it makes my hair stand on end and my body shiver."[6] When a Bolshevik dwelt on the autonomous aspect of his life, he was usually describing his "prerevolutionary illicit existence." In reference to that phase of his biography, he could be boasting of detachment, having been completely unmoved by official ideology. But when turning to the period after 1917 the autobiographer had to become quite willing to surrender in the contest between Party influence and his inner self. An autonomous self was an imperfect self. He who kept a part of himself to himself "failed to write himself into the new order," "detached himself" (*otorvalsia*), became a "dissenter" (*otshchepenets*).

The January 1924 application by a Leningrad State University student named Lopatnikov bemoans the loss of a sense of complete fusion with the Party. Lopatnikov contrasted his Civil War sense of belonging to his vacuous present:

During my service in the Red Army I made various contributions to the cultural front. At that time I had the orders and advice of my comrades and commissars to follow. At present I can hardly do any good. After my demobilization, I became an isolated being, longing to contribute to a larger whole but unable to. This tiny unit—myself—is a subject of distrust by Party members. [. . .] I need somebody who will lead me. Only the Party collective can effectively guide my work. I am familiar with the program of the Communist Party and this program corresponds to my political convictions. I have a great longing to take part in the rebuilding of the Soviet Union.

Lopatnikov cursed the gulf that had opened between him and the collective. Emphasizing that he had no masters but the Party, he promised "to carry out all the decisions of the Party organs."[7]

If history was the Bolshevik grand narrative, autobiography was its application to a particular life. While the promise of universal emancipation inspired each autobiographical story, the Bolshevik's individual conversion foreshadowed the proletarian emancipation as a whole. Such parallels explain the resemblance between the outcome of history and the conclusion of Bolshevik autobiographies. Bolshevik self-realization was absolutely impossible without attuning the individual self to the general course of history. The drama of the Bolshevik autobiography hinged on the author's recognition that the life story of a singular and autonomous individual had to be shattered and recreated as the story of a life lived for the sake of the proletarian movement. Converted to Bolshevik collectivism, the autobiographer typically placed his life experience within the broad metaphorical structure the Party was advancing, thereby suggesting that the Bolshevik story was relevant to his own self-understanding and everyday conduct.

Acutely aware that admission to the brotherhood of the elect depended on his capacity to identify with the Bolshevik narrative and accept this narrative as his own, Belokosterov, a student at Smolensk Institute, recapitulated in his autobiography the basic layout of the Bolshevik master story.[8] And from the very beginning, Belokosterov's life and the political process were closely linked. The autobiography opened thus: "My father, a peasant, was a victim of the conditions the [old] regime created in the army. After his death my mother went to the city to earn a living, leaving me with my grandparents." Since his summers were spent laboring and his winters studying, the narrator quickly learned that he who does not work shall not eat. "Upon arriving in the city, I knew that I must either look for a job or starve." Though the situation in the city's labor market prevented his holding any job that did not require his being at "the beck and call of another," Belokosterov left no doubt in the reader's mind that he had experienced the class struggle from the workers' side of the barricade. Concomitant class resentment soon appeared: "It was in the city that I first encountered the most shameless exploitation. It so offended my still unfortified soul that I started to loathe the existing order with every ounce of my being. In the meanwhile, the Revolution was beginning to mature." Carefully following the rules of the autobiographical genre, Belokosterov insisted that objective development and his subjective transformation could not be separated. As the objective economic tensions between capitalism and labor became more acute, the autobiographer's proletarian identity crystallized.

Belokosterov's autobiography is exceptional in its sensitivity toward the experiential aspects of the protagonist's development. Eloquent descriptions trace the injuries to a young, impressionable soul made by bloodsuckers, prompting the growth of an immeasurable hatred toward the tsarist order. While objective conditions are certainly part of the narrative, the accompanying inner movements of Belokosterov's soul are carefully detailed. The autobiographer begins by experiencing life "unconsciously"; then, with the growth of the revolutionary movement, his deep-seated worker's identity blossoms. The parallels between the move of the proletarian class from potentiality to actuality on the objective, universal level as well as on the subjective, particular level were the pivot around which Belokosterov's narrative revolved. Nowhere in his autobiography did the author celebrate either himself or his own autonomy. Discovering his personal self was only a vehicle to a higher end, which was the celebration of the Communist movement.

When the Revolution erupted, Belokosterov's eyes were opened, he came to know who he really was, and applied to the Party. Thus, the revolutionary consciousness of one man and the consciousness of the entire Russian working class evolved in tandem. His fate and the fate of the Revolution became one: "When the accursed time came, when the circle of our foes—Kolchak, Iudenich, Denikin, surrounded the workers' republic from all directions—I, together with my Party cell, volunteered to go to the front." The fusion of the autobiographer with the Party community was now complete: as soon as he saw that the republic was in danger, Belokosterov went off to wage the Bolshevik war "together with his comrades."

It is tempting to read Belokosterov's autobiography in a psychological key, interpreting the text as a symptomatic composition by an exceptionably vulnerable young individual. Desperate to overcome his insecurity and to find a firm anchor in life, so this reading goes, Belokosterov was drawn to embrace the Party, which promised him the sense of warmth and belonging he so badly needed. This sort of emphasis on the supposedly immutable psychological features of the individual, however, turns the tropes that went into the construction of the autobiographer's self-image into psychological truisms. Whereas for the psychologist the psyche is an immutable given that adapts only slightly to its environment, for the Bolshevik the self is open to a radical deconstruction. The smooth transposition of the psychological subject of an autobiographical text (the author) into its literary subject (its protagonist) is always disrupted in one way or another.[9] Belokosterov needed Bolshevik poetics to construct his neurosis. His autobiography tells us little about the psychological deficiencies of Soviet men and women and a great deal about the core Bolshevik assumption that no individual could possibly feel fulfilled outside the proletarian community.

The Party expected its members to submerge themselves in the Bolshevik community without leaving any residue of individuality. It was the collectivity that would provide the model for individual self-construction, and the official discourse never praised loners. Since the autobiographers willingly sacrificed their autonomy, the model Bolshevik self can be described as profoundly "illiberal." The central values of liberalism—all tied to the Romantic celebration of the individual—were the despised sins of student autobiographies. But the Bolshevik never feels hemmed in by a prescriptive mould, never has the occasion to lament not being permitted to be him- or herself.[10] There was no sense of falsifying one's own nature. "Every Communist, every participant in the Revolution," wrote Viktor Serge, "feels himself to be the humblest servant of a limitless cause. The highest praise that can be bestowed on him is to say that he has 'no private life,' that his life has fused totally with history."[11] Or, as Trotsky put it, "Great events taught us to subordinate our subjectivity to the objective rhythm of history."[12]

It is little wonder that the Bolshevik autobiographies are so conspicuously uniform. Uniformity should be expected when the self is conceived as something that develops according to rational laws, so that what was present in *nuce* from the very beginning of life gradually unfolds by a necessary, predetermined sequentiality. The Bolshevik individual was a part of a predestined historical process designed to enable him to regain his proper, authentic relation to society. The protagonist of the autobiography functioned according to his historical role. Naturally the Bolshevik autobiography was depersonalized. What counted was not the individual as such, but the active presence of the Communist light in the individual. Since the Communist message was indivisible, the more conscious the Party member, the less individualized he was.

Maksim Gorky's autobiographical stories of the 1920s were written as a reaction against Rousseau's celebration of unique individuality. A subject of much ridicule among Bolshevik literary critics, Rousseau's *Confessions* opens with these words: "I am constituted in a special way, differently than anybody I have ever met. I dare to think that there is no one like me under the sun. Though I may not be better than others, I am certainly unlike all others." Calling Rousseau the "apostle of individualism [. . .] with its odious cult of social alienation," Gorky preferred to see himself as someone "born from within the popular mass." Criticizing all "illusion of the independence of individual consciousness from the conditions of the epoch and the influences of class environment," he shied away from the notion that he was a "unique" (*iskliuchitel'nyi*) and totally "original" (*original'nyi*) creature. Gorky was proud to have fashioned himself upon the "collective worldview of Communism, with its scorn for a self which considers itself a pinnacle of the enormous pyramid of popular experience." His multiple autobiographical narratives "tried to substitute for the lyrical accent of the autobiographical genre an epic one," dedicating much space not just to the protagonist's own, "individual self," but also to the description of "the world around me."[13]

That the liberal quest for personal uniqueness was completely alien to the Bolshevik notion of the self does not mean, however, that all sense of individuality was absent. Since each Party applicant would find his own way to the light, particularizing his life story, Bolshevik autobiographies were never absolutely identical. As we have had plenty of opportunity to see, some room for variation within the genre always remained. Insofar as no model for the self could ever be filled out to the last detail or provide guidelines for every single aspect of human existence, the Bolshevik writer could always find room for his idiosyncrasies in the spaces unfilled by the basic structure of the autobiographical genre. In fact, students whose self-presentations mechanically reproduced official schemes and turns of phrase without enriching these with inner substance risked the accusation of "hiding behind formulas" and, ultimately, of shielding from the public eye a self hostile toward Bolshevism.

Was the autobiography not a genre that was supposed to enable the individual to break loose from the crowd? And was Bolshevik autobiography not anomalous in that it had the opposite effect of strengthening the bond between the individual and the collective? Gusdorf has proposed a distinction between "public" and "private" autobiographical types. The confessional, "private" type of autobiography, Gusdorf claims, appears only in cultures that possess a self-consciousness due to a phenomenon akin to the Christian ascetic tradition of self-examination. Suggesting Saint Augustine's *Confessions* as the locus classicus of the private autobiography, Gusdorf points out that in confessional Christianity each man was accountable for his own behavior, and intentions weighed as heavily as acts. Inversely, in cultures with a taboo even on viewing one's own image in a mirror, the "public autobiography" developed. Here the perspective was external to the Self and the autobiographical text centered not on self-exploration but on making an impression on posterity. The autobiographer recorded the events of his own life as a biographer would and the text he produced was a public document that projected a certain positive image of its author as an actor on the historical stage. Gusdorf's example of a public autobiography was the memoir of the Cardinal de Retz, who reconstructed all of the battles he had actually lost as victories.[14]

What has been said so far of the illiberal self suggests, however, that Bolshevik autobiographies did not lend themselves easily to this kind of typology. Bolshevik autobiographies cannot be described as belonging to either the private or the public autobiographical type because they straddled both types. The substantial degree of elision of the boundaries between the public and the private in defining the self sets the Bolshevik autobiography apart from traditional autobiographical writing. Unlike "private" autobiographers, the Bolshevik autobiographer's notion of individual emancipation was strongly related to the larger political project defined by Communism. Distinguishing the self as well as integrating it in history constituted two basic functions in a permanent state of tension. This tension was one of the primary forces behind the "activism" characteristic of the Bolshevik autobiography, and behind the sense of its protagonist's direct personal involvement in the course of events. In its function of giving relevance to the particular and of providing a sense of individuality, the Bolshevik myth gave a prominent role to the individual self as the agent of History.[15]

The demand placed on the Party applicant to link his or her individual conversion with the proletarian awakening forced him or her to compose an autobiography that transcended individual history and pertained to the history of the revolutionary movement in general. Nikolai Skrypnyk, a prominent Ukrainian Bolshevik, stated in the concluding pages of his autobiography: "My work after February, like that of every Party member who participated in all the revolutionary events, was so closely bound up with the Revolution that if I were to describe it, I would have to write the history of the Revolution itself."[16] Aleksandr Shliapnikov, a prominent Party leader, concluded his autobiography with a similar elision of all distinction between his private self and the history of the Party. "This is the tally of my activities up to 1920: to get into details would mean to enumerate a large part of events that have to do with the Revolution, events in which I participated."[17]

In such an autobiography, the most intimate events had to have a public significance because every personal tribulation either facilitated conversion or retarded it. Inversely, it was impossible to omit world historical developments concurrent with the autobiographer's private life because they could not but influence one's consciousness in one way or another. Contingent historical events were never presented as insignificant or external or as a force that interfered with inner transformations; rather, they had to be built into the life story as enriching elements. Bourgeois victories propelled the autobiographical plot forward by awakening the author's class anger and proletarian victories did the same by filling the author's soul with enthusiasm. The flow of history itself was a central formative element in the life of an admirable individual.[18]

APPENDIX

The Case of Fiodor Fiodorovich Raskol'nikov:
Bolshevik Autobiography Across the 1917 Divide

THE FLOOD OF PERSONAL DOCUMENTS emerging from the Soviet archives suggests that the Bolshevik regime engendered one of the largest collective autobiographical projects undertaken in modern history. The tsarist government did not sponsor autobiographical writing, and if we do find pre-1917 autobiographies they belong to the narrow circles of writers and artists who emulated west European manners of self presentation. Memoirs and even privately held diaries existed outside the state's data-collecting project and can hardly be seen as a direct precursor of the Bolshevik autobiography. What was new in the Soviet era was not just the contents of the autobiographies but the fact that they were demanded by the Party. It would have been fascinating to compare autobiographical narratives crossing the 1917 divide and to study the changing poetics of individual self-presentation.

I was able to find only one example of a Bolshevik autobiography that has a prerevolutionary variant, but since this is such a rare specimen it is worth looking into at length. The autobiography in question belongs to Raskol'nikov, the pen name of Il'in, a prominent Bolshevik writer turned naval commander known for his role as the commander of the Kronstadt fortress in 1917. When writing his first autobiography in 1913 for Vengerov's *Biographical Dictionary of Russian Writers and Scholars*, Raskol'nikov was a student at the St. Petersburg Imperial Archeological Institute. Applying himself to a similar task in 1926, he was a prominent Soviet proselytizer and a member of the editorial boards of the prestigious Soviet publications *Molodaia gvardiia and Kransnaia nov'*.

It is futile to ask what version of Raskol'nikov's autobiography is closer to the truth. Both texts were composed in a particular context and must be read as products of the regime of truth regnant at the time of their composition. The author does not merely adapt himself to circumstances; it is equally possible that he conceives of himself differently at different times. In 1913, Raskol'nikov presents himself as a young, progressive writer who aims to become a serious scholar. Thirteen years later, he has his reputation as a revolutionary hero to defend. Now he is a man of action, less a thinker.

Certain aspects of Raskol'nikov's autobiographies demonstrate consistency, others point to changes in outlook. Most notably, Raskol'nikov modifies—and sometimes completely alters—his tone toward the old regime and its system of values. If in the Soviet period he presents himself a staunch anti-monarchist, thirteen years earlier he is more ambivalent. To be sure, Raskol'nikov is a Marxist who is already demanding a radical transformation of the social order at the earlier date, but in 1913 he is also thankful for the help the tsarist administration extended to him and his family. The autobiographer is mindful of what the empire had done for Russia's glory in the recent and not so recent past. While the 1926 narrative directs itself exclusively toward the future, in 1913 the life of the protagonist is situated in tradition.

Raskol'nikov was born on January 28, 1892 (old style) at the outskirts of Petersburg. His 1913 autobiography states that he was born to a clerical family, which means he must have identified himself in official papers either as a *popovich* (a son of a priest who left the clergy) or a *raznochinets* (a person of various ranks") , a category that included individuals who did not fit into the traditional estate categories.

When he returned to the story of his life in 1926, Raskol'nikov was reluctant to go on categorizing himself in estate terms. He was aware that identity is made or unmade depending on whether one described oneself in the language of class or in that of estate. The autobiographer built on the Soviet shift from estate to vocation that appeared and was embodied in groupings such as "students," "physical workers," "pedagogical workers," and "mixed occupation," and described himself as a professional revolutionary and thus a member of the new intelligentsia. Of course, every alteration in one's class affiliation necessitated the production of a narrative incorporating one's old identity, a story of transformation, and an explanation of how the current class identity had been determined. Raskol'nikov was about to spin such a story, but in the meantime he dwelled on his economic hardships as a youngster to hint that his lower-class self presentation was not without a basis.

"Generally, my family was in need," Raskol'nikov wrote in his Soviet autobiography, and went on to complain about his frustrating inability to receive a decent education—a privilege preserved for the rich under the old regime. "My mother's salary, 60 rubles a month, was entirely consumed by everyday expenses," he explained. It took her heroic efforts to give the future Bolshevik columnist a chance to acquire minimal writing skills.

"Getting into debt, she managed to pay for my secondary education," although authorities "occasionally relieved me of tuition payments due to my difficult economic situation."

It is worth emphasizing that the 1913 reader found a very different description of the family's material situation in those same years. In this account, Raskol'nikov not only wrote that his parents lived comfortably enough but also that they owed their well-being to the tsar and were thankful for it. When his father died "and mother remained with two sons to look after," the paternalistic state did not leave her in the lurch. "Mother got a position as a vendor at the state shop at the Vyborg side. . . . In addition to the 750 rubles she earns she also has a three-room state apartment at her disposal and free light and heat."

Raskol'nikov's earlier autobiography is much more effusive about his parents' social characteristics. "I am a son out of wedlock of the archdeacon of the Sergeevsk Artillery Synod and a daughter of a general-mayor. My parents were not united by the bond of a religious marriage because my father, a widowed servant of the cult, did not have the right to remarry. Both of my parents were fairly religious people and they spent the nineteen years of their life together living in concord." In this rendition of his past, Raskol'nikov is not embarrassed by the devout atmosphere regnant in his family during childhood. Quite the contrary: his parents' spiritual intimacy gave him comfort and emotional security for which he is clearly thankful.

In 1913, Raskol'nikov speaks fondly of his father, priest or no priest. This is all the more striking as his father died an ignoble death in the middle of a very embarrassing scandal. While the Soviet version of his autobiography only mentions dryly that "my father died in 1907," the earlier text is generous with the gory details. "On April 12, 1907, father committed suicide. His servant complained to the St. Petersburg district court that he raped her. Fearing a house search and a juridical persecution that would follow he cut his carotid artery with a shaving knife." The 1913 autobiographer is clearly heartbroken. "The complaint had no basis. [. . .] According to the lawyers, the case was hopeless for the prosecution because no witnesses or material evidence could substantiate the charges. But father could not wait until the hearing and put an end to his life at the age of 62." Far from the image of a superstitious priest, his father is presented as an emotional anchor. "Everybody remembers that he had a soft character and a wonderful voice."

Of course, parents were a mandatory topic in the post-1917 autobiographies as well. Most if not all the autobiographers dedicate a sentence, and sometimes even a full paragraph, to their occupation, character, and political orientation. When Raskol'nikov describes his father in 1913, however, he speaks not about class but about heritage, virtue, and similar values associated with the tsarist ideology.

Pedigree is especially important to the autobiographer. At first, the Marxist writer seems determined to present himself as an autonomous, self-sufficient subject.

> Regarding the history of my clan (*rod*): though I am interested in the genealogy of my family tree I never pride myself on my ancestors' activity. The golden words of Sumarokov (or was it Kheraskov?) to the effect that "The one who boasts about his ancestry is boasting about something that does not belong to him" (*kto rodom khvalitsia – tot khvalitsia chuzhim*) are always on my mind. I prefer to direct my personal and social activity so that it will be fruitful in itself. My self-satisfaction must have nothing to do with the intoxicating pride of those who rely on the brave actions of their forefathers.

Considering this solemn pontification in his prerevolutonary autobiography, it is all the more surprising that Raskol'nikov dwells on his old family relations in excruciating detail immediately in what follows:

> From father's side, my ancestors have done nothing extraordinary: for over 200 years they served God in the Petropavlovsk Church of the village of Keikino, Iamburg district Petersburg province. [. . .] Father's predecessors (*predshestvenniki*) come from the noble clan of Timiriazevs. They later received the surname Ostorozhnye and only recently became Petrovs, named so after one of the saints sanctifying the Keikino church.

Even more words are spent on "my lineage from the side of my mother, whose surname I carry." More famous in Russian history, this lineage harks back to the prince Dmitrii Andreevich of Galich.

> In the fifteenth and sixteenth centuries my ancestors held court positions and served as court officers (*stol'niki*), cupbearers (*chashniki*), chamberlains (*postel'nichii*) and so on. My great-great-grandfather, Dmitrii Sergeevich, distinguished himself during Catherine II's reign, courageously sinking a number of Turkish vessels at the battle of

Chesmensk (1770). A ship from the Baltic fleet was named after him *Lieutenant Il'in*. [. . .] My great-grandfather, Mikhail Vasilevich Il'in, was a lieutenant colonel of the marine artillery; he authored a number of scholarly studies and his name is mentioned in the critical-biographical dictionary of Russian writers and scholars and in numerous other publications.

Raskol'nikov goes on and on speaking about his grandparents, uncles, and aunts. Testing the patience of the reader who wants to hear about the autobiographer's own life story, he spares no detail describing their exploits.

This narratological choice does not mean, however, that Raskol'nikov remained firmly in the traditionalist orbit. He rejected unequivocally what was doubtlessly most dear to his parents: orthodoxy. Even in his autobiography from 1913, where his parents appeared in a favorable light, he made it clear that he respected their humanity despite their clericalism, not because of it. Raskol'nikov's first autobiography took a somewhat facetious tone toward religion: "I was baptized according to the Orthodox ritual but in reality I am an unquestionable and resolute atheist for ten years now. Needless to say, I never fast and never visit the church." The autobiographer's sorry experience with religious education further underscored his distance from clerical ideology. He tells us that his mother sent the young Raskol'nikov to the Shelter of Prince Ol'denburg—a respectable *realschule* of a religious bent. The young boy had a full stipend and came home only on Saturdays. Having spent eight years of his life in this institution, he graduated in 1908 "with distinction."

The Soviet version of the autobiography is not only more detailed on the protagonist's school days but places his conversion to Marxism in that period. Here orthodoxy acquires its typical post-1917 negative connotations: authoritarianism, brainwashing, even sadism. Raskol'nikov's description of his school days could not be more negative. He wrote about the the "nightmarish morals and manners" of the "bursa," a collective term for both primary and secondary levels of ecclesiastical education—and, more specifically, a colloquial reference to the dormitories in which the young pupils lived. "In the bursa, flagging pupils were put on their knees before the entire class. Lisitsin, the priest, used to publicly pull me by the ears." The young boy had a visceral reaction: "In the seventh grade, I became an atheist." A dose of materialist propaganda helped. "In that year, I came across the creations of Maksim Gorky, Leonid Andreev, and others. This newest literature solidified my atheism."

When the narratives reach the subject of the First Russian Revolution and its impact on the psyche of the young protagonist, their emphasis varies. The divergences between the two texts are slight, but would not have been missed by contemporary readers. According to his 1913 autobiography, Raskol'nikov converted to the revolutionary cause under the influence of political events. "The revolutionary period of 1905–1906, which caught me in my fifth year of studies, made a huge, truly enormous impression on me. I immediately submerged myself in the thick of political life. In my social orientation I identified with the Marxist current, and I am dedicated to the Marxist ideas until this day."

In his autobiography from 1926, the events of 1905 are also told in the context of the "few words that must be said about the formation of my political attitudes." By this time the Bolshevik view of the past had stabilized considerably and personal narratives had to fit current historiography. Raskol'nikov's emphasis was no longer on the liberation movement and the role of the urban intelligentsia therein but on the marvelous appearance of a new type of state institution, the "soviet," and on the growing phenomenon of workers' strikes. Still an urchin, as he tells the story in 1926, Raskol'nikov

> participated in strikes, not once but twice. On one such occasion, I was even elected as a member of the pupils' delegation that presented the schoolmaster with demands regarding the improvement of our everyday conditions. I was nearly expelled from school for that. [. . .] My sympathy toward the downtrodden and exploited was sustained by the literary creations of Sheller-Mikhail. I was especially impressed by his novel, *When Trees are Cut – Splinters Fly*. The political tribulations during the Revolution of 1905, and the acute consciousness of social injustice drew me to socialism spontaneously (*stikhiino*).

Raskol'nikov did not lose interest in revolutionary theory despite Stolypin's coup d'état that nullified almost all the constitutional achievements of 1905. His earlier autobiography mentions that in 1909 he enrolled in the economics department of the St. Petersburg Polytechnic Institute—a known hotbed of Marxist thinking, or so the narrator claims. As a student Raskol'nikov was reading a lot. "The literary creations of Plekhanov and Bernatskii exerted a huge influence on me. They strengthened my worldview." The later autobiography belabors the same arguments but in a higher key. "During the first course of study I familiarized myself with the literary work of George Plekhanov and they turned me into a Marxist. In the summer of 1910, I studied [Marx's] *Capital* carefully. All remaining doubts evaporated, and in December of that year I enrolled in the Party." Raskol'nikov added two facts that solidify his Bolshevik record in those difficult years: "I worked shoulder to shoulder with Viacheslav Molotov in the institute's Bolshevik faction," and, "I was the liaison man with the Party committee."

Both versions of his autobiography agree that Raskol'nikov committed himself to radical journalism wholeheartedly. "When the first issue of the legal Bolshevik newspaper *Zvezda* came out, I announced my full solidarity with the newspaper's direction to the editorial board and offered my services," he boasted in 1926. "Beginning with eyewitness accounts, I gradually moved to writing articles." In April 1912, Raskol'nikov joined the editorial board of *Pravda* but he spent only one month at this: on the night of May 21–22 he was arrested.

In his earlier autobiography Raskol'nikov wrote that he faced several charges: "membership in the Russian Social Democratic Workers' Party, affiliation with the city coalitional student committee, and contributing to a workers' newspaper." Returning to the story of his arrest after the Revolution, he prefered to focus on the first charge exclusively: "I was charged with membership in RSDRP based on article 102." The Ministry of Internal Affairs sentenced the protagonist to a three-year administrative exile in the Archangel'sk Province but the sentence was soon commuted to compulsory emigration. Raskol'nikov went to Germany but was arraigned at the border in October 9, 1912.

If the reasons for this arrest remain unstated in his first autobiography, in returning to the subject in 1926 Raskol'nikov portrayed himself as a professional revolutionary who was exposed. "The German gendarmes took me for a Russian spy. Their main evidence was a schematic plan of the immigrants' quarter in Paris drawn for me by Ermeev before I left Petersburg." Released in few days, Raskol'nikov tried to sneak back into Russia "in order to engage in underground activity." He was caught, but the tsarist police soon realized he could not face criminal charges: our hero had lost possession of himself.

Obliged to be apologetic regarding his radicalism in 1913 lest his literary career be interrupted, Raskol'nikov wrote about a mysterious nervous breakdown. His medicalized account justified his unruly behavior on the basis of psychological weakness. He mentioned psychological "fatigue" (*utomlenie*) and "depression" (*udruchenie*). For a brief period of time, so the autobiographer implied, a psychological malady could overcome the mind, prompting an individual to act improperly. In the jerking puppet that behaved irresponsibly, the reader was asked to recognize Raskol'nikov's flesh. In view of his "sickly condition" (*boleznenoe sostoianie*) and "prolonged exhaustion of the organism" Raskol'nikov was sent to a hospital instead of a jail. His mother managed to obtain permission for Raskol'nikov to recuperate in his native city. In Petersburg, he was diagnosed at the clinic of professor Gerveg with "neurasthenia," an illness that consisted in "general weakness of the nervous apparatus." Well treated, "soon I was healthy again."

Temporary dementia does not befit a firm, omniconscious Bolshevik of 1926, so Raskol'nikov is less verbose about his state during his 1912 arrest in his second autobiography. When he does mention that "the nervous breakdown induced by incarceration announced itself" he links his infirmity to revolutionary sacrifice: only when energies completely abandoned him did the autobiographer cease working for the Revolution. This explains why there was no mention of revolutionary activity from 1913 until 1917 on his part.

On February 21, 1913, Raskol'nikov qualified for the amnesty associated with the tercentennial of the Romanovs "as a student." Administrative limitations and police surveillance came to an end, and in the autobiography he composed only a few months later he noted that he could finally "resume his scholarly and literary activity." Raskol'nikov enrolled in the Imperial Archeological Institute and destined himself to the academic world. Again, his later narrative is slightly different. Here he is a resolute revolutionary, not a bookish literatus. "Naturally, I immediately resumed work for *Pravda*," a risk mentioned to prove deep revolutionary commitment. "Due to censorship restrictions, *Pravda* was coming out under different, often changing names in those days," Raskol'nikov explained, and added that "my cooperation with the newspaper intensified in the spring of 1914, following Kamenev's return from abroad."

Here we have already moved beyond the period Raskol'nikov described in his first autobiography. What can we say about the two authors who emerge in texts separated by a mere thirteen years, but that these were years filled with so many wars and revolutions? Perhaps the best way to distinguish Raskol'nikov's two life stories is to examine their account of his conversion. It is difficult to identify the moment of conversion in the prerevolutionary autobiography with precision. The narrator does not distance himself from his parents but he does break with religion—a step that can be described as a reinvention of the self. And he does openly declare his adoption of Marxism, though by Marxism he may well have meant a scholarly version of it, perhaps a commitment to the amelioration of workers' conditions and not a revolutionary creed. At the same time, the prolonged account of the tsarist amnesty in the first autobiography can be read as a reverse conversion: Raskol'nikov's psyche heals, he leaves his revolutionary pranks behind, and the old regime accepts him back. He can live where he likes and study what he chooses.

In his account from 1926, conversion appears as a dramatic, one-time event, belonging to the distant past. The amnesty Raskol'nikov received in 1913 was an opportunity to continue revolutionary activity unhindered, not a token of royal forgiveness he truly identified with. Indeed, at that time Raskol'nikov is already rubbing shoulders with the fathers of Bolshevism. His contribution to the illegal press also cannot be interpreted in two ways.

The final part of his autobiography, appearing in the later version only, attempts to construct a persuasive portrayal of a zealous Bolshevik. Raskol'nikov's commitment became evident when the war broke out. "From the first days of the imperialist manslaughter (*imperialisticheskaia boinia*) I assumed an internationalist, Leninist position," he writes. "I took part in drafting the collective response to Vandervelde"—the treacherous leader of the Second International who sanctioned the Social Democratic endorsement of World War I.

What the autobiographer has to say next must therefore be described as nothing less than astonishing: "The war turned me, like my contemporaries, into a military man. Always drawn to the sea, I chose the fleet and became a navel cadet. When the February Revolution erupted I was just about to take my exams at the cadet school." Raskol'nikov is not a Bolshevik internationalist but a young officer and he contributes to the imperialist war, inadvertently or not. Having met Raskol'nikov in the spring of 1915 at the funeral of the historian Bogucharskii, Gorky ridiculed his cadet overcoat: "They dressed you up well, didn't they?!"

No amount of shrewd poetic maneuvering could dissipate the cloud that hung over the autobiographer. Only his future exploits in Kronstadt, which he knew were on the mind of all his Soviet readers, could redeem his lapse. The autobiographer insisted he retained revolutionary time-reckoning and his true self reemerged as soon as the monarchy fell. Raskol'nikov had never betrayed Bolshevism deep down in his soul. His abandonment of the

Leninist ranks had been caused by circumstances beyond his control. When February 1917 came around, "I immediately contacted the Party committee. I was happy to leave the moldy barracks and join the rebelling masses," he writes in his *Kronshtadt and Petrograd in 1917*, a text than can be read as his third autobiography, albeit one divested of an individual protagonist—Raskol'nikov's life fused with the revolutionary cause to such an extent that his biography had become the biography of the Party.

Sources: F. Raskol'nikov, *O vremeni i o sebe* (Leningrad: Lenizdat, 1989), pp. 19–23. *Deiateli SSSR i revoliutsionnogo dvizheniia Rossii: entsiklopedicheskii slovar' Granat* (Moscow: Sov. entsiklopediia, 1989), pp. 189–190. The quote from Gorkii is from Z. Grebel'skii, *Fedor Raskol'nikov* (Moscow: Moskovskii rabochii, 1988), p. 13. The diagnosis of "neurasthenia" is taken from Doctor L. Merel'zon, *Nevrasteniia. Ee istochniki, preduprezhdenie i lechenie* (Krasnodar, 1927), pp. 8–10, and Doctor A. Kholetskii, *Polovaia zhizn' i nevrasteniia* (Krasnodar, 1927), pp. 3–5.

NOTES

Sources cited in the following notes.

GANO: *Gosudarstvennyi arkhiv Novosibirskoi oblasti* (Novosibirsk Oblast Government Archive)

PATO: *Partiinyi arkhiv tomskoi oblasti* (Tomsk Oblast Party Archive)

PSS: V. I. Lenin, *Polnoe Sobranie Sochinenii*, fifth edition (Moscow, 1963-1977)

RGASPI: *Rossiiskii gosudarstvennyi arkhiv sotsial'no-politicheskoi istorii* (Russian State Archive of Socio-Political History)

TsGA IPD: *Tsentral'nyi gosudarstvennyi arkhiv istoriko-politicheskikh dokumentov*

TsGAODM: *Tsentral'nyi gosudarstvennyi arkhiv obshchestvennykh dvizhenii goroda Moskvy* (Central State Archive of Social Movements of Moscow)

WKP: Smolensk Party Archive

INTRODUCTION

1. Stephen M. Kotkin, *Magnetic Mountain: Stalinism as a Civilization* (Berkeley: University of California Press, 1995), p. 23.
2. Mark D. Steinberg, *Proletarian Imagination: Self, Modernity, and the Sacred in Russia, 1910–1925* (Ithaca: Cornell University Press, 2002), pp. 2-9, 102-146.
3. In the field of Russian history, the pioneer in the study of ego documents was Reggie Zelnik. See his "Russian Bebels: An Introduction to the Memoirs of Semen Kanatchikov and Matvei Fisher," Parts 1 and 2, *Russian Review* 35 (July and October) (1976) pp. 249-289, 417-447, as well as R. Zelnik, ed. and trans., *A Radical Worker in Tsarist Russia: The Autobiography of Semen Kanatchikov* (Stanford, CA: Stanford University Press, 1986). Zelnik supervised numerous theses that touched on the subject in one way or another. See a comprehensive list in *Reginald E. Zelnik, Perils of Pankratova: Some Stories from the Annals of Soviet Historiography* (Seattle: University of Washington Press, 2005), 117-137.
4. Stephen M. Kotkin, "1991 and the Russian Revolution: Sources, Conceptual Categories, Analytical Frameworks," *Journal of Modern History* 70 (1998), pp. 384-485.
5. Glennys Young, "Fetishizing the Soviet Collapse: Historical Rupture and the Historiography of (Early) Soviet Socialism: Historians of the Soviet Union," *Russian Review* 66 (2007), pp. 100-101.
6. Sheila Fitzpatrick, "Lives under Fire: Autobiographical Narratives and their Challenges in Stalin's Russia," in *De Russie et d'ailleurs: Mélanges Marc Ferro* (Paris: Institut d'études slaves, 1995); C. Pennetier et B. Pudal, eds., *Autobiographies, autocritiques, aveux dans le monde communiste* (Paris: Belin, 2002); and Brigitte Studer, et al., *Parler de soi sous Staline: La construction identitaire dans le communisme des années trente* (Paris: Fondacion Maison des sciences de l'homme, 2002).

7. Stephen E. Hanson, *Time and Revolution: Marxism and the Design of Soviet Institutions* (Chapel Hill: University of North Carolina Press, 1997).
8. Peter Holquist, " 'Information Is the *Alpha* and *Omega* of Our Work': Bolshevik Surveillance in Its Pan-European Context," *Journal of Modern History* 69 (1997), pp. 415-450.
9. Michel Foucault, *The Care of the Self* (New York: Vintage, 1988), p. 42. See also his theoretical statements, collected in Paul Rabinow, ed., *Power* (New York: The Free Press, 2000). For a critical examination of the impact of Foucault on the study of the Russian Revoltion see, Laura Engelstein, "Culture, Culture, Everywhere: Interpretations of Modern Russia, across the 1991 Divide," *Kritika* 2 (2001), 363-393; Ronald G. Suny, "Revision and Retreat in the Historiography of 1917: Social History and its Critics," *American Historical Review* 53 (1994) pp. 165-182.
10. Kotkin, *Magnetic Mountain*, 623, 683, 694.
11. In a series of innovative works, Jochen Hellbeck explored the self-expressive, Romantic aspect of the Bolshevik ego documents. See his most recent: Hellbeck, *Revolution on My Mind: Writing a Diary Under Stalin* (Cambridge MA: Harvard University Press, 2006).
12. Of course, in examining the Bolshevik self I am not making exclusive claims about how Soviet people actually conceived of themselves. Indeed, Soviet citizens may well have had alternative ways of self-identification. Thus we should not be surprised that those Soviet refugees who found their way to the West after the Second Word War venerated "personal autonomy" and "freedom of conscience," proving to be adepts of liberal self-presentation. Such rapid transformation of identity does not unmask the Bolshevik self as contrived because my core assumption is that individuals can articulate themselves along a number of linguistic axes and take part in a plurality of identity games. However, as long as someone lived in the Soviet Union, he or she could not ignore the ways in which the Bolshevik discourse engaged their sense of self on pain of turning them into outcasts. See Raymond A. Bauer and Alex Inkeles, *The Soviet Citizen: Daily Life in a Totalitarian Society* (Cambridge, MA: Harvard University Press, 1959).
13. For the spiritual dimension of Bolshevik autobiographies see, Richard L. Hernandez, "The Confessions of Semen Kanatchikov: A Bolshevik Memoir as Spiritual Autobiography," *Russian Review* 60 (2001), pp. 16-17.
14. The records of student interrogations, their autobiographies, and the recommendation letters that comprise the source base for this study are located in personal files of individual students, local Party cell application dossiers, and files containing purge-related materials. The "standard Party card," a personal booklet of thirty-three pages that all Communists had to carry in the 1920s, included basic details of the holder's autobiography. *Izvestiia TsK RKP*(b), August 18, 1920; *Spravochnik partiinogo rabotnika*, vyp.1 (Moscow, 1921), pp. 69-70; *Partiinyi arkhiv tomskoi oblasti*, PATO. f.17, op.1, d.631, l.5.
15. For characterizations of the aquisition of revolutionary consciousness by Russian workers as something like a conversion see, Reginald Zelnik, "To the Unaccustomed Eye: Religion and Irreligion in the Experience of St. Petersburg Workers in the 1870s," *Russian History*, 16 (1989), pp. 316-318; Dave Pretty, "The Saints of the Revolution: Political Activists in 1890s Ivanovo-Voznesensk and the Path of Most Resistance," *Slavic Review* 54 (1995): p. 300; Mark D. Steinberg, "Workers on the Cross: Religious Imagination in the Writings of Russian Workers, 1910-1924," *Russian Review* 53 (1994), pp. 213-215.

16. *Dvenadtsatyi s"ezd RKP(b) 17-25 Aprelia 1923 goda. Stenograficheskii otchet* (Moscow: Gospolitizdat, 1968), p. 160.

17. Pierre Hadot, "Forms of Life and Forms of Discouse in Ancient Philosophy," in Arnold Davidson, ed., *Foucault and His Interlocutors* (Chicago: University of Chicago Press, 1997).

18. Saint Augustine, Bishop of Hippo, *Confessions*, trans. R. S. Pine-Coffin (Baltimore: Penguin, 1986); P. Abelard, *Heloise and Abelard*, trans. Betty Radice (Harmondsworth, UK: Penguin, 1978); Saint Teresa of Avila, *The Life of Saint Teresa of Avila by Herself*, trans. J. M. Cohen, (London: Penguin, 1987).

19. A. S. Mandel, "Le process inquisitorial comme acte autobiographique: Le cas de sor Maria de San Jeronimo," In *L'autobiographie dans le monde hispanique*, pp. 155-169 (Paris: Diffusion H. Champion, 1980); Antonio Gomez Moriana, "Autobiographie et discourse ritual: La confession autobiographique au tribunal de l'Inquisition," *Poétique 56*, (1983). This view of the subject was useful to historians, especially John H. Arnold, *Inquisition and Power: Catharism and the Confessing Subject in Medieval Languedoc* (Philadelphia: University of Pennsylvania Press, 2001).

20. A. G. Tartakovskii, *Russkaia memuaristika XVII-pervoi poloviny XIX v. Ot rukopisi k knige.* (Moscow: Nauka, 1991).

21. Michel Foucault, *Religion and Culture*, ed. Jeremy Carrette (New York: Routledge, 1999), p. 180. For the genesis of this self-affirmation see, Michael Mascuch, *Origins of the Individualist Self: Autobiography and Self Identity in England, 1591–1791* (Stanford. CA: Stanford University Press, 1996); Karl J. Weintraub, *The Value of the Individual: Self and Circumstance in Autobiography* (Chicago: University of Chicago Press, 1978); Charles Taylor, *The Sources of the Self. The Making of Modern Identity* (Cambridge MA: Harvard University Press, 1989), pp. 127-142.

22. It was not unusual for political movements eager to construct the New Man to encourage autobiographical self-narrativization. Not only do the affinities in the practices employed to affect individual self-transformation leap to the eye in this connection, but also important differences in terms of the way the end product was conceived: some versions of the new Self stressed universal values, others national values; some emphasized aesthetics and form, others ethics and consciousness. See for example the interesting collection of German workers' autobiographies, Wolfgang Emmerich, *Proletarische Lebensläufe: Autobiographische Dokumente zur Entstehung der Zweiten Kultur in Deutschland*, 2 vols. (Hamburg: Rowohlt, 1974-75). For a sample of early Nazi autobiographies, see Theodore Abel, *Why Hitler Came into Power* (New York: Prentice-Hall, 1938). For the centrality of personal narratives in Soviet Russia, see Golfo Alexopoulos, "The Ritual Lament: A Narrative of Appeal in the 1920s and 1930s," *Russian History/Histoire Russe* 24 (1997).

23. I follow here the argument in Peter Fritzsche, "Where Did All the Nazis Go? Reflections on Collaboration and Resistance," *Tel Aviver Jahrbuch für deutsche Geschichte* 23 (1994).

24. Smolensk Party Archive (henceforth: WKP), 326, l.19.

25. For the official stance on the brutalities of the Civil War, see Glennys Young, "Terror in Pravda, 1917–1939: All the News That Was Fit to Print," in Catherine Evtukhov and Stephen Kotkin, eds., *The Cultural Gradient: the Transmission of Ideas in Europe, 1789–1991* (Lanham, MD: Rowman & Littlefield, 2003), pp. 169-170.

26. On the subject of resistance, see Jeffrey Rossman, "Weaver of Rebellion and Poet of Resistance: Kapiton Klepikov (1880–1933)," and "Shop-Floor Opposition to Bolshevik Rule," *Jahrbücher für Geschichte Osteuropas* 44, no. 3 (1996), pp. 374-408; and Tracy McDonald, "A Peasant Rebellion in Stalin's Russia: The Pitelinskii Uprising, Riazan, 1930," in Lynn Viola, ed., *Contending with Stalinism: Soviet Power and Popular Resistance in the 1930s* (Ithaca: Cornell University Press, 2002).

27. James C. Scott, *Domination and the Arts of Resistance: Hidden Transcripts* (New Haven, CT: Yale University Press, 1990), p. 138. This approach is brilliantly critiqued in Susan Gal, "Language and the 'Arts of Resistance,' " *Cultural Anthropology* 10 (1995), pp. 407-424.

28. Colin Morris, *The Discovery of the Individual* (London: S.P.C.K., 1972), pp. 7-8.

29. Erving Goffman, *The Presentation of Self in Everyday Life* (New York: Anchor, 1959), p. 81.

30. Ibid., p. 81.

31. Ibid., pp. 169-170.

32. A. Fil'shtinskii, "Priemnye ispytaniia v sverdlovskom universitete," *Zapiski kommunisticheskogo universiteta imeni Sverdlova* (Moscow, 1924), p. 300.

33. TsGA IPD, f.984, op.1, d.126, ll.35-39. The merit of the poetical reading of historical documents is defended in the following classics: Hayden White, "The Value of Narrativity in the Representation of Reality," in W. J. T. Mitchell, ed., *On Narrative* (Chicago: University of Chicago Press, 1981); Michael J. Toolan, *Narrative: A Critical Linguistic Introduction* (London: Routledge, 1988); Larry J. Griffin, "Narrative, Event-structure Analysis, and Causal Interpretation in Historical Sociology," *American Journal of Sociology* 98 (1993), pp. 1094-1133.

34. The following information and citations are from Slesar's autobiography, in WKP, 326, l.87.

35. The following information and citations are from Rabinovich's autobiography in WKP, 326, ll.247-250.

36. Hayden White, *The Content of the Form. Narrative Discourse and Historical Representation*, (Baltimore: Johns Hopkins University Press, 1987), pp. 47-48.

CHAPTER 1

1. On the importance of decentering the Bolshevik project geographically, see Donald J. Raleigh, *Provincial Landscapes: Local Dimensions of Soviet Power, 1917–1953* (Pittsburgh: University of Pittsburgh Press, 2001).

2. Dominic LaCapra maintains that close reading of questions and answers may provide a concrete understanding of the "skewed reciprocity of speech" during public interrogations. See LaCapra's review, "The Cheese and the Worms: The Cosmos of a Sixteenth-Century Miller," *History and Criticism*, (Ithaca: Cornell University Press, 1985), pp. 45-69.

3. N. Krupskaia, "Partiia i studenchestvo," *Krasnaia molodezh'* no. 1 (1924), ; N. Derzhavin, *Vysshaia shkola i revoliutsiia* (Moscow-Petrograd, 1923); E. Gorodetskii, "Sovetskaia reforma vysshei shkoly 1918 goda i Moskovskii universitet," *Vestnik MGU. Ser. obshchestvennykh nauk*, vyp. 1 (Moscow, 1954); I. Meseniashin, "Petrogradskaia gruppa 'Levoi professury.' " *Vestnik vysh. shkoly* no. 9 (1958); and E. Brusnikin, "Iz istorii bor'by Kommunisticheskoi partii za vuzovskuiu intelligentsiiu v 1917-1922 gg.," *Voprosy istorii KPSS* no. 8 (1972).

4. Sheila Fitzpatrick, *The Commissariat of Enlightenment: Soviet Organization of Education and the Arts under Lunacharsky, October 1917–1921* (Cambridge, UK: Cambridge University Press, 1970); Lynn Mally, *Culture of the Future: The Proletkult Movement in Revolutionary Russia* (Berkeley: University of California Press, 1990).

5. Michael David-Fox, *Revolution of the Mind: Higher Learning among the Bolsheviks, 1918–1929* (Ithaca: Cornell University Press, 1997); Peter Konecny, *Builders and Deserters: Students, State and Community in Leningrad, 1917–1941* (Montreal: McGill-Queen's University Press, 1999).

6. Kurt Widenfeld, *The Remaking of Russia* (London: Labour Publishing Company, 1924), p. 113; L. Livshits, "Rabfaki i vysshaia shkola," *Znamia rabfakovtsa* no. 1 (1922); N. Vikhirev, "Politicheskaia istoriia rabfakov," *Znamia rabfakovtsa* no. 4-5 (1922), pp. 38-43; *Piat' let Leninskoi ucheby: iubileinyi sbornik (1922–1927)* (Leningrad, 1925).

7. N. Popov, "O Sotsial'nom sostave RKP(b) i o Leninskom prizyve," *Krasnai nov'* no. 3 (1924), pp. 310-311.

8. *Tsentral'nyi gosudarstvennyi arkhiv obshchestvennykh dvizhenii goroda Moskvy* (henceforth, TsGAODM), f.67, op.1, d.97, l.6ob.

9. *Pravda*, November 12, 1921.

10. In February 1920 the Petrograd Party organization issued a circular stating that: "uniform and careful statistical work is indispensable in order to control and correctly distribute the resources of the Party," TsGA IPD, f.138, op.1, d.1g, l.21.

11. *Instruktsiia organizatsiiam RKP(b) o edinom bilete* (Moscow, 1920).

12. Popov, "O Sotsial'nom sostave RKP(b)," p. 311.

13. *Desiatyi s"ezd RKP(b), Mart 1921 goda* (Moscow, Gospolitizdat, 1963), p. 695.

14. For divergent assessments of NEP, see V. Brovkin, *Russia After Lenin: Politics, Culture and Society, 1921–1929* (London: Routledge, 1998), and Lewis H. Siegelbaum, *Soviet State and Society Between Revolutions, 1918–1929* (Cambridge, UK: Cambridge University Press, 1992). For official accounts of the mutiny, see A. Slepkov, *Krontshtadtskii miatezh* (Moscow-Leningrad, 1928) and A. Pukhov, *Kronshtadskii miatezh v 1921 godu* (Leningrad, 1931).

15. *Odinnadtsatyi s"ezd RKP(b), Mart-Aprel' 1922 goda. Stenograficheskii otchet (Moscow, Gospolitizdat, 1966), pp. 395, 546-547; T. H. Rigby, Communist Party Membership in the U.S.S.R., 1917-1967* (Princeton, NJ.: Princeton University Press, 1968), p. 95.

16. *Dvenadtsatyi s"ezd RKP(b)*, l. 248.

17. *Biulleten' TsKK RKP(b) i NK R-KI SSSR* 22 (November 15, 1924), p. 6.

18. PATO, f.17, op.1, d.747, l.21.

19. PATO, f.115, op.2, d.11, ll. 28-29.

20. Meijer, Jan M., ed., *The Trotsky Papers, 1917–1922*, vol.2, (The Hague: Mouton, 1971), p. 650. *Desiatyi s"ezd RKP(b)*, pp. 571-576.

21. Popov, "O Sotsial'nom sostave RKP(b)."

22. *Odinnadtsatyi s"ezd RKP(b)*, p. 404

23. L. Kopelev, *I sotvori sebe kumira*, (Ann Arbor, MI: Ardis, 1971), p. 162.

24. TsGA IPD, f.1085, op.1, d.10, l.25.

25. In spring 1923 the Twelfth Party Congress reduced the number of recommendations required for worker recruits and put a moratorium on promoting nonworkers to full Party membership that was to last until the Thirteenth Party Congress (1924). *KPSS v rezoliutsiiakh* (Moscow, 1970), p. 452; Rigby, *Communist Party Membership*, pp. 101-102; TsGA IPD, f.138, op.1, d.1g, p. 44.

26. TsGA IPD, f.138, op.1, d.1g, l.44.
27. TsGA IPD, f.984, op.1, d.129, l.17.
28. Mark Von Hagen, *Soldiers in the Proletarian Dictatorship: The Red Army and the Soviet Socialist State, 1917–1930* (Ithaca: Cornell University Press, 1989); Roger R. Reese, *The Soviet Military Experience: A History of the Soviet Army, 1917–1991* (London: Routledge, 2000), pp. 7-25, 52-60.
29. Oskar Anweiler, *Geschichte der Schule und Pädagogik in Russland, vom Ende des Zarenreiches bis zum Beginn der Stalin-Ära* (Berlin, 1964); G. Z. F. Bereday, ed., *The Politics of Soviet Education* (Westport, CT: Greenwood Press, 1976); W. Berelowitch, *La soviétisation de l'école russe: 1917–1931* (Lausanne: L'Age d'Homme, 1990; Sheila Fitzpatrick, *Education and Social Mobility in the Soviet Union, 1921–1934* (Cambridge, UK: Cambridge University Press, 1979).
30. I. Strugatskii, "Dumki v golos," *Student revoliutsii* no. 5 (1927), p. 83.
31. I. Stukov, "Trevozhnoe iavlenie," *Pravda*, December 22, 1921.
32. Z. Lozinksii, "Normal'noe iavlenie," *Pravda*, December 24, 1921.
33. M. Mironov, "Lozhnaia trevoga," *Pravda*, January 3, 1922.
34. E. Preobrazhenskii, "Nauka dlia rabochego klassa," *Pravda*, January 1, 1922.
35. "Otkliki chitatelei," *Pravda*, January 1, 1922.
36. PATO, f.115, op.2, d.6, l.4.
37. Varlen L. Soskin, *Vysshee obrazovanie i nauka v Sovetskoi Rossii: Pervoe desiatiletie (1917-1927)* (Novosibirsk: Novosibirskii Gosudarstvennyi Universitet, 2000).
38. J. R. Adelman, "The Development of the Soviet Party Apparat in the Civil War: Center, Localities, and National Areas," *Russian History* no. 9 (1982), p. 102.
39. The workers' faculty in the Tomsk State University was formed in September 1920; 75 percent of its students were either Party or Komsomol members. *Krasnaia molodezh'* no. 7-8 (1923), p. 57; *Krasnaia molodezh'* no. 2 (1924), p. 90; *Vestnik professional'no-tekhnicheskogo obrazovaniia* no. 9 (1921), p. 46; P. Zaichenko, *Tomskii gosudarstvennyi universitet imeni V. V. Kuibysheva* (Tomsk, 1960), p. 230; and *Tomskii universitet, 1880–1980* (Tomsk, 1980), p. 120.
40. In spring 1923, the nascent Party cell in the Tomsk Technological Institute boasted 63 members; following the 1923 admission, however, its membership reached 116; see P. Zaichenko, *Tomskii gosudarstvennyi universitet imeni V. V. Kuibysheva* (Tomsk, 1960), p. 268. "Ocherki po istorii revoliutsionnogo dvizheniia studenchestva TTI (1900-1925)," *Tomskii technologicheskii universitet za 25 let svoego sushchestvovaniia* (Tomsk, 1928), p. 120.
41. *Sbornik materialov PK RKP(b)*, vyp.2 (Petrograd, 1921), p. 38. During the 1920–21 academic year, Party members in the Moscow workers' faculties strongly outnumbered Party members in Moscow's regular universities. N. Babenkova, "Ukreplenie partiacheek vuzov v pervyi period nepa," *Studenchestvo v obshchestvenno-politicheskoi zhizni* (Moscow, 1979), p. 54.
42. *Pravda*, November 23, 1923; *Krasnyi student* no. 7-8 (1923), p. 60; *Sbornik materialov Petrogradskogo komiteta RKP(b)*, vyp.2 (Petrograd, 1921), p. 38, and vyp.4 (Petrograd, 1922), p. 23; *Biulleten' deviatnadtsatoi Petrogradskoi gubernskoi organizatsii RKP(b)*, no. 1 (1923), pp. 8, 17.
43. TsGA IPD, f.1085, op.1, d.10, l.4, d.16, l.15. From September 1922 to February 1923, only only 4 Party applications were submitted to academic Party cells in Volodarsk district (compared with 88 applications submitted in the factories during the same time). *Sbornik materialov Leningradskogo komiteta RKP*, vyp.6 (Petrograd, 1923), pp. 173, 201.

44. TsGA IPD , f.1085, op.1, d.12, l.65.
45. "Dushevnoe nastroenie uchashcheisia molodezhi," *Krasnyi student* no. 4 (1923),
    pp. 13-14; "Dukhovnyi lik studenchestva," *Student-proletarii* no. 6-7 (1924),
    p. 69; *Upadochnoe nastroenie sredi molodezhi*, pp. 143-144; A. Zharov, *Protiv
    upadochnichestva. Protiv "eseninshchiny"* (Moscow: "Pravda," "Bednota," 1926),
    pp. 6-7; I. Borybshev, *Melkoburzhuaznye vliianiia sredi molodezhi* (Moscow, 1928),
    p. 94.
46. Eric Naiman, *Sex in Public: The Incarnation of Early Soviet Ideology* (Princeton, NJ:
    Princeton University Press, 1997), pp. 170-171.
47. *Rossiiskii gosudarstvennyi arkhiv sotsial'no-politicheskoi istorii* (henceforth, RGASPI)
    f.613, op.3, d.161, l.30.
48. Texts found to contain "ambiguity" (*dvumysel*) were forwarded to the control
    commission for closer investigation. PATO, f.17, op.1, d.1065, l.4. TsGA IPD, f.408,
    op.1, d.1175, l.59.
49. Lionel Trilling, *Sincerity and Authenticity* (London: Oxford University Press, 1972),
    pp. 5-6.
50. TsGA IPD, op.1, d.116, l.72.
51. TsGA IPD, op.1, f.197, d.116, l.75. Shkliarovskaia's autobiography drew no less fire.
    According to her own version of her past, she was born to a poor family but somehow
    managed to spend her early years at a study bench. "Having graduated from a parish
    school in 1911 I enrolled in a higher elementary school where I remained until the
    outbreak of World War I. [. . .] In 1917, I joined the Bolsheviks.[. . .] I became a
    member of a Party committee during the Civil War. [. . .] The Whites accused me of
    belonging to the Bolsheviks -- I was summoned to the counter-intelligence department
    and my house was searched." On the face of it, this was an impressive narrative:
    Shkliarovskaia claimed she had "accepted the October Revolution internally,"
    According to her classmates, however, "some details just do not mesh (*ne viazhutsia*),"
    The story of Shkliarovskaia's education was the Achilles' heel of her self-presentation.
    "One cannot help noticing her unusual background," her ill wishers stated. It simply
    did not correspond to the education known to be offered in the schools where she
    supposedly studied. Talking to Shkliarovskaia's roommate from her Siberian period a
    certain Ermires found out that the autobiographer "had a high school education -- a
    biographical detail that classified her as a member of the intelligentsia" and explained
    why the head of the Khabarovsk Party agitation department was "stunned that she
    might be accepted into the Communist University," The conclusions of Strishchuk,
    speaking next, were blunt: "I believe Shkliarovskaia's autobiography is incorrect
    (*nevernaia*); her education must be more extensive than higher elementary school. [.
    . .] She would have us believe that she studied physics and geometry from the fourth
    grade on," Strizchuk believed he had caught Shkliarovskaia red-handed: "she does
    not even know the structure of the high school curriculum she supposedly went
    through." Another denouncer, Remz, corroborated this suspicion: "Shkliarovskaia
    told me herself that she moved from higher elementary school to a gymnasium,"
    Sverzhev tried to intercede on behalf of the defendant: "There are no grounds to claim
    Shkliarovskaia graduated a gymnasium – she could have forgotten the curriculum,"
    But when the issue was put to a vote the harsher view – "It is doubtful whether the
    information in her questionnaire is true" – won a majority (11 for, 7 abstained.)
    TsGA IPD, op.1, f.197, d.116, l.75.

52. M. Foucault, *Power/Knowledge: Selected Interviews and Other Writings, 1972–1977* (New York, 1977), pp. 131-132.

53. Renza concludes that what is at stake in autobiography is not the recreation of the past of the writer but an interpretation of his present. See his article "The Veto of the Imagination: A Theory of Autobiography," *New Literary History* 9 (1977), pp. 2-3. For the tension between "fictionality" and "truth" in autobiography see also Roy Pascal, *Design and Truth in Autobiography* (Cambridge, MA: Harvard University Press, 1960).

54. *Izvestiia TsK RKP(b)* no. 45, September 1922.

55. RGASPI f.613, op.1, d.3, ll.120, 133.

56. TsGA IPD, f.984, op.1, d.126, ll.158-162.

57. *Desiatyi s"ezd RKP(b)*, p. 232.

58. V. I. Lenin, *Polnoe Sobranie Sochinenii*, fifth edition (henceforth, PSS) (Moscow, 1963-1977), vol. 44, p. 123.

59. PATO, f.17, op.1, d.1065, ll.6-7.

60. O. Obichkin, *Kratkii ocherk istorii ustava KPSS* (Moscow, 1986), p. 83.

61. TsGA IPD, f.258, op.1, d.29, ll.10, 17.

62. TsGA IPD, f.984, op.1, d.28, ll.17-18.

63. TsGA IPD, f.258, op.1, d.111, l.43.

64. TsGA IPD, f.984, op.1, d.125, l.12.

65. TsGA IPD , f.1085, op.1, d.24, l.197.

66. TsGA IPD, f.138, op.1, d.1g, l.1; d.11, l.2; PATO, f.17, op.1, d.470, ll.12-36.

67. RGASPI f.613, op.1, d.3, l.105; TsGAODM f.64, op.1, d.74, l.29ob.; d.78, l.18.

68. *Chetyrnadtsatyi s"ezd vsesoiuznoi kommunisticheskoi partii(b). Stenograficheskii otchet* (Moscow-Leningrad, 1926), pp. 600-601.

69. TsGA IPD, op.1, f., d.101, l.219.

70. Sheila Fitzpatrick and Robert Gellately, "Introduction to the Practices of Denunciation in Modern European History," *Journal of Modern History* 68, 1996.

71. For the role of denunciations in Soviet society, see S. Popov, "Sistema donositel'stva," *Klio* 1 (1991); S. Korolev, *Donos v Rossii. Sotsial'no-filosofskie ocherki* (Moscow, 1996); V. Kozlov, "Fenomen donosa," *Svobodnaia mysl'* no. 4, 1998, pp. 100-112.

72. *Izvestiia TsK KPSS*, (1990), no. 5, p. 116, and (1991), no. 4, p. 223.

73. David-Fox, *Revolution of the Mind*, p. 116.

74. RGASPI f.613, op.1, d.3, l.138.

75. Lenin, PSS, vol. 37, p. 535.

76. *Pravda*, October 13, 1921; Gosudarstvennyi arkhiv Novosibirskoi oblasti, (henceforth, GANO), f.288, op.1, d.104, l.102; *Leningradskaia pravda*, May 25, 1924.

77. TsGA IPD, f.138, op.1, d.34, l.93.

78. TsGA IPD, f.138, op.1, d.34, l.72.

79. TsGA IPD, f.984, op.1, d.58, l.39.

80. TsGA IPD, f.1085, op.1, d.13, l.46.

81. TsGA IPD, f.984, op.1, d.188, ll.38-45.

82. RGASPI f.17, op.67, d.187, l.21.

83. TsGAODM, RGASPI f.80, op.1, d.58, l.21.

84. TsGA IPD, f.984, op.1, d.148, l.148.

85. TsGA IPD, f.188, op.1, d.188, l.11.

86. *Izvestiia TsK RKP(b)*, December 2, 1919. Lenin, PSS, vol. 37, p. 46 and vol. 39, p. 361. *Vos'maia konferentsiia RKP(b)* (Moscow, 1961), p. 140. TsGA IPD, f.1, op.1, d.332, ll, 1-2.

87. RGASPI f.45, op.1, d.1, l.18; TsGA IPD,f.138, op.1, d.1g, ll.1-2.
88. TsGA IPD, f.138, op.1, d.34, l.72.
89. TsGA IPD, f.197, op.1, d.71, ll.59-60; Lenin, *PSS*, vol. 39, pp. 225-226.
90. TsGA IPD,f.138, op.1, d.1g, ll.1-2.
91. TsGA IPD,f.138, op.1, d.1g, ll.1-2.
92. The events surrounding the case of Bushinskii, a student at the Smolensk Institute, show the importance of a correct stance toward the Kronstadt mutiny. Bushinskii portrayed himself as a loyal and steadfast Bolshevik. He always sympathized with Lenin and was class conscious and ready to sacrifice for the victory of the Revolution. But when a letter was received in 1921 claiming that at the first sight of trouble Bushinskii had withdrawn his application materials, storm clouds began to gather. The applicant's nemesis, a certain Nikiforov, stated: "During the days of the uprising, Bushinskii used to come to me and ask 'How are things with Kronstadt?' He begged me to report to the cell that his application had been handed in 'by accident.' I was supposed to say that it was I who had sent in his application and that he, Bushinskii, had initiated nothing." Nikiforov's denunciation was supported by other students who recalled that "during the Kronstadt days Bushinskii was in hiding, avoiding the military alert regulations." Even the rumor of such a step by Bushinskii generated considerable anxiety. After all, his contemporaries were well aware of mass departures from the Party, sparse as the information flowing out of Kronstadt might have been. (Here are few examples: Shisheleva, a worker at the Kronstadt artillery shop, petitioned in March 1921 "not to be considered a Party member any longer. I came to realize that Communists are akin to bloodthirsty beasts who take no pity on their prey." Shatel', a teacher, also regretted joining the Bolsheviks in 1920. "Following the first salvo at the peaceful Kronstadt population [. . .], I dread the thought of being considered an accomplice in spilling innocent blood." In a curious inversion of the official rhetoric, the inhabitants of Kronshtadt justified their ill-advised enrollment in the Party by "lack of consciousness" and "inability to grasp basic things.") Could Bushinskii also be an apostate? Did he not hide in his apartment waiting to see which way things would go? When Soviet power emerged victorious in Kronstadt, he resurfaced, grasped his rifle, and went to the Cheka detachment to push his enrollment forward. What counted, when all was said and done, was Bushinskii's state of mind. It seemed as if "Bushinskii wanted to become a Bolshevik "only in order to get closer to the source of power," someone said. Bushinskii countered: "I remained in the barracks [for the duration of the Kronstadt mutiny] and slept there embracing my rifle"—but he could not recall the names of his commanding officers. He was also forced to admit that the cowardly remarks Nikiforov reported were "a fact." Yet, he pleaded, "I could say back then things I would not say now. Comrades, I have been reborn (*pererodilsia*)!" Bushinskii hoped to pass off his mistakes as part of a learning process but his claims were rejected. WKP, 326, l.17; *Izvestiia vremennogo revoliutsionnogo komiteta* (Kronshtadt), March 10, 1921; V. P. Naumov and A. Kosakovskii, eds., *Kronshtadt. 1921*, (Moscow, 1997), pp. 151-153. RGASPI f.613, op.1, d.3, l.18. TsGAODM f.64, op.1,d.78, l.9. On the impact of Kronstadt on Smolensk, see *Ocherki Istorii Smolenskoi Organizatsii KPSS*, p. 117. For the Smolensk garrison's participation in the supression of the Kronstadt rebellion, see *Pravda*, March 27, 1921.

93. PATO, f.17, op.1, d.747, l.20. When information about such dilemmas reached its offices, the Party apparatus noted that "bureau members are often under the erroneous impression that they have to be unanimous in their decisions on Party admissions and that presentation of minority opinions before the Party cell is prohibited. Cases were brought to our attention where the bureau's majority erroneously denounced the bureau's minority for infringement of Party discipline dealing with dissenting bureau members as factionists." The bureau's resolutions had only a recommendatory value, allowing it to speak in multiple voices. *Obichkin, Kratkii ocherk istorii ustava KPSS*, pp. 74-75; PATO, f.17, op.1, d.631, l.3.
94. PATO, f.320, op.1, d.13, ll.21-22.
95. In 1921, a certain Saraev attributed to himself party standing going back to 1919. When the fraud was discovered he was immediately purged. RGASPI f.613, op.1, d.6, l.124.
96. *Odinnadtsatyi s"ezd RKP(b)*, p. 399.
97. A. Kirilina, *Neizvestnyi Kirov* (Moskow: Olma-Press, 2001), p. 100.
98. TsGA IPD, f.138, op.1, d.1g, l.27.
99. TsGA IPD, f.197, op.1, d.21, l.15.
100. TsGA IPD, op.1, d.447, l.9.
101. TsGA IPD, op.1, d.447, l.7.

CHAPTER 2

1. Sheila Fitzpatrick, "Ascribing Class: The Construction of Social Identity in Soviet Russia," *Journal of Modern History* 65 (1993).
2. Siegelbaum, *Soviet State and Society*, pp. 85-94. Alan M. Ball, *Russia's Last Capitalists: The Nepmen, 1921-1929* (Berkeley: University of California University Press, 1987), pp. 15-37.
3. G. Vinokur, *Kul'tura iazyka* (Moscow: Federatsiia, 1925), pp. 60-61.
4. Stephen F. Cohen, *Bukharin and the Bolshevik Revolution: A Political Biography, 1888–1938* (New York: Oxford University Press, 1980), pp. 135-136; Lynne Viola, *The Best Sons of the Fatherland: Workers in the Vanguard of Soviet Collectivization* (New York: Oxford University Press, 1987), p. 9; James W. Heinzen, *Inventing a Soviet Countryside: State Power and the Transformation of Rural Russia, 1917–1929* (Pittsburgh: University of Pittsburgh Press, 2004), p. 73.
5. Filled in by about half a million Party members during the 1922 Party census, such questionnaires became a vast database against which autobiographical claims could be verified. *Spravochnik partiinogo rabotnika*, vyp. 3 (Moscow, 1923), pp. 128-130.
6. Anne E. Gorsuch, " 'NEP be Damned!' Young Militants in the 1920s and the Culture of Civil War," *Russian Review* 56, 1997.
7. V. I. Lenin, "What Is to Be Done?" *Selected Works* (Moscow: Progress Publishers, 1977), vol. 1, p. 233.
8. *KPSS v rezoliutsiiakh i resheniiakh*, vol. 2, p. 189.
9. *Desiatyi s"ezd RKP(b)*, p. 281.
10. "Ob ukreplenii partii v sviazi s uchetom opyta proverki lichnogo sostava ee. Rezoliutsiia vserossiiskoi konferentsii," *Sputnik kommunista* no. 10 (1922), pp. 88-90.
11. V. Solntsev, *Obshchestvennye klassy* (Petrograd, 1923), p. 203; *Pod znamenem marksizma* no. 10 (1923), p. 243.

12. Ian Hacking, "Biopower and the Avalanche of Printed Numbers," *Humanities in Society* 3-4, (1982), p. 293.

13. Roughly corresponding to the French *état* and the German *Stand*, the term *soslovie* designated such hereditary groups in Imperial Russia as the nobility, clergy, townspeople, and peasantry. Gregory L. Freeze, "The Soslovie (Estate) Paradigm and Russian Social History," *American Historical Review* 91 (1986), pp. 11-36.

14. PANO, f.2, op.1, d.330, l.52

15. PANO, f.2, op.1, d.330, l.58.

16. PANO, f.2, op.1, d.330, l.60. Another Siberian Communist University applicant, Kuznestov, was described as a "son of a worker not tempted by NEP." PANO, f.2, op.1, d.330, l.96; d.261, ll.200-201.

17. GANO, f.1053, op.1, d.589, ll.210, 297; d.1000, l.27; E. Piatigorskii, "Tak vot oni kto!" *Znamia rabfakovtsa* no. 6 (1922), pp. 117-118.

18. Michel Foucault, "The Subject and Power," *Critical Inquiry* 8 (1982), pp. 777-797.

19. PATO, f.17, op.1, d.631, ll.6-149.

20. PATO, f.17, op.1, d.631, l.58. d.608, l.50.

21. TsGA IPD, f.80, op.1, d.11, l.271; TsGA IPD, f.138, op.1, d.55, ll.18, 22.

22. "Obrashchenie M. Gor'kogo k trudovoi intelligentsii," *Intelligentsiia i sovetskaia vlast'. Sbornik statei* (Moscow, 1919), p. 24.

23. M. Liadov, *Voprosy byta* (Moscow, 1925), pp. 21-22.

24. *Sud'by sovremennoi intelligentsii* (Moscow, 1925), p. 44.

25. TsGA IPD, f.138, op.1, d.34, l.10.

26. *Odinnadtsatyi s"ezd RKP(b)*, p. 376.

27. *Izvestiia TsK RKP(b)* no. 33 (1921), p. 39.

28. Exploring the Bolshevik degeneration anxieties, Eric Naiman shows how the Soviet regime used medical, sexual, and corporeal metaphors to represent and contest the ideological/political meaning of NEP. Naiman, *Sex in Public*, pp. 79-123.

29. Adelman, "Development of the Soviet Party Apparat," p. 108.

30. *Odinnadtsatyi s"ezd RKP(b)*, pp. 403-404.

31. TsGA IPD, f.984, op.1, d.72, l.17.

32. *Dvenadtsatyi s"ezd RKP(b)*, p. 789.

33. Instructions on the Lenin Levy were published in *Pravda* on February 9 and February 12, 1924; the impact of the Lenin Levy is summarized in *Partiia v tsifrovom osveshchenii. Materialy po statistike lichnogo sostava partii* (Moscow-Leningrad, 1925), pp. 43, 69, 73.

34. *KPSS v rez, vol. 1, p. 822*; Rigby, *Communist Party Membership*, pp.130-131; Obichkin, *Kratkii ocherk istorii ustava KPSS*, p. 78.

35. *Dvenadtsatyi s"ezd RKP(b)*, pp. 37-38.

36. Nina Tumarkin, *Lenin Lives! Lenin Lives! The Lenin Cult in Soviet Russia* (Cambridge, MA: Harvard University Press, 1983), pp. 119-120.

37. *U velikoi mogily* (Moscow, 1924), p. 25.

38. Arthur Jay Klinghoffer, *Red Apocalypse: The Religious Evolution of Soviet Communism*, (University Press of America, 1996) p.59.

39. Popov, "O Sotsial'nom sostave RKP(b)," pp. 315-316; A. Stepanov, "Zadachi proletarskogo studenchestva-rabochikh ot stanka, v sviazi s verbovkoi v partiiu," *Student-rabochii* no. 6 (1924), pp. 43-44.

40. O. Cullmann, *Salvation in History*, (New York, 1967), p. 182.

41. Klinghoffer, *Red Apocalypse*, p. 59.

42. J. Stalin, "Po povodu smerti Lenina. Rech' na II vsesoiuznom s'ezde sovetov, 26 ianvaria 1924 goda," *Sochineniia* vol. 6 (Moscow, 1952), p. 46.

43. TsGA IPD, f.80, op.1, d.11, ll.124-161. The evidence below may be compared with the material in *Leninskii prizyv v RKP(b)* (Moscow-Leningrad, 1925); "Otkliki rabochikh i krest'ian na smert' Lenina," *Krasnyi arkhiv* no. 1 (1934); and "Trudiashchiesia skorbiat o vozhde," *Sovetskie arkhivy* no. 2 (1969).

44. Leszek Kolakowski, "Marxist Roots of Stalinism," in Robert C. Tucker, ed., *Stalinism. Essays in Historical Interpretation* (New York: Norton, 1977), p. 294.

45. TsGA IPD f.3, op.1, d.32, l.81; f.984, op.1, d.68, l.4; f.1085 op.1, d.6, l.3; f.80, op.1, d.54, l.7.

46. *Sbornik materialov Leningradskogo komiteta RKP*, vyp.7 (Leningrad, 1924), p. 236; *Student-rabochii* no. 8 (1924), p. 64; *KPSS v rezoliutsiiakh i resheniiakh* (Moscow, 1970), vol. 1, pp. 771-778; PANO, f.2, op.1, d.17, ll.36, 82, 233; f.1, op.2, d.380, ll.13, 22; PATO, f.1, op.1, d.1154, l.8.

47. *Sibirskaia partiinaia organizatsiia v tsifrakh* (Novosibirsk, 1928), p. 23; A. Makaeva, "Leninskii prizyv v partiiu v Tomskoi gubernii," *Sibir' i dal'nii vostok v period vosstanovleniia narodnogo khoziaistva* (Tomsk, 1963), vyp. 2, p. 41; PATO, f.320, op.1, d.6, ll.1-6.

48. *Rabochii student* no. 1 (1924), p. 33; *Tomskii technologicheskii institut za 25 let svoego sushchestvovaniia*, p. 122; PATO, f.320, op.1, d.5, ll.1-18.

49. This massive enrollment was not blocked by the intensification of the discrimination against "semi-proletarians" by the Party apparatus. Thus the Fourteenth Party Conference split the first membership category, "workers," in two: "industrial workers regularly occupied in physical labor for wages" (obliged to produce recommendations from only two Communists with only one year of Party standing), and "non-industrial workers" (who needed the recommendations of at least two Party members with two years' standing)—a fine-tuning of the Party's classification methods that obviously damaged student chances of admission. Furthermore, the Central Committee resolved that whereas induction into the Party of a "worker from the bench" required ratification by the district committee only, in case of the second and the third Party membership categories (to which all students belonged), additional approval by the circuit committee or the provincial committee was needed. *Izvestiia*, October 26, 1925; *Izvestiia TsK RKP(b)* no. 6 (1925), p. 3; *O rabote iacheek RKP(b) vyshikh uchebnykh zavedenii. materialy soveshchaniia vuzovskikh iacheek pri TsK RKP(b) 25-27 fevralia 1925 goda* (Moscow, 1925), p. 136. *KPSS v rezoliutsiiakh i resheniiakh*, vol. 3 (Moscow, 1970), pp. 100, 117; Obichkin, *Kratkii ocherk istorii ustava KPSS*, pp. 81, 88; Edward Hallett Carr and R. W. Davies, *Foundations of a Planned Economy*, vol. 2 (London: Macmillan, 1969), pp. 109, 183-184; TsGA IPD, f.984, op.1, d.72, l.17; d.120, ll.18, 44.

50. TsGA IPD, f.6, op.1, d.224, l.66.

51. For the examination of Marxist veneratrion of the proletariat see, David Lovell, *Marx's Proletariat. The Making of a Myth* (London: Routledge, 1996), pp. 17-56; Leonard P. Wessell, Jr., *Prometheus Bound. The Mythic Structure of Karl Marx's Scientific Thinking* (Baton Rouge: Louisiana State University Press, 1984), pp. 144-170.

52. For workers' stance toward the Soviet power, see Maurice Brinton, *The Bolsheviks and Workers' Control 1917–1921* (Montreal: Black Rose Books, 1975); and discussion in William G. Rosenberg, "Workers and 'Workers' Control' in the Russian Revolution," *History Workshop* 5 (1978). For the official Bolshevik view of anarchism during the revolutionary years, see E. Yaroslavsky, *History of Anarchism in Russia* (New York: International Publishers, 1937); for a Western apparaisal see, Paul Avrich, "Russian Anarchists and the Civil War," *Russian Review* 27 (1968), pp. 296-300.
53. TsGA IPD, f.80, op.1, d.11, l.271.
54. PANO, f.2, op.1, d.17, l.233.
55. TsGA IPD, f.1085, op.1, d.26, l.276.
56. WKP, 326, l.170.
57. WKP, 326, ll.172-173.
58. WKP, 326, l.59.
59. Language, some scholars would say, is important, but it does not exist in a vacuum and does not operate independently—language is spoken by living people with their own backgrounds and circumstances. Yet it is my claim here that to account for one's capacity to act it is not necessary to postulate a subject prior to that which would capture it; here a capacity for action emerged out of a specific Bolshevik technology of self. Rejecting the view of language as exteriorized social or political interest, I show how meaning was activated by other meanings, and how political behavior was modified in and by the revolutionary process itself. Rather than presupposing the existence of a multilayered social structure that language somehow expresses, as Leopold Haimson and a number of his disciples tend to do, I treat language as a constitutive force that brings society into being in the first place. Leopold Haimson, "The Problem of Social Identities in Early Twentieth-Century Russia," *Slavic Review* 47(1) (1988), pp. 1-38.
60. See the trailsetting criticism of social history in Stephen Kotkin, "One Hand Clapping: Workers in 1917," *Labor History* 32(4) (1991), pp. 604-620.
61. This issue is discussed in Mark D. Steinberg, "The Urban Landscape in Workers' Imagination," *Russian History* (1996), pp. 47-66.
62. TsGA IPD, f.197, op.1, d.71, ll.48-49.
63. For background, see Jonathan Aves, *Workers Against Lenin: Labour Protest and the Bolshevik Dictatorship* (London: I. B. Tauris Publishers, 1996). Historians who believe in "workers" as a pre-linguistic social given tend to examine workers' resistance to the Bolshevik power sympathetically; see, among others, John E. Marot, "Class conflict, political competition and social transformation," *Revolutionary Russia* 7 (1994), and Jeffrey J. Rossman, *Worker Resistance Under Stalin Class and Revolution on the Shop Floor* (Cambridge, MA: Harvard University Press, 2005).

CHAPTER 3

1. TsGAODM f.64, op.1,d.78, l.8.
2. *Dvenadtsatyi s"ezd RKP(b)*, p. 522.
3. Susan G. Solomon, *The Soviet Agrarian Debate: A Controversy in Social Science, 1923–1929* (Boulder, CO: Westview Press, 1977); Terry Cox and Gary Littlejohn, eds., *Kritsman and the Agrarian Marxists* (London: Frank Cass, 1984).
4. WKP, 326, pp. 153-154.
5. TsGA IPD, f.197, d.116, l.71.
6. TsGA IPD, f.3, op.1, d.841, ll.1-12; PATO, f.320, op.1, d.6, ll.1-63; d.114, ll.24-25, 65.
7. Rigby, *Communist Party Membership*, p. 97.
8. TsGA IPD, f.1085, op.1, d.24, l.4.
9. TsGA IPD, f.1085, op.1, d.26, ll.6-8.
10. "The second Lenin Levy," is a phrase that does not appear to have been applied at the time except in one Leningrad newspaper article, *Leningradskaia pravda*, February 19, 1925. In April 1925, the Tomsk State University Party cell reported it had eighteen "peasants" on its rolls. However, in terms of "profession" only ten of them could be classified as "land tillers"; the remainder were either "medical assistants" or "school teachers," that is, individuals who could also be defined as "employees." PATO, f.115, op.2, d.8, l.146.
11. TsGA IPD, f.1085, op.1, d.24, l.53.
12. TsGA IPD, f.984, op.1, d.137, l.175.
13. TsGA IPD, f.197, d.117, l.76ob.
14. PATO, f.320, op.1, d.19, l.10.
15. TsGA IPD, f.1085, op.1, d.23, l.47.
16. PATO, f.19, op.1, d.465, ll.27-28.
17. In Smolensk, ballot N.3 was manned by SR candidates. L. M. Spirin, *Rossiia, 1917: Iz istorii bor'by politicheskikh partii* (Moscow, 1987), p. 310. *Ocherki istorii Smolenskoi organizatsii KPSS* (Moscow, 1985), p. 70.
18. TsGA IPD, f.984, op.1, d.126, ll.89-93.
19. Bolshevik attitudes to the peasants are discussed in Moshé Lewin, *Russian Peasants and Soviet Power* (Evanston, IL: Northwestern University Press, 1968), and Cohen, *Bukharin and the Bolshevik Revolution*.
20. The question of peasant conversion to atheism is examined in Glennys Young, *Power and the Sacred in Revolutionary Russia: Religious Activists in the Village* (University Park, PA: Pennsylvania State University Press, 1997), pp. 132-135.
21. But see also Edward E. Roslof, *Red Priests: Renovationism, Russian Orthodoxy, and Revolution, 1905–1946* (Bloomington: Indiana University Press, 2002).
22. TsGA IPD, f.197, op.1, f.116, l.75.
23. WKP, 326, ll.14, 68.
24. TsGA IPD, f.566, op.1, d.271, ll.21-40; TsGA IPD, Personal file no. 663708 (Leven's).
25. Leven's mention of his attentive reading of the Bible for "contradictions and nonsense" invokes an official strategy, endorsed by the League of the Godless, of acquiring knowledge of Christianity in order to expose its inconsistencies. It also calls to mind antireligious disputes in which the Godless were to use such knowledge against the "enemy." Young, *Power and the Sacred*, pp. 96-100. Daniel Peris, *Storming the Heavens: the Soviet League of the Militant Godless* (Ithaca: Cornell University Press, 1998), pp. 19-20.

CHAPTER 4

1. Alain Besançon, *The Intellectual Origins of Leninism* (Oxford, UK: Basil Blackwell, 1981); Ernest L. Tuveson, "The Millenarian Structure of *The Communist Manifesto*, ïn C. A. Patrides and Joseph Wittreich, eds., *The Apocalypse in English Renaissance Thought and Literature* (Ithaca: Cornell University Press, 1984).
2. WKP, 326, l.26.
3. The literature on the "intelligentsia" in Russia is enormous. See Hugh Seton-Watson, "The Russian Intellectuals," *Encounter* (Sept. 1955), pp. 42-50; M. Malia "What is the Russian Intelligentsia?" in Richard Pipes, ed., *The Russian Intelligentsia* (New York: Columbia University Press, 1961); Vladimir C. Nahirny, *The Russian Intelligentsia: From Torment to Silence* (New Brunswick, NJ: Transaction Books,1983); Jane Burbank, "The Intelligentsia," in Edward Acton, Vladimir Iu. Cherniaev, and William G. Rosenberg, eds., *Critical Companion to the Russian Revolution 1914–1921* (London: Arnold, 1997), pp. 515-528.
4. A. V. Lunacharskii, *Intelligentsiia v ee proshlom, v nastoiashchem i budushchem.* (Moscow, 1924), p. 127.
5. Lenin, *PSS*, vol. 8, pp. 392-393.
6. Diane P. Koenker and Ronald D. Bachman, eds., *Revelations from the Russian Archives* (Washington, DC: Library of Congress, 1997), pp. 58-61. *Pravda*, October 28, 1921. TsGAODM f.64, op.1,d.78, l.18. For the decision to embark on the purge see, *Pravda*, June 30, 1921; the national results of the purge are summarized in *Pravda*, December 18, 1921.
7. *Spravochnik partrabotnika* no. 2 (Moscow, 1922), pp. 77-78.
8. *Desiatyi s"ezd RKP(b)*, p. 274.
9. TsGAODM f.64, op.1,d.78, l.18.
10. J. Arch Getty, *The Origins of the Great Purges* (New York: Cambridge University Press, 1985), p. 46.
11. G. Zinov'ev, "Doklad na vserossiiskom s'ezde nauchnykh rabotnikov 23-go noiabria 1923 g.," in V. Soskin, ed., *Sud'by russkoi intelligentsii: Materialy diskusii, 1923–25 gg.* (Novosibirsk, 1991), pp. 137-138.
12. *Deviataia konferentsiia RKP(b)* (Moscow, 1972), p. 144.
13. Rigby, *Communist Party Membership*, pp. 96-97; *Pravda*, October 28, 1921. PATO, f.1, op.1, d.981, l.72.
14. *Pravda*, November 29, 1921.
15. *Odinnadtsatyi s"ezd RKP(b)*, p. 373.
16. In agricultural provinces like Smolensk, 23.8 percent of the purged were described as "responsible workers"; 13.4 percent were Razdobreev-type "specialists." *Pravda*, October 11 and December 18, 1921; *Odinnadtsatyi s"ezd RKP(b)*, p. 746.
17. *Pravda*, October 9, 1921.
18. *Pravda*, October 28, 1921.
19. The plenipotentiaries could collect negative material against Communists independently of the cell. While it was the cell's vote that was binding, their assessments played a role when the cell's decisions were reviewed by the higher Party organs. *Pravda*, October 9, 1921; N. Rodionova, *Gody napriazhennogo truda* (Moscow, 1963), p. 69.
20. WKP, 326, l.16.
21. L. Trotskii, "Ob intelligentsii," *Sochineniia*, vol. 20 (Moscow, 1925), p. 336.
22. WKP, 326, ll.1-7.

23. *Izvestiia TsK RKP(b)* no. 33, pp. 39-40.
24. *Odinnadtsatyi s"ezd RKP(b)*, p. 372.
25. TsGAODM f.1673, op.1,d.48, l.8; *Leninskii sbornik*, vol. XXXV, p. 179.
26. *Pravda*, October 12 and November 30, 1921.
27. *Pravda*, October 28 and November 30, 1921. PATO, f.1, op.1, d.981, l.57.
28. WKR, 326, ll.9-10.
29. *Spravochnik partrabotnika* no. 3 (Moscow, 1923), pp. 105-108; WKP, 326, ll.9, 15-16.
30. WKP, 326, l.17.
31. The purge protocols from the Smolensk Technological Institute are all the more valuable if we take notice of Kalinin's regret that "for the most part minutes of Party meetings dedicated to the 1921 purge are not kept." *Pravda*, October 27, 1921.
32. For the intelligentsia's hatred of the "intellectual, curious, and cerebral side of themselves" see Richard Stites, *Revolutionary Dreams* (New York: Oxford University Press, 1989), pp. 72-73.
33. PANO, f.2, op.1, d.17, l.233.
34. Rigby, *Communist Party Membership*, pp. 102-117; *KPSS v rezoliutsiiakh i resheniiakh* (Moscow, 1970), p. 452; TsGA IPD, f.138, op.1, d.1g, l.44.
35. *Sbornik Materialov Leningradskogo Komiteta RKP*, vyp. 6 (Petrograd, 1923), pp. 173, 201.
36. TsGA IPD, f.1085, op.1, d.10, l.4.
37. TsGA IPD, f.1085, op.1, d.12, p.65; d.16, l.15.
38. PANO, f.2, op.1, d.17, p.233; d.24, l.318; PATO, f.320, op.1, d.7, l.29.
39. PATO, f.115, op.2, d.3, ll.6-16; d.4, l.41.
40. There were, however, instances when that was out of the question. A number of students had to be categorized as "intelligentsia" despite their "peasant" origins: comrade Zudilov became a mental laborer due to his "clerical work," while Toletukhina and Kletkina were so categorized "while teaching in school." When the transition to intellectual labor took place before the student enrolled in the Party, his or her "degeneration" could not be overlooked. GANO, f.1053, op.1, d.589, l.51; PATO, f.320, op.1, d.19, ll.126-127. PATO, f.115, op.2, d.3, ll.6-27.
41. PANO, f.2, op.1, d.963, l.4.
42. Only thirteen university Communists were "workers" with real experience in production; ten other Communists were "land tillers" (*khleboroby*). PATO, f.115, op.2, d.8, l.146.
43. TsGA IPD, f.1085, op.1, d.23, l.199.
44. PATO, f.17, op.1, d.747, l.21.
45. PATO, f.17, op.1, d.747, p.21
46. TsGAODM, f.67, op.1,d.97, l.6ob.
47. TsGA IPD, f.1085, op.1, d.24, l.14.
48. TsGA IPD, f.984, op.1, d.188, ll.143-144.
49. PATO, f.115, op.2, d.12, l.62.
50. *Trinadtsatyi s"ezd RKP(b), Mai 1924 goda. Stenograficheskii otchet* (Moscow: Gospolitizdat) p. 711.
51. The prerevolutionary mystique of the intelligentsia did not go away easily. Thus Nikolai Chaplin, the head of the Komsomol in the 1920s, refused to put "employee" as his social position, always preferring, "member of the intelligentsia." D. Poliakova, "Poka serdtsa dlia chesti zhivy ..." in A. Afanas'ev, *Oni ne molchali* (Moscow, 1991), p. 358.

52. Although "others" was a highly anomalous category since it also subsumed "professional revolutionaries." No less than 35 delegates to the summer 1924 Thirteenth Party Congress, for example, were classified as "others." TsGA IPD, f.984, op.1, d.249, ll.1-2, 5.

53. In 1927, about every forth Leningrad student was enrolled in the Komsomol (1,542 out of 6,501). TsGA IPD, f.6, op.1, d.224, l.206. TsGA IPD, f.984, op.1, d.244, l.27; f.K-141, op.1, d.1a, l.5.

54. TsGA IPD, f.984, op.1, d.120, l.33; Komsomol members younger than twenty could apply for Party membership only through the Komsomol district committee. TsGA IPD, f.138, op.1, d.1g, p. 17; *Spravochnik partiinogo rabotnika*, vyp. 3 (1923), pp. 124-125. On measures curtailing admissions of Komsomol students into the Party, see *Student revoliutsii* no. 5 (1927), pp. 21-22; O. Dubatova, A. Tuliak, "O rabote Komsomola v vuze," *Krasnoe studenchestvo* no. 8 (1927-28), p. 38.

55. Carr, *Foundations of a Planned Economy*, pp. 100-101; Rigby, *Communist Party Membership*, p.163.

56. PATO, f.76, op.1, d.114.

57. Hellbeck, *Revolution on My Mind*, p. 311.

58. TsGA IPD, f.984, op.1, d.126, ll.35-39.

59. TsGA IPD, f.1085, op.1, d.26, ll.142-143.

60. *Deiateli SSSR*, p. 570.

61. *Deiateli SSSR*, p. 623.

62. *Deiateli SSSR*, p. 624.

63. *Deiateli SSSR*, p. 624.

64. *Deiateli SSSR*, p. 626.

65. *Deiateli SSSR*, p. 775.

66. TsGA IPD, f.984, op.1, d.126, ll.66, 69, 73-77.

67. *Volna. Ezhemesiachnyi organ federatsii anarkho-kommunisticheskikh grupp* no. 48 (1923), pp. 38-39.

68. On *makhaevshchina* as a pejorative term, see L. Syrkin, "Chto takoe makhaevshchina?" *Krasnaia letopis'* (1929), no. 6 and (1930) no. 1,.

69. For the Menshevik stance after 1917, see Abraham Ascher, ed., *The Mensheviks in the Russian Revolution* (London: Thames & Hudson, London, 1976), pp. 111-117, and discussion in L. H. Haimson "The Mensheviks after the Bolshevik Revolution," Part I, *Russian Review* 38 (October 1979) and 39 (April 1980); Part II, *Russian Review* 39 (October 1980).

70. "Sotsial'naia fizionomiia intelligentsii," *Biulleteni literatury i zhizni* no. 1 (1924), p. 5.

71. A. Lunacharskii, "Intelligentsiia i ee mesto v sotsialisticheskom stroitel'stve," *Revoliutsiia i kul'tura* no. 1 (1927), pp. 25, 33-34.

72. *Sud'by sovremennoi intelligentsii*, p. 45.

73. "Revoliutsiia i melkaia burzhuaznaia demokratiia. Rech' Lenina na sobranii otvetstvennykh rabotnikov-kommunistov 27-go Noiabria 1918 goda." *Intelligentsiia i sovetskaia vlast'*, p. 18. Robert C. Tucker, ed., *The Lenin Anthology* (New York: Norton, 1975), p. 379.

74. Elise Kimerling, "Civil Rights and Social Policy in Soviet Russia, 1918–1936, *Russian Review* 41(1) (January 1982). A. Dobkin, "Lishentsy: 1918–1936," *Zven'ia: istoricheskii al'manakh'*, 2 vols. (Moscow-St Petersburg, 1992), vol. II; Golfo Alexopoulos, *Stalin's Outcasts: Aliens, Citizens, and the Soviet State, 1926–1936* (Ithaca: Cornell University Press, 2003).

75. TsGA IPD, f.197, op.1, d.115, l.30.

76. PATO, f.17, op.1, d.747, l.21.

77. WKP, 326, l.211.

78. RGASPI, f.17, op.8, d.396., l.17.

79. For a general outline of Russian politics during the Revolution, see L. Semennikova and V. Blokhin, *Politicheskie partii Rossii: pervaia chetvert' XX v: spravochnik* (Briansk: Grani, 1993); and *Politicheskie partii Rossii. Konets XIX-pervaia tret' XX veka. Entsiklopediia* (Moscow, 1996).

80. TsGA IPD, f.1085, op.1, d.26, l.58.

81. TsGA IPD, f.1085, op.1, d.26, l.61.

82. On the Kadets, see Melissa Stockdale, "The Constitutional Democratic Party," in Anna Geifman, ed., *Russia Under the Last Tsar* (Oxford, UK: Blackwell Publishers, 1999), pp. 164-169. For a more comprehensive discussion see William G. Rosenberg, *Liberals in the Russian Revolution: The Constitutional Democratic Party, 1917–1921* (Princeton, NJ: Princeton University Press, 1974).

83. M. Vasser, "Razgrom anarkho-sindikalisticheskogo uklonay v partii," *Voprosy istorii KPSS*, no. 3 (1962), p. 64.

84. For "internationalists," see TsGA IPD, f.5247, op.1, d.2-3; for "Revolutionary Communists" see TsGA IPD, f.501, op.1, d.1.

85. Taking its name from the central organ of the party—the newspaper *Borot'ba* (Struggle)—the Borotba Party arose in May 1918 after the split in the Ukrainian Socialist-Revolutionary Party on the basis of supporting Soviet power in Ukraine. In March 1919 it assumed the name Ukrainian Party of Socialist-Revolutionary-Borotbists (Communists), and in August the same year the name was changed to Ukrainian Communist Party (Borotbists). As the Borotbists' conference in the middle of March 1920 resolved to heed the call of the Communist International and join the Bolsheviks of Ukraine, members of this party were enrolled into the Bolshevik ranks automatically. RGASPI f.613, op.1, d.3, l.7.

86. Leonard Schapiro, *The History of the Communist Party of the Soviet Union*, (London,1960), pp. 180-181; *Izvestiia TsK RKP(b)* no. 22 (September 18) and no. 24 (October 12), 1920; TsGA IPD, f.408, op.1, d.1179, ll.133-134.

87. TsGA IPD, f.197, op.1, d.115, l.25.

88. TsGA IPD, f.197, op.1, d.115, l.30.

89. TsGA IPD, f.4000, op.5, d.4478, ll.3-4.

90. Zvi Y. Gitelman, *Jewish Nationality and Soviet Politics* (Princeton University Press, 1972), pp. 444-445.

91. Zivah Galili and Boris Morozov, *Exiled to Palestine: The Emigration of Zionist Convicts From The Soviet Union 1924–1934* (London: Frank Cass, 2006), pp. 41-66.

92. Iu. Margolin, *Kak bylo likvidirovano Sionistskoe dvizhenie v Sovetskoi Rossii* (Jerusalem, 1988).

93. For evidence of the expulsion of students who were associated with Poalei Tsion, see David-Fox, *Revolution of the Mind*, p. 149.

94. Grusman's Party application from 1931 was rejected on procedural grounds: he failed to obtain a sufficient number of recommendations. TsGA IPD, f.984, op.1, d.519, ll.101-102.

95. *Desiatyi s"ezd RKP(b)*, p. 254. I. Smilga, *Na povorote* (Moscow: Gos.izd., 1921), p. 5.

96. Edward Hallett Carr, *The Bolshevik Revolution: 1917-1923*, vol. 1 (London: Macmillan, 1950), p. 213; *Pravda*, October 13 and 28, 1921. The Party added, though, that the investigation of former members of petit-bourgeois parties "has to be carried out with tact, so that an unnecessarily gloomy mood would not engulf those who, working hand in hand with us, have proved their sincerity and loyalty to the Communist cause." PATO, f.1, op.1, d.981, l.75.

97. Alexander Dallin and Nicolaevsky, pp. 175-176, 206; George Legget, *The Cheka: Lenin's Political Police* (Oxford, UK: Clarendon Press, 1981), pp. 344-346; *Pravda*, October 21, 1921; *Pravda*, December 2, 1921; *Pravda*, April 17, 1923. *Vserosiiskaia perepis' chlenov RKP(b) 1922 goda*, vyp. 4 (Moscow, 1923), p. 26; PATO, f.17, op.1, d.631, l.35. For a more general Bolshevik treatment of "petit-bourgeois parties," see M. Ravich-Cherkaskii, *Anarkhisty* (Khar'kov, 1929); B. Gorev, *Anarkhisty v Rossii* (Moscow, 1930); I. Vardin, *Revoliutsiia i Men'shevizm* (Moscow-Leningrad, 1925); D. Erde, *Men'sheviki* (Khar'kov, 1929); S. Chernomyrdik, Esery, *(partiia sotsialistov-revoliutsionerov)* (Khar'kov, 1930).

98. *Odinnadtsatyi s"ezd RKP(b)*, p. 374.

99. *Odinnadtsatyi s"ezd RKP(b)*, p. 437.

100. *Odinnadtsatyi s"ezd RKP(b)*, p. 392.

101. *Odinnadtsatyi s"ezd RKP(b)*, p. 545.

102. The 1925 Regulations went even further, allowing only productivist cells to enroll former members of petit-bourgeois parties, and even that pending the ratification of the Central Committee itself. *Programy i ustavy KPSS* (Moscow, 1969), pp. 260, 276.

103. For the classic studies on the Social Revolutionaries see, Oliver H. Radkey, *The Sickle Under the Hammer: The Russian Socialist Revolutionaries in the Early Months of Soviet Rule* (New York: Columbia University Press, 1963); Manfred Hildermeier, *The Russian Socialist Revolutionary Party Before the First World War* (New York: St. Martin's Press, 2000); Michael Melancon, *The Socialist Revolutionaries and the Russian Anti-War Movement, 1914–1917* (Columbus: Ohio State University Press, 1991). For the Bolshevik attitude toward the party after the consolidation of power, see Marc Jansen, "A Show Trial Under Lenin," *Russian Review* 43(1) (January 1984), pp. 85-86. It should be noted, however, that for the purposes of our discussion the mythologized histories of the Socialist Revolutionaries are most useful. See, for example, the official Soviet account in K. Gusev, *Partiia eserov* (Mysl, 1975).

104. TsGA IPD, f.566, d.274, ll.29-30.

105. For the Left SRs and their complex relations with the Bolsheviks see, Michael Melancon "The Left Socialist Revolutionaries, 1917-1918," in Edward Acton, Vladimir Iu. Cherniaev, and Wiliam G. Rosenberg, eds., *Critical Companion to the Russian Revolution, 1914–1921* (Bloomington: Indiana University Press, 1997); Iu. Fel'shtinskii, *Bol'sheviki i levye esery, oktiabr' 1917-iiul' 1918 na puti k odnopartiinoi diktature* (Paris: YMCA-Press, 1985); A. Litvin and L. Ovrutskii, *Levye esery: programma i taktika (nekotorye voprosy)*, (Kazan': Izdatel'stvo Kazanskogo Universiteta, 1992).

106. TsGA IPD, f. 4000, op.5, d.4399, l.1.

107. TsGA IPD, f.1085, op.1, d.26, l.240; PATO, f.1, op.1, d.97.

108. Historical research shows that the Mensheviks and the Bolsheviks were not always at odds during the revolutionary years. See for example André Lebich, *From the Other Shore: Russian Social Democracy after 1921* (Cambridge, MA:: Harvard University Press, 1997), p. 60; Abraham Ascher, *Pavel Axelrod and the Development of Menshevism* (Cambridge, MA: Harvard University Press, 1972), p. 382; Leopold H. Haimson et al., *The Making of Three Russian Revolutionaries. Voices from the Menshevik Past* (New York: Cambridge University Press, 1987), pp. 312-313. An important sociological perspective is provided in David S. Lane, *The Roots of Russian Communism: A Social and Historical Study of Russian Social Democracy, 1898–1907* (Assen: Van Gorchum, 1969).

109. Frederick C. Corney, *Telling October: Memory and the Making of the Bolshevik Revolution* (Ithaca: Cornell University Press, 2004), pp. 37-38, 47-48.

110. TsGA IPD, f.984, op.1, d.58, l.56.

111. TsGA IPD, f.984, op. 1, d.72, l.17.

112. TsGA IPD, f.197, op.1, d.116, ll.72-74.

113. Former members of other parties were the first to be purged: a staggering 23 percent were purged by the checkup commissions nationally. The final purge frequency was much lower, only 8 percent, but still three times higher than the general purge frequency. *Itogi proverki*, p. 42; TsGA IPD, f.7, op.2, d.1242, l.146.

114. TsGA IPD, op.1, f.197, d.117, l.37.

115. TsGA IPD, f.1085, op.1, d.435, l.94a.

116. TsGA IPD, f.1085, op.1, d.437, l.14.

117. TsGA IPD, f.984, op.1, d.119, ll.63-64.

118. Doctor L. Merel'zon, *Nevrasteniia. Ee istochniki, preduprezhdenie i lechenie* (Krasnodar, 1927), pp. 8-10.

119. PATO, f.17, op.1, d.631, l.47.

120. TsGA IPD, f.197, op.1., d.217, l.17.

121. M. Basov, "Volia," *Bol'shaia sovetskaia entsiklopediia*, 1st ed. (Moscow, 1929), vol. 13, pp. 106, 100.

122. Hannah Arendt, *The Life of the Mind*, vol. 2 (London: Secker & Warburg 1978), p. 74.

CONCLUSION

1. Clifford Geertz, *The Interpretation of Cultures* (New York: Basic Books, 1973), pp. 3-30.

2. Igal Halfin, ed., *Language and Revolution: The Making of Modern Political Identity* (London: Frank Cass, 2002).

3. Mike Hepworth and Brian S. Turner, *Confession. Studies in Deviance and Religion,* (London: Routledge & Kegan Paul, 1982), pp. 85, 93.

4. N. S. Antonova and N. V. Drozdova, eds., A. A. Bogdanov (Malinovskii), *Stat'i, doklady, pis'ma i vospominaniia, 1901-1928* (Moscow, 1995), vol. 1, pp. 23-24.

5. Karl Weintraub, "Autobiography and Historical Consciousness," *Critical Inquiry*, vol. 1 (1975), pp. 838-839.

6. N. Kozlova, "Zalozhniki slova?" *Sotsiologicheskie isledovaniia* (1995), p. 134.

7. TsGA IPD, f.984, op. 1, d.72, l.17.

8. WKP, 326, ll.61, 124-126.

9. Paul Jay, *Being in the Text: Self-Representation from Wordsworth to Roland Barthes* (Ithaca: Cornell University Press, 1984), p. 29.

10. Weintraub, "Autobiography," p. 837.

11. Victor Serge, *The Year One of the Russian Revolution* (Chicago: Holt, Rinehart, and Winston, 1972), p. 367.

12. *Biulleten' oppozitsii*, nn. 68-69 (1938), p. 19.

13. E. Tager, "Avtobiograficheskie rasskazy Gor'kogo 20-kh godov," *Gor'kovskie chteniia*, (Moscow, 1954), pp. 283-286. Gorky's autobiographical stories were published in *Krasnaia nov'*, nn. 1–6 (1923).

14. George Gusdorf, "Conditions and Limits of Autobiography," in James Olney, *Autobiography: Essays Theoretical and Critical* (Princeton, NJ: Princeton University Press, 1980), p. 33.

15. John T. Marcus, "The World Impact of the West," in Henry A. Murray, ed., *Myth and Mythmaking* (Boston: Beacon Press, 1968), p. 225.

16. Georges Haupt and Jean-Jacques Marie, eds., *Makers of the Russian Revolution: Biographies of Bolshevik Leaders* (London: Allen and Unwin, 1974), 232.

17. *Deiateli SSSR*, p. 770.

18. Weintraub, "Autobiography," pp. 832-833.